DESTROYER
AT WAR

DESTROYER AT WAR

THE FIGHTING LIFE AND LOSS OF HMS
Havock
FROM THE ATLANTIC TO THE MED 1939 – 1942

DAVID GOODEY AND
RICHARD OSBORNE

Frontline Books

DESTROYER AT WAR
The Fighting Life and Loss of HMS *Havock*
From the Atlantic to the Med 1939 – 1942

First published in 2017 by Frontline Books,
an imprint of Pen & Sword Books Ltd,
47 Church Street, Barnsley, S. Yorkshire, S70 2AS.

ISBN: 978-1-52670-900-4

CIP data records for this title are available from the British Library

For more information on our books, please visit
www.frontline-books.com
email info@frontline-books.com
or write to us at the above address.

Printed and bound in Great Britain by TJ International Ltd

"One of the Navy's Most Famous Destroyers"
Daily Mirror, 8 April 1942

"Cry Havoc, and let slip the dogs of war"
Julius Caesar by William Shakespeare

In memory of my father, Stoker Albert W. Goodey
David Goodey

Contents

Foreword by David Goodey

My father, Albert William Goodey, joined the Royal Navy on 26 April 1938, at the age of twenty. From a poor background in Brentwood, Essex, England, he had worked as a steam railway locomotive fireman on the London Liverpool Street to East Anglia line. He tired of this and joined the Navy well before the outbreak of the Second World War. He served in many theatres of war from Spain in 1938 to post-war Palestine and was demobbed on 23 May 1950.

Having completed training at Chatham, as a Stoker Rating in the engineering division, he took his first commission in the new 'Hero' class destroyer HMS *Havock* on 29 September 1938. After three years, he left her on 14 November 1941, just five months before she was lost.

The first ship with the name *Havock* was built in 1893 and was the first vessel designed, built and designated as a torpedo boat destroyer (TBD) which was soon abbreviated to "destroyer". The name *Havock* commemorates the capture of the Dutch ship *Havik*, which means Hawk, in 1796, and according to the *Aberdeen Journal* of 8 September 1937, *Havock* is a corruption of *Havik*. The second *Havock* was authorised in the 1934 Naval Programme, ordered on 12 December 1934, and laid down at William Denny and Brothers Ltd of Dumbarton, near Glasgow, on 15 May 1935. Her machinery was installed in the same yard. She was duly launched on 7 July 1936 and completed on 16 January 1937, at a total cost of a £248,468 and 10 shillings.

On completion *Havock* joined the Second Destroyer Flotilla, referred to in this history as the DF2, and commonly known at the time as 'The Fighting Seconds'. Of the *entire* flotilla of nine, only *Hotspur* and *Hero* survived the war.

The 2nd Destroyer Flotilla
(Pennant Numbers and Launch Dates)
Hardy (H87) (Leader) 7/36

Hunter (H35)	2/36	*Hero* (H99)	3/36
Hostile (H55)	1/36	*Hereward* (H93)	3/36

| *Hotspur* (H01) | 3/36 | *Hyperion* (H97) | 4/36 |
| *Havock* (H43) | 7/36 | *Hasty* (H24) | 5/36 |

Havock was always a lucky and very happy ship and her first 'Captain', Lieutenant Commander Rafe Edward Courage, was much revered by the crew as a courageous and very capable destroyer captain. He typically slumped over the compass with a lugubrious, unflustered look but offered an approach to the enemy which was as robust and as wild as his red hair, from which his nickname 'Nutty' came.

I traced over fifty of *Havock*'s crew during the 1980s and arranged several reunions. My interest in her was crowned in 2003 when eighty-five-year-old Albert Goodey unveiled a monument in Narvik's Ofotfjord, at Skjomnes, Norway, to those that died and served at the naval Battles at Narvik. Attending were President Cosmo of Norway, Admiral of the Fleet Jonathon Band, British Ambassador Mariot Leslie, the Polish Attaché, the Minister for Veterans Ivor Caplin MP as well as a number of Norwegian Admirals and Veterans. We laid wreaths from Norwegian Naval Coastguard Vessels in the fjord and visited graves at Ballangen, including that of Captain Bernard Armitage Warburton-Lee VC of *Hardy*. Albert was a Stoker for his entire naval career, but on that day, he represented British Naval history for not only the battles in Norway but also the whole of the Second World War. He was proud, I was proud, Britain and Norway were proud. Albert died in 2006 aged eighty-eight.

There were over 500 British and Allied destroyers in the Second World War and this work records the history of a short-lived but very active, heroic, celebrated and quite famous one. Destroyers were dispensable workhorses and therefore were used in most high-risk situations and sometimes were unfortunately sacrificed to save capital ships or important convoys. In fact, it was one such convoy that was the beginning of the end for *Havock*. Despite their fragility, destroyers were fast, agile greyhounds of the sea and packed a big punch – truly the dogs of war.

Like any other ship *Havock* had her moments of inspiration and glory, but was also often mechanically unsound as damage compounded over time. She fought surface ships, submarines, aircraft and shore installations. She picked up literally thousands of troops, survivors and refugees. She protected the Fleet, ran supplies night and day to some of the hottest spots and was often called upon to do other disparate duties. Wherever she went she invariably met danger and suffered considerable damage, some even self-inflicted, and casualties, whilst taking her toll of the enemy.

Havock spent little time in harbour unless under repair. She ran and ran as this diary of events shows. Her crew was equal to any. When she was wrecked in April 1942 the national newspapers reported the loss with the words; "Havock, Britain's No. 2 Destroyer of this war – second only in fame and glory to the Cossack – has been wrecked off the coast of Tunisia.", and "One of the Navy's most famous destroyers, a ship which survived bombs, torpedoes and full scale battles, has been wrecked".

In two and a half years *Havock* was awarded a staggering total of eleven battle honours. These, which exclude the Spanish Civil War, graphically track her progress through the war until her slow death in April 1942.

Atlantic	1939	Matapan	1941
Narvik	1940	Greece	1941
Norway	1940	Crete	1941
Cape Spada	1940	Libya	1941-42
Mediterranean	1940-41	Malta Convoys	1941-42
Sirte	1942		

We owe, in part, our freedom to ships and crews such as this and they in turn deserve to be remembered.

David Goodey,
Chelmsford, Essex,
February 2017.

Foreword by Richard Osborne

I have always been a keen student of naval history with interests in warship design, operational performance and service histories and, in particular, the naval war in the Mediterranean during 1940-1943. While researching into the life and death of the cruiser HMS *Manchester*, I also became reacquainted with HMS *Havock* and started to compile her service history. By 2013, my researches were such that I was able to give a presentation entitled *The Slow Death of HMS Havock* at the World Ship Society's Annual Naval Meeting at Bristol in June of that year. David Goodey was in the audience present and, during subsequent discussions, we realized that we had complementary information and decided to collaborate. Consequently, we have been able to use eyewitness accounts, newspaper reports, official documents and court martial proceedings to piece together *Havock's* exploits which included the battles of Narvik, Matapan, and Second Sirte. Thanks to having access to several personal accounts, we have able to describe the trials and tribulations experienced by her crew during their imprisonment in the notorious Vichy internment camp at Laghouat.

The aim of this book was to provide a detailed account of the rigours to which an over-worked and barely-maintained Fleet destroyer was exposed while serving with the Mediterranean Fleet. Cunningham was perennially short of destroyers and he kept them running until they had to be taken in hand for the minimum repairs required to return them to active service. Unsurprisingly, by April 1942 *Havock* had become worn out mechanically and was in desperate need of her first proper refit since completion in January 1937. The seemingly endless operations also placed intense pressures on the destroyer's officers and men and there is evidence in the Court Martial documents that the resultant fatigue must have been a contributory factor to her loss on 6 April.

In this book, we have attempted to address the problems facing *Havock's* commanding officer and the alternative actions that he could have taken while, at the same time, honouring the brave men who manned one of the Royal Navy's most famous destroyers of the Second World War.

Richard Osborne,
Nailsea, Bristol,
February 2017.

Acknowledgements

O ur first thanks go to contributors from the *Havock*'s crew-members, all of whom have now 'crossed the bar', who were there. They witnessed first-hand the events in the fighting life and loss of HMS *Havock* and after and without their input this work would have been impossible. They were:

Lieutenant Commander Rafe Edward Courage RN, Lieutenant Commander Geoffrey Robert Gordon 'Robin' Watkins RN, First Lieutenant John Blackmore Burfield RN, Lieutenant Michael Baillie-Grohman RN, Midshipmen Derek William Napper and David Masterman Ellis, Warrant Officer Leslie Millns, Chief Petty Officers Frederick Richard Kemp, George William Clarke Carter and John Thomson, Petty Officer Alex 'Bugs' Levene, Stoker Petty Officer George Shuttleworth, Chief Stoker Albert Victor Phillips, Leading Seaman Alfred John 'Jack' Surridge, Leading Signals Telegraphist Frank 'Nobby' Hall, Telegraphist Fred Buckingham, Able Seamen, James Arthur 'Buster' Brown, John Edmund Dodds, Maurice Douglas, Harry George Jenkins, A. 'Ginger' Humphries, Griff 'Jess' Gleed-Owen, Sidney 'Wiggie' Bennett, Hugh 'Bob' Langton, Albert Wilford and Roy Howard, Stokers Albert William Goodey and Jock Burt and last, but not least, 'The Anonymous *Havock* Diarist'.

There are many others who without their help and support, large and small, this project would not have succeeded. First and foremost, my co-author, Dr Richard Osborne, is profoundly thanked because without him this book would never have reached publication. Others who have made substantial contributions are Geirr Haarr, Bob Wilford, Jill Kingsbury, John Whithouse, Ian McLeod, Don Kindell, Rear-Admiral Kit Layman, Mike Harris, Richard Gleed-Owen, Ron Cope and Kim Langton. Forgive me if a name or two is missing.

The Imperial War Museum Sound Archives and the staff at The National Archives at Kew are sincerely thanked as is Frontline books which have given me the opportunity to make public, from half a life time collecting information from disparate sources, the history of one of the Royal Navy's hardest working, most celebrated and battle honoured destroyers. Finally, my wife Jan who has patiently accepted my long-time obsession with getting this project finished as a dedication to my father – a very ordinary man like so many others, who could have given his life at any moment but survived to live to the grand age of eighty-eight.

David Goodey

I thank my co-author David Goodey for his part in this most enjoyable and fruitful collaboration that has led to the publication of this work. We also are indebted to Andrew Smith, whose linguistic skills enabled him to delve into and translate Italian sources thereby providing information on Axis forces off Tunisia on the night of 5th/6th April 1942. Dave Sowdon, Harry Spong and Stephen Hacker are thanked for their advice and constructive criticism. We thank the World Ship Society for allowing us to use photographs from their extensive collection. We are also indebted to John Grehan for his editorial role in this work – any mistakes that remain are ours and ours alone.

Finally, I thank my wife Chris, once again, for her patience and support throughout the many months of research and writing that were required to bring this project to a conclusion.

Richard Osborne

Glossary of Technical Terms and Abbreviations

AA	Anti-Aircraft
AB	Able Seaman
Abaft	A relative term used to describe the location of one object in relation to another in which the object described is farther aft than the other.
Abeam	The bearing of an object 90 degrees from ahead (in a line with the middle of the ship).
AMC	Armed Merchant Cruiser
AR.RDF	Aerial Ranging Radio Direction Finding
A/S	Anti-submarine
ASDIC	Usually claimed to stand for Anti-Submarine Detection Investigating Committee but Willem Hackman ("Seek & Strike: Sonar, anti-submarine warfare and the Royal Navy 1914-54, HMSO 1984) could find no evidence for the existence of such a committee. He believed that the acronym stood for Anti-Submarine Division-ics – the Department that initiated research into underwater detection during 1914-1918. Today ASDIC is known as SONAR.
Athwartships	Across the ship, at right angles to the centreline.
AW.RDF	Air Warning Radio Direction Finding.
Beam	The registered breadth of a vessel measured at the outside of the hull amidships, or at its greatest breadth.
Bearing	The direction of an object with reference to you, your ship or another object.
Bulkhead	A vertical structural partition in a vessel's interior dividing it into various

	compartments for strength and safety purposes.
Bulwark	Barrier of stiffened plating at the outboard edge of the main or upper deck to prevent or inhibit the entry of the sea.
Cable (length)	100 fathoms or 600 feet.
CAFO	Confidential Admiralty Fleet Order.
Capstan	Steel warping drum rotating on a vertical axis for the handling of mooring lines and, optionally, anchor cable.
CERA	Chief Engine Room Artificer
C-in-C	Commander-in-Chief
CO	Commanding Officer
Coaming	Any vertical surface on a ship designed to deflect or prevent entry of water.
CPO	Chief Petty Officer
CS	Cruiser Squadron
Deck	A platform or horizontal floor which extends from side to side of a vessel.
Displacement	The weight of the water displaced by a ship. This weight is the same as the weight of the ship when afloat. Standard displacement is the displacement of a warship complete, fully manned and equipped ready for sea including all ammunition, equipment, provisions, miscellaneous stores and fresh water for the crew but without fuel or reserved boiler water on board. Full load is standard displacement plus fuel and reserve boiler water on board.
DCT	Director Control Tower
DCNS	Deputy Chief of Naval Staff
DF	Destroyer Flotilla
DIP	Direct Impact Percussion (shell)
DNC	Director of Naval Construction
DF	Destroyer Flotilla
DG	Degaussing, the process of decreasing/eliminating the magnetic field of a ship.
DNI	Director of Naval Intelligence
DNO	Director of Naval Ordnance
Draft (draught)	The depth of a vessel below the waterline measured vertically to the lowest part of the hull, propellers or other reference point.

DSC	Distinguished Service Cross
DSM	Distinguished Service Medal
DSO	Distinguished Service Order
Engine Room	Space where the main engines of a ship are located.
ERA	Engine Room Artificer
FAA	Fleet Air Arm
Fathom	A seagoing unit of measure equivalent to six feet.
FO	Flag Officer
Forecastle	A structure at the forward end of a vessel formed by carrying up the ship's shell plating at deck height above the level of the uppermost complete deck and fitting a deck over the length of this structure
Forecastle deck	A deck over the main deck
Forefoot	The forward end of a vessel's stem which is stepped on the keel.
Forepeak	The narrow extremity of a vessel's bow. Also the space within it.
Foul	Jammed, not clear
Frames	The ribs of a ship
Freeboard	Vertical measurement from the vessel's side amidships from the load waterline to the upperside of the freeboard deck.
Gunner	Warrant Officer given training as a gunnery instructor with particular emphasis on Direction. Their skills and training also helped to ensure high levels of availability of weapons.
Gunner (T)	Warrant Officer trained as a gunnery instructor but with the emphasis on torpedoes
HA	High Angle (gunnery)
HA.DCT	High Angle Director Control Tower
HATF	High-Angle Timed Fuze (AA shell)
Halliards or Halyards	Ropes used for hoisting gaffs, sails and signal flags
Hawse	The part of a ship's bow in which are the hawse holes for the anchor chains
HE	High explosive.
Heel	Inclination of a vessel to one side.
HF/DF	High Frequency Direction Finding

HMAS	His Majesty's Australian Ship
HMS	His Majesty's Ship
IFF	Interrogator Friend or Foe
Inboard	Towards the centreline of a ship
LA	Low Angle (gunnery)
LA.DCT	Low Angle Director Control Tower
LS	Leading Seaman
Lt	Lieutenant
Lt Cdr	Lieutenant Commander
List	To lean to one side
MAS	Motoscafo Armato Silurente
Mile	Where 'mile' is used in this book as a distance at sea, the nautical mile or sea mile should be assumed – one minute of latitude, equivalent to 6,080 feet (usually rounded off to 2,000 yards in naval practice and 1.8532 kilometres. The English land mile is 1,760 yards (5,280 feet).
MTB	Motor Torpedo Boat
nm	nautical mile
oa	Length measured from the foremost point of the stem to the aftermost part of the stern
Outboard	In a direction towards the side of the ship
OS	Ordinary Seaman
NOIC	Naval Officer In Charge
Paravane	A type of water kite which is towed with wire rope from a fitting on the forefoot of a vessel, operates to ride out from the ship's side and deflect mines which were moored in the path of the vessel and to cut them adrift so that they rose to the surface where they could be seen and destroyed.
Pitching	The oscillatory vertical motion of a vessel forward and aft
Plot clock	Used in navigation in conjunction with nautical charts in the chart house or plotting room
PO	Petty Officer
Port side	The left hand side of the ship looking forward
pp	Length between the perpendiculars from the forward side of the stem to the aft

	side of the stern part of the designed waterline
Quarter	A side of a ship between the main midship frames and the stern
Quarterdeck	The after portion of the weather deck and allotted for the use of officers
RADAR	RAdio Detection and Ranging
RAF	Royal Air Force
RCNVR	Royal Canadian Navy Volunteer Reserve
RDF	Radio Direction Finding (RADAR)
Ring Main	An electrical wiring technique used in electricity supply
RM	Royal Marine
RN	Royal Navy
RNR	Royal Navy Reserve
RNVR	Royal Navy Volunteer Reserve
Roll	Motion of a ship from side to side, alternatively raising and lowering each side of the deck
RPC	Remote Power Control
SAP	Semi-Armour Piercing (shell)
SHP	Shaft Horse Power
S/M	Submarine
SNOIC	Senior Naval Officer In Charge
SPO	Stoker Petty Officer
SONAR	SOund Navigation and Ranging
SR.RDF	Surface Ranging Radio Direction Finding
SS	Steam Ship
Starboard side	The right hand side of the ship looking forward
S/Lt	Sub Lieutenant
SW.RDF	Surface Warning Radio Direction Finding
TSDS	Two Speed Destroyer Sweep. TSDS comprised a pair of davits on the quarters to hoist out paravanes, stowed on the quarterdeck, and winches to haul and veer on the wires, plus stowages for said wires, and for the other minesweeping apparatus (kites, otters). The equipment was designed to sweep moored mines
Type 271	Surface warning radar.
Type 286	Air warning radar.

Ultra	Code name and message prefix for Special Intelligence from codes and cyphers.
USS	United States Ship
USW	Ultra Short Wave (radio)
VALF	Vice-Admiral Light Forces
VAM	Vice-Admiral Malta
VC	Victoria Cross
WO	Warrant Officer
Working up	A period spent in exercises working up the efficiency of a ships' company of ships newly commissioned after building or refit.
W/T	Wireless Telegraphy
'Y' work	The interception of enemy signals including direction finding
Zig zag patterns	Strict navigational evolutions involving changes of courses at pre-determined intervals so as to make submarine attacks more difficult. Each ship in the group was given precise instructions prior to the commencement of an operation and specific zig zag patterns would be initiated in response to a signal from the group commander. Zig Zag Plan 10, 110 would mean base course 110 degrees with a 15 degree turn to port after twenty minutes, a 20 degree turn to starboard after thirty minutes, a 25 degree turn to port fifteen minutes later and then a 10 degree turn to starboard after twenty-five minutes. Repeat *ad nauseum* until ordered to stop.

Chapter 1

A Ship is Born

HMS *Havock* was a destroyer of the H or Hero class whose construction was foreshadowed in the autumn of 1933 when the First Lord of the Admiralty[1] circulated his construction proposals[2] for 1934. These included the aircraft carrier *Ark Royal*, three Town class and one Arethusa class cruisers and another flotilla of destroyers, the H class. The latter was the penultimate class of a series of seventy-seven destroyers constructed to a largely standardised design derived from that of the V and W class destroyers and Scott and Shakespeare class flotilla leaders which were beginning to enter service shortly before the Armistice on 11 November 1918.

British destroyer development 1908-16

The early British destroyers were designed to protect the battlefleet from attack by enemy torpedo boats and consequently were known as Torpedo Boat Destroyers (TBD). In order to be effective, the latter had to be faster, more seaworthy and have a heavier gun armament than contemporary torpedo boats. The TBDs were also equipped with torpedoes and consequently could also be employed offensively against an enemy battlefleet but this was considered to be very much a secondary function. However, developments in torpedo technology led to a reappraisal of TBD capabilities and functions.

Thus, compared to earlier TBDs, the vessels of the G or Beagle class of the 1908-09 programme displaced 950 tons with a top speed of twenty-seven knots and had a much-improved armament consisting of one 4-inch and three 12-pounder guns plus two tubes for 21-inch torpedoes. The latter weapon was not only considerably more destructive than earlier torpedoes but also had a range of 12,000 yards at thirty knots which equated to the effective gun range of battleships of the period. The introduction of the 21-inch torpedo meant that one fleet could fire torpedoes into the centre of an oncoming opposing fleet which was six miles away. It was argued[3] that, although these so-called 'browning'[4] shots were unlikely to hit specific ships, they had a good chance of hitting some of the closely spaced ships in the enemy battlefleet and thereby could force the latter to fight at longer ranges which would favour the British with their superior gunnery control.

The incremental improvements in subsequent classes were shown to good effect in the L class of 1912 which had a full load displacement in excess of 1,000 tons and carried three 4-inch guns as well as four 21-inch torpedo tubes. The Ls set the pattern for subsequent 235 M, R and S class destroyers built during the First World War. Completed with either two or three funnels, their bridge was no more than sixty feet from the bow and consequently was very wet in a seaway. Furthermore, the bridge was so far forward that personnel manning this flimsy structure were subjected to violent movements in quite moderate weather and their performance declined as the sea state increased.

The larger Kempenfelt class flotilla leaders, which were armed with four 4-inch guns and entered service in 1915-16, fared no better and the desirability of the bridge positions being as far aft as practicable caused this design to be reviewed again at the Admiralty in March 1916. A new design was prepared in which the bridge moved aft by about thirteen feet, the first and second funnels were combined and the forecastle deck extended aft. No. 2 gun, formerly on a platform between the first two funnels, was moved to a position on the forecastle on a deckhouse, a blast screen being provided to protect the crew of No. 1 gun. The deckhouse was utilised to provide further accommodation for officers. Right-ahead fire for two guns was thus secured, and the upper gun became capable of being manned in weather which would preclude the fighting of No. 1 gun[5]. These modifications were effected in the six-strong Grenville class which had been ordered in 1915 and entered service in 1917.

Enter the V class

Probably the most innovative and iconic destroyer design of the period owes its existence to the adoption of geared turbines in the R Class destroyers then building. Because the latter were likely to be significantly faster than the Kempenfelt class leaders, this led to the design, in April 1916, of a new flotilla leader utilising the same machinery as the R Class TBDs so as to expedite construction[6]. The smaller machinery power enabled the Kempenfelt class armament to be carried on a vessel 15 feet shorter. Furthermore, the V class leaders were faster than the Kempenfelts because the saving in weight obtained by having a shorter vessel with lower-powered machinery coupled with the increase in machinery and propeller efficiency due to the adoption of geared turbines. Compared with the Grenville class, the bridge in these new leaders was fifteen feet further aft, accommodation was increased and they were £50,000 cheaper to build. The V leaders carried the same number of guns as the Kempenfelt and Grenville classes but they had higher velocity and increased range, namely four 4-inch QF Mark V on C.P. II mountings with 30° elevation. Two 4-inch guns were superimposed forward in 'A' and 'B' positions two 4-inch superimposed aft in 'X' and 'Y' positions. One 3-inch 20-cwt Mark III high-angle gun was mounted on a platform aft of the funnels for anti-aircraft purposes. Two pairs of 21-inch double revolving torpedo tubes and four torpedoes were carried, except in *Vampire*, which had two sets of triple 21-inch torpedo tubes and six torpedoes.

Five vessels, *Valkyrie*, *Valorous*, *Valentine*, *Valhalla* and Vampire were ordered during April to July 1916 with delivery scheduled to begin from June 1917. The new leaders were a great improvement over earlier designs, with good seakeeping and a powerful gun armament, with their superimposed guns in 'B' and 'X' positions being able to fight in very heavy weather. They had a distinctive appearance with a tall thin fore funnel and a shorter fatter second funnel.

In response to reports that the Germans were building large destroyers the Admiralty Board decided in June 1916 that it was necessary to have destroyers of greater gun power than the R Class. Compared with the latter, the enhanced gun power was to be obtained by adding a fourth 4-inch gun as well superimposing two of the four guns. In order to obtain such destroyers within the minimum time of construction, twenty-five vessels were ordered to be of the same dimensions, form and arrangement as the V Class flotilla leaders already designed but with modification to their bridge and accommodation to render them more suitable for destroyer work[7]. Decks were strengthened to take triple 21-inch torpedo tubes, and bridges were strengthened with canvas screens being replaced by steel plating. The first of the class entered service in August 1917 and the last in June of the following year. In December 1916 orders were placed for twenty-three repeat V class but equipped with the triple 21-inch torpedo tubes which had not been available earlier. Known as the W class, two ships were cancelled in April 1917 and remainder were completed between November 1917 and October 1918.

The proven superiority of the V and W classes of destroyers at sea over the R class together with a perceived need for a longer-range gun armament for these vessels, led to the placing of the orders in January and April 1918 for a further fifty-four vessels to the V Class design. It was decided that the 4-inch QF Mark V guns of the V and W Classes should be replaced by 4.7-inch guns as mounted in the Scott and Shakespeare class flotilla leaders. The armament therefore consisted of four 4.7-inch BL guns, one 3-inch HA gun and two sets of triple tubes for 21-inch torpedoes[8]. Only sixteen of these ships were completed, mostly between April 1919 and June 1920, with the thirty-eight being cancelled after the Armistice between November 1918 and September of the following year.

Scott and Shakespeare class flotilla leaders

In early 1916, at the time the V class leaders were being designed, Admiral Jellicoe indicated the need for a flotilla leader of greater size and displacement in order to combat the severe weather conditions experienced in the North Sea. At about the same time there were also reports that German destroyers mounting 5-inch guns were being constructed and consequently the DNC was instructed to design ships capable of meeting this new challenge. Fortuitously, Thornycroft had submitted a design for a new flotilla leader and the DNC reported that, if fitted with 5-inch guns, it would meet this new requirement. Because the Navy did not have a 5-inch gun in its inventory the Army's 4.7-inch gun was utilised instead in the new Admiralty design which was to become the Scott class. The result was an armament consisting of five 4.7-inch BL Mk I guns on C.P. VI mountings arranged as in the V Class but with an extra gun on top of fan intakes between funnels plus two sets of 21-inch triple torpedo tubes[9]. This made them the most heavily armed destroyers in the world which together with the addition of a nine-foot rangefinder as well as torpedo sights on the bridge resulted in a massive improvement in fighting efficiency.

One vessel only, *Scott*, was ordered to this design in April 1916, but two similar vessels, *Shakespeare* and *Spenser*, were ordered about the same date from Thornycroft to their form, the general arrangement being similar to the Admiralty design. The large flat-sided funnels of the Thornycroft vessels made them appear larger than those completed to the Admiralty design. Subsequently, repeat Scotts were ordered in December 1916 (*Bruce & Douglas*) and April 1917 (*Campbell, Mackay, Malcolm, Montrose* and *Stuart*). One repeat Shakespeare (*Wallace*) was ordered in April 1917, followed by six more in April 1918 (*Barrington, Hughes, Keppel,*

Rooke, Saunders and *Spragge*). After the Armistice *Rooke* was renamed *Broke* while *Barrington, Hughes, Saunders* and *Spragge* were cancelled.

Thus it was that the Royal Navy ended the First World War with the finest destroyers afloat as represented by the 1,325 ton V /W and Modified V/W classes and the 1,500 ton Leaders of the Shakespeare and Scott classes all of which had an endurance of 3,200-3,500 nautical miles at fifteen knots. Unsurprisingly, these ships set the style of the destroyers in service with many navies in the 1920s and early 1930s.

Post War Destroyer Construction

The huge number of destroyers built during the conflict meant that there was no urgency to recommence destroyer construction in the early 1920s. Great War experience showed that fleet destroyers required a large fuel capacity and endurance for screening purposes while a heavy torpedo armament was considered to be of primary importance for fleet action. The Admiralty envisaged that the next generation of destroyers would be about the same size as the Scott class leaders, armed with four 4.7-inch and two 2pdr guns and at least six 21-inch torpedoes and equipped with Asdic and depth charges. Endurance was expected to be about 5,000 nautical miles at twelve knots. However, the designs offered to the Admiralty in November 1923 specified ships which were 300-600 tons greater than the Scott class leaders with an endurance of 4,500-5,000 nautical miles at twelve knots.

In the event, the Admiralty felt that these proposed destroyers would be too large and when the prototypes were ordered in 1924 the Admiralty specified ships similar to the most recent design available, namely Thornycroft's Modified W class. The two foremost destroyer builders, Thornycroft and Yarrow, were selected and given a free hand within the Admiralty's broad specifications to evolve a standard type. Consequently, the prototypes *Amazon* and *Ambuscade* were generally similar to the Modified W class but with two knots more speed, all-steel bridges, improved habitability and a wider radius of action. From them stemmed the seventy-nine ships of A to I classes which formed eight full flotillas of nine vessels, a half flotilla of five vessels plus two additional vessels for the RCN.

The central British destroyer tactical concept of the inter-war period remained the long-range browning shot. Consequently, in July 1926, during discussion of the requirements for a class of destroyers to be built under the 1927 Estimates, it was agreed that emphasis should be placed on torpedo attack. This requirement, which dominated British destroyer design into the Second World War and beyond, seems strange in light of the lack of success of ship-launched torpedoes during the Great War. However, it can be argued that fear of torpedo attack may have had an effect out of all proportion to the results actually achieved[10].

At about this time the Royal Navy believed that the antidote to the submarine was an Asdic-equipped destroyer armed with depth charges while the antidote to mines laid in the path on the oncoming fleet was the Two-Speed Destroyer Sweep (TSDS). The latter could be used as a search sweep ahead of the fleet, as a protective sweep, or as a clearance sweep and was effective against simple moored mines at twelve knots and above. However, it was felt that a destroyer equipped with both would suffer from a congested quarterdeck and therefore it was envisaged that flotillas of destroyers would be alternately equipped with Asdic or TSDS. In 1928 it was decided that all destroyers would be built with trunks and offices so that Asdic could be installed even if completed as TSDS ships. Turning to the 4.7-inch gun armament of these new destroyers, it was decided that their mountings had to be hand-operated because loss of power would cause their inactivation. In comparison, hand-worked guns could remain in action as long as there was a man alive to load them.

A major factor influencing British naval policy and construction programmes was budgetary economy which, of course, accorded with the contemporary Government policy of orthodox and deflationary finance. Another factor that further reduced naval construction was the notorious 'Ten Year Rule' which was instituted in 1919 and assumed that there would be no major war for ten years from that date. Unfortunately, in June 1928 the Chancellor of the Exchequer, Winston Churchill, made this rule self-perpetuating. Add to that baleful influence of the politically naïve naval treaties of the period and one can well imagine why, with the limited funds at their disposal, the Admiralty deliberately built medium-sized destroyers which showed only minimal improvement over the Scott class leaders.

The A – I classes

The replacement programme began with the leader *Codrington* and eight A class destroyers of the 1927-8 programme. Their displacement was 1,330 (standard) tons and they measured 312 feet between the perpendiculars, with a beam of 32 feet 3 inches and a draft of 8 feet 6 inches. Their machinery developed 34,000 shp to give a top speed of 34.5 knots and a range of 5,000 nautical miles at fifteen knots. The Leader *Codrington* was 200 tons heavier and armed with a fifth 4.7-inch gun between the funnels. However, *Keith*, *Kempenfelt* and *Duncan*, the leaders of the subsequent B, C and D classes respectively, were the same size as the destroyers and armed with four 4.7-inch guns.

The B class of the 1928-9 programme was a slightly modified version of the A class being fitted with Asdic rather than TSDS, while the C class of the following year had a separate rangefinder and Director Control Tower (DCT) on the bridge. The subsequent D class of 1930-1 were essentially repeats of the earlier Cs but had a single 3-inch HA gun between the funnels. The ships of the E class (1931-2 programme), which were fitted with TSDS, Asdic and depth charge throwers, had a close range AA armament of a pair of quadruple 0.5-inch machine-gun mountings. The elevation of the 4.7-inch in the CP Mk XIV mounting in the A to D classes was 30 degrees but this was increased to 40 degrees in the E to G classes with the MK XVII mount by raising the trunnions four and a half inches and dropping the mount into a pit with flaps which could be closed for low angle fire. Two ships, *Esk* and *Express*, were intended to serve as minelayers, having landed their A and Y guns and torpedo tubes, but were convertible to TSDS ships at short notice. The Leader *Exmouth* was a derivative of the earlier *Codrington* and was armed with a fifth 4.7-inch gun between the funnels. The destroyers of the F class (1932-3 programme) introduced 40 degree 4.7-inch mountings, Asdic and TSDS as well as the Mk IX torpedo while the leader, *Faulknor*, was a repeat of *Exmouth*.

The provisions of the London Treaty of 1930 meant that it was essential to save tonnage on each ship of the G class of 1933-4 programme and this was achieved by reducing the lengths of the engine and boiler rooms as well as machinery power. Torpedo batteries were an essential component of the tactical doctrine of the Royal Navy's destroyers and one of the class, *Glowworm*, introduced the quintuple torpedo tube and carried ten 21-inch torpedoes. The leader *Grenville* was forty tons lighter than *Faulknor* but still carried five 4.7-inch guns.

Havock and her sisters

On 13 July 1934 the Admiralty Board decided that the 1,350 ton H class of the 1934-5 programme would be repeats of the G class but with extensive use of welding to save weight.

The H class were fitted with the heavier CP XVIII 4.7-inch gun mounting which permitted 40 degree elevation without the need for pits. *Hereward*, acted as a trials ship for the large, powered experimental twin 4.7-inch gun mountings which were to be installed in the Tribal class destroyers which were then being designed. The mounting was fitted in B position and this necessitated a new bridge structure with angled faces. When the prototype twin 4.7-inch gun mounting was removed in 1937 single 4.7-inch guns were mounted in A and B positions. *Hero* was also completed with the new style bridge which proved to be both simpler and more efficient than in previous classes and was adopted by the subsequent I class of 1935-6 and all subsequent classes until the post-war Darings. The leader *Hardy* was a repeat of *Grenville* with three inches more beam and a tripod foremast.

The I class of 1936 was the last of eight-and-a-half flotillas constructed to what had by then become an outdated and obsolescent design. In many ways, these destroyers were as good as any in the category in the world with outstanding all-round and weatherly qualities but they suffered from two serious defects. The first was the Staff preoccupation with warfare in the North Sea and Mediterranean which led to inadequate endurance and the second was their negligible anti-aircraft capability. British destroyers of the inter-war period are often criticised rightly for their poor AA capability, it being believed during the mid-1920s-30s that a rapidly manoeuvring destroyer was an impossible target for a bomber. That being the case, the Admiralty was satisfied that a pair of single 2-pounder pompoms or quadruple 0.5-inch machine-guns would provide adequate defence. Although their medium calibre guns could contribute to the long-range defence of the battle fleet, for which an elevation of 30 to 40 degrees was quite sufficient, the Admiralty had chosen the wrong AA system by rejecting a tachymetric control system in favour of a guessed estimate of aircraft movements. The lack of a suitable dual-purpose gun and high-angle control system for destroyers was keenly felt and, although the 4-inch AA gun was available with an elementary high-angle fire control system, there was a natural reluctance to drop to a smaller calibre when many foreign destroyers were mounting 5-inch and heavier guns. Far less explicable was the Admiralty's rejection of the 20mm Oerlikon and the 40mm Bofors guns, both of which had been available pre-war.

Tenders for the H class destroyers had been invited on 15 August 1934, received on 25 September and the vessels ordered on 13 December of that year. The contracts for *Havock* and her sister *Hasty* were awarded to William Denny and Brothers of Dumbarton, the *Dundee Courier* of 26 December 1934 reporting that:

> Dennys has received a contract for two destroyers of the 1934 programme and work will commence on these early next year.

Havock was laid down on 15 May 1935, launched on 7 July 1936 and completed on 6 January of the following year. The Portsmouth Evening News of 20 January 1937 reported that:

> HMS Havock, completed by Messers Denny & Brothers, Dumbarton, receives her full crew at Chatham today for service with the 2nd Destroyer Flotilla. She is to leave for Portland on 2 February 1937.

Chapter 2

Spanish Civil War
(January 1937 – March 1939)

On Saturday 31 January 1937, only two weeks after her completion and trials, *Havock* prepared to sail from Chatham to the Mediterranean, her designated theatre of operation, to take part in exercises and visits. A new crew and a new ship would surely take time to shake down into an effective and efficient naval unit and most of the following months were used for just this purpose, but perhaps not well enough, as we shall see.

During the course of the week before departure from Chatham, stores and ammunition were loaded and the shield of 'B' gun was painted with red, white and blue stripes to allow immediate identification as a neutral in the Spanish Civil War zone[1].

On Friday 6 February, *Havock* slipped her moorings at Chatham and arrived in Portland the next day before subsequently sailing on for Gibraltar, the gateway to the Mediterranean. She stopped briefly to refuel at Gibraltar, before sailing on to Malta, quite unaware of the close ties she would form with that brave island. She was now formally assigned to the Second Destroyer Flotilla (DF2) and her home station, despite involvement in much activity elsewhere, would be the Mediterranean until the end of her days.

As soon as she arrived at Malta *Havock* found herself in at the deep end in the Spanish Civil War. Many of the typically superstitious sailors were quick to note that it was Friday the 13th, and therefore doom and disaster were bound to strike before they could get a suntan! They were almost proved right when the one-month-old ship, not many days out of Chatham and quite unprepared for a first taste of action, was bombed on 13 February while en route to Malta with her fellow destroyer *Gipsy*.[2] Lieutenant Commander Courage submitted his secret report to Admiral Pound two days later.

H.M.S *Havock*, at Malta
15 February 1937

Secret

No A/41 - I have the honour to submit the following report on the bombing (13 February) of H.M. Ships *Havock* and *Gipsy* while on passage between Gibraltar and Malta.

2 - At 16.15 H.M.S. *Havock* and *Gipsy* had completed picking up lifebuoys and were proceeding on a course of 083 degrees. *Gipsy* at 14 knots *Havock* at 17 knots to take up position for T.D. 55.

3 - At 1637 an aeroplane was sighted bearing 150° and as *Havock* was in position 37 degrees 00' N 01' 10' E, it was assumed to be a French Mail or Military plane.

4 - The plane passed slightly ahead of *Havock* on a course of 350 degrees and at 1640 two large bombs assumed to be 250 lbs. fell on the port beam of *Havock* abreast 'B' Gun and about 50-70 yards away.

5 - Action Stations were immediately sounded and ammunition provided at all guns.

6 - H.E. ammunition had been struck down earlier as ships were well clear of Spanish Waters and bad weather was expected

7 - AT 1640 H.M.S. *Gipsy* reported that she was ready to open fire and I ordered her to carry on, though her Commanding Officer had already exercised his initiative and commenced with his machine guns. At 1642 he fired two rounds of S.A.P. which was the only ammunition he had on deck to indicate that he was being engaged. At the same time both ships hoisted White Ensigns at the masthead and spread Union Flags on the Torpedo Tubes.

8 - At 1643 the aeroplane circled round to port to 180° and steered to pass astern of *Gipsy*.

9 - At 1645 when astern of *Gipsy* the aeroplane altered to the same course obviously preparing another attack. Both ships altered course to Starboard and increased to full speed.

10 - Fire was opened with 0.5 machine guns. The aeroplane altered course to counteract *Gipsy's* manoeuvre and about 1646 ½ four bombs were seen to leave the machine.

10a - *Gipsy* promptly altered course further to Starboard and *Havock* to Port and the bombs fell between the two ships about 100 yards from Gipsy and 300 from *Havock*.

11 - As the bombs fell the aeroplane altered course to the North and steered towards Majorca.

12 - The markings on the under wing of the aeroplane appeared to be light and dark bands running fore and aft which were

assumed to be the Insurgent Markings as confirmed by *Gipsy* who has seen these before.

13 - The aeroplane was a four-engined Junker Type monoplane and was proceeding about 90 m.p.h. at a height of 6,000 feet. throughout the attack.

14 - The bombs dropped in the second attack were at first thought to be two 400-500 lb. bombs and two light bombs, but it is possible that all were of 250 lbs. and that the two 'heavy ones' burst further under water and gave an impression of greater weight, while the two lighter ones failed to explode.

15 - No damage was sustained by either ship, nor did the fire of our guns appear to effect the machine.

16 - H.M.S. *Gipsy's* report is enclosed and also her diagram which is concurred in.

Of the incident, John Thomson, *Havock* Signals Telegraphist, remembered[3]:

I happened to be off watch at the time. It was a fine sunny day and I was on the upper deck. I don't recall anyone seeing the aircraft until it was quite close. When it did finally drop its load nobody was more surprised than us. We experienced a problem in firing the 4.7s as no one knew where the keys to the ready-use locker ammunition were. Perhaps this is something not talked about too much! After all, we had only just sailed from Gibraltar for our first look at the Med.

Frank 'Nobby' Hall, *Havock* Signals Telegraphist, recollected[4]:

As regards the bombing of *Havock* and *Gipsy* a follow-up occurred. Must have been sometime during the last dog watch when a number of darkened ships were sighted ahead of *Havock* on a reciprocal course. Emergency alteration of course was made to starboard. The ships were illuminated by searchlight. No reply to our signals. The ships were observed to be a Spanish Government cruiser and destroyers. Was the bombing a case of mistaken identity?

Another crew member, Able Seaman Griff 'Jess' Gleed-Owen, wrote a letter home to his mother, covering the period Friday 12 to Monday, 15th of February 1937, revealing the unpreparedness of the 'green' crew for its intervention duties[5]:

> Well I've been under fire at last! I expect you'll hear all about it on the wireless tonight. The *Gipsy* and us were doing an evolution pretending that a man had fallen overboard and seeing which of us could have the life-buoys over and lower a whaler to pick him up first. We'd just 'rescued' the man and raised the boats and were still on the upper deck when suddenly we heard a terrific explosion. I thought at first that we had fired a gun to denote that we had completed the manoeuvre, then someone said 'Blimey, we've been bombed' and sure enough, less than 50 yards off our port bow was a terrific splash in the water and above us was a monoplane.
>
> There were tons of excitement on board and the 0.5 gun crews were piped to close up. Then we were piped to actions stations and we rushed up to the guns and started clearing away for action. I was pretty scared. I felt like doing an Ostrich and bunging my head in a funk hole. It's a horrible feeling to see a 'plane dropping bombs on you and you've got no ammo ready to your guns. We could feel the wind from that bomb it was so close. It was a pretty good shot, and if the wind hadn't blown it off to one side we'd have got it right on our foc'sle and it would have gone right through our decks down to the fore' magazine and sunk us for certain.
>
> As we're a new ship's company we have never done any drill yet in supplying ammunition to the guns and as it all has to be hoisted up from the mags below decks by means of hoists it takes a lot of organisation and coop-eration to maintain a constant and immediate supply of ammo to the guns. Well we, or rather the ammo supply party, had to hunt around for hoists, keys to unlock mag-azines, etc, and it was about three quarters of an hour before we could get even 20 rounds up to the guns. Well after dropping her first bomb off our bow the plane cir-cled away to the horizon, she was about 6,000 ft. and as she went the *Gipsy* opened up with her 'B' Gun and one 0.5 inch.
>
> The *Gipsy*, in common with all British ships in the Med, had all her ready use lockers round the guns ready filled with ammunition and so she could open up imme-diately. But she only had S.A.P. (semi-armour piercing)

shell for use against ships and that's no good against an
aeroplane unless a direct hit is scored, which is unlikely.
So of course, the *Gipsy* missed the plane and by that time
I'd run aft to get our gun telescopes it was starting to
circle back. The organisation was very bad, I had to look
for the G.I. because he had the key of the keyboard and
then I had to find the key of the telescope cupboards and
get the gun telescopes out and up to the gun, by then I
heard that the plane had dropped 4 more bombs at the
Gipsy and I came up just in time to see it disappearing.
I found later that the first she dropped at us was really
two together and they landed about 40 yards ahead of us
and 30 yards off to port. The officer of the watch had seen
the bombs dropping and had swerved to miss them. The
next two were just ahead of and either side of the *Gipsy*'s
bows and the other two between the ships. As that type
of plane, a German Junkers, only carries 6 bombs she
had to buzz off after unloading. We remained at the
guns until supper and then started cruising stations in 4
watches all the night through.

Sunday: I had the morning watch at defence stations
on 'B' Gun, from 4 a.m. until 8 a.m. We sat around the
gun straining our eyes for signs of enemy planes or ships
because at about 8 p.m. last night, just when we were
congratulating ourselves on having got away with losing the plane the first watchmen reported a ship without
any lights ahead and sure enough when I went to look
we'd trained our searchlights on it, a damn great Spanish
Government Cruiser[6] on our port quarter and another
to starboard. I was expecting them to think we were
insurgent destroyers and open fire on us, and our 4.7s
wouldn't have had much chance against their 6-inch,
and we carried no warheads on our torpedoes.

The general opinion is that had we been carrying no
lights we'd have been fired upon. They have lost their
harbour lately you see and now have nowhere to go
so just sail about the Med like the Flying Dutchman.
Everyone was scared when we saw the cruisers and we
heard gunfire ahead at about the same time.

We get to Malta tomorrow p.m. Last night the Skipper
spoke to the POs of the supply parties and told them that
they had been as poor as haddock water at organising
the supply of ammo. He said he blamed himself also
for not having had a supply of ammo ready at the guns

before as the other ships had. Because we really did put up a shocking show, we weren't cleared for action for at least half an hour which of course is terrible even for a new ship and ship's company.

We're in sight of Malta, we'll be in soon. I'm the buoy jumper i.e. I've got to go in the whaler, hop off onto the buoy and shackle our cable to it. The last jumper was pulled into the 'drink' by the cable but I'll have a life line round my guts.

After recovering from the bombing incident, *Havock* spent the rest of February and March in and around Malta, lapping up the sun and the beer, known as 'Blues' from its label. For most of the crew this was their first trip abroad and they were going to make the most of it. *Havock* continued to work up with her flotilla mates until on 14 April, *Hardy* (D2 Leader), *Hotspur*, *Hereward*, *Hasty* and *Havock* were anchored in St Paul's Bay where platoons, plus mouth-organ band, were landed for a route march while the remainder were left behind to exercise General Drill.

The week of 26 April, found *Havock* in Sliema Creek, Malta. This was the land of the 'Blues', the 'Gut'[7], Tony's Bar, Sliema Wanderers Supporters Club and many more regular haunts. Following this period of 'tiring' relaxation *Havock* left Malta on 3 May, with the Commander-in-Chief and Rear Admiral (Destroyers) for patrols off the coast of Spain in connection with more Spanish Civil war non-intervention duties. On the 5th *Hostile* was sent to patrol off Barcelona and on the 7th the remainder of the flotilla split to monitor various Spanish ports, *Hunter* to Almeria, *Hyperion* to Malaga, *Hero* to Huelva and *Hasty* to Cadiz, while *Hardy*, *Hotspur* and *Havock* fell on the stony ground of Gibraltar.

After more patrolling *Havock* fuelled and stored left Gibraltar on 30 May, to relieve *Vanoc* off Malaga for patrol duties from 31 May to 8 June. On 10 June, *Havock* returned to Gibraltar from Malaga to refuel and re-store having completed her patrol. No sooner was this done than she returned again on 12 June to the Malaga patrol. This process of patrol and relief was finally broken when on 15 June, the DF 2 was relieved of patrol duties by the DF1 after which DF2 sailed for Malta spending four days exercising with the fleet on passage. They arrived in Malta on the 20th rested and practiced in turn

The days of 8-14 July was spent cleaning the ship and exercising 'Action Stations'. On 28-30 of the month it was out to sea again for minesweeping and concentration firing practice.

By 14 August, on arrival in Spanish waters, DF2 parted company with *Havock* and *Active*, which were sent to Valencia. A week later on the 20th *Havock* again joined *Active* at Marseilles, via Barcelona. Two days later on the 22nd *Havock* retraced her steps to Barcelona and Palma and, eventually, her roaming brought her to Valencia on the 28th. This whole period had allowed a green crew to work together with their machinery, weapons and flotilla compatriots all of which was to be very useful when the 'fun' of the war commenced.

Meanwhile, the influx of Soviet arms and equipment into Republican Government territory during the summer of 1937 had resulted in Mussolini ordering the so-called 'pirate submarine' campaign during the summer of 1937. Thus, from 6 August to 13 September Italian submarines undertook fifty-nine missions across the entire Mediterranean to interdict Soviet merchant ships supplying Republican forces. The most famous incident of this campaign was the unintentional attack by the submarine *Iride* on the destroyer *Havock* on the night of 31 August/1 September. Suddenly the tranquillity of never-ending patrolling was shattered by a signal from *Havock* which read 'Attacked by S/M in 38.46M, 00.31E; am hunting S/M'[8].

Whilst steaming at night between Valencia and Cartagena, *Havock* spotted a torpedo, evidently meant for her, passing astern. Strenuous hunting with depth charges followed to bring the submarine to the surface before the search was abandoned. The submarine was the Italian Perla class *Iride*[9] commanded by 'Prince' Junio Valerio Borghese[10], and was damaged by the depth charging. The Italians allegedly lost two men killed during the incident. Later the Italians claimed it was a mistake and had intended attacking a Spanish Government destroyer[11]. Newspapers reported that the submarine was believed to have been sunk by depth charges from *Havock*. The incident was widely reported in various newspapers with the following stories:

THE EVENING NEWS
(Wednesday September 1, 1937)

BRITISH WARSHIP ATTACKED OFF SPAIN
Unknown Submarine Fires in the Night – Her Torpedo Misses

WHY DESTROYERS LEFT GIBRALTAR
Ordered to Go at Once to Scene of New Attack

HAVOCK FIRED AT OFF SPAIN'S EAST COAST

Britain's Destroyer Havock, previously the target of aerial bombs in the Mediterranean, was, it was revealed today, attacked off the east coast of Spain last night by an unknown submarine.

Havock was on patrol off Cape San Antonio, in Spanish Red Government territory between Alicante and Valencia, when she was attacked. News of the attack was received at the Admiralty in London today.

It was stated at the Admiralty that the submarine fired at the Havock – with a torpedo it is believed, but she was not hit.

Two British Destroyers – the Flotilla leader Hardy and the Hyperion – are speeding to the scene of the attack.

Hardy and Hyperion left Gibraltar last night in a hurry and sailed eastwards. Officers and men had suddenly been recalled, aboard the two ships, from cafes and hotels.

Why the Hardy and Hyperion were sailing, where they were sailing, none of the Commanders knew. News of the attack on the Havock gave the answer.

Rear Admiral J.F. Somerville, in the Cruiser Galatea, Rear Admiral commanding destroyer flotillas of the Mediterranean Fleet, had ordered the Hardy and Hyperion to leave Gibraltar at once for the scene of the attack on Havock.

Last February the Havock and the destroyer Gipsy were bombed by a big warplane about 20 miles off Cape Tenes on the Algerian coast. Six bombs were dropped near the warships, but neither was hit.

The Destroyers opened fire on the plane, which then made off in the direction of the Balearic Islands. It was believed to be Spanish, an anti-Red machine.

Havock was launched in July last year. She is of 1,335 tons belonging to the Hero class of destroyers and carries an armament of four 4.7 inch guns and eight 21-inch torpedo tubes. Lieut-Commander R.E. Courage has commanded her since last January, when she was completed.

On Thursday, 2 September 1937, following the incident, *Havock, Active* and *Hasty* arrived back at Gibraltar. The *Daily Mirror* of 1 September 1937 noted that:

DESTROYERS RETURN TO GIBRALTAR

The Destroyer Havock returned to Gibraltar today. She was accompanied by Hasty, which had been assisting in the search for the unknown submarine.

Men of the crew of HMS Havock state that they saw torpedoes approaching. Thereupon the Havock zig-zagged and dropped depth charges. She signalled to the Cruiser Galatea and other British men of war.

Watch was kept by the warships for several hours over a 1-15 miles' radius, but no submarine came to the surface. The men believed, however, that the submarine had sunk, as oil was seen on the surface soon after.

On Thursday, 2 September1937 the *Daily Express* staff reporter in Gibraltar wrote:

RAIDER SUNK, CREW SAY

Lieutenant-Commander Rafe Courage, of the Destroyer Havock, brought his ship into Gibraltar early today and stepped ashore for an urgent conference with Rear-Admiral Evans, Gibraltar naval chief.

This I understand is the tenor of the report he made:

The Havock was steaming past San Antonio (midway between Valencia and Cartagena) in the darkness of Tuesday night when a submarine, about to submerge, was seen a few hundred yards away to port.

There was no clue to the nationality of the submarine, but the fact that it was about to attack was apparent and the Havock went into action.

By the time the Destroyer had swung round, the submarine was totally submerged. Its periscope, then its conning tower, reappeared on the starboard side and while the Havock was slewing round to face in the new direction a torpedo fired from the submarine began cutting across the calm sea.

It passed harmlessly by Havock's stern and exploded when about three hundred yards away.

Havock, now cleared for action, raced towards the spot where the submarine was submerging again.

It sank too quickly to be attacked on the surface, but the Havock's submarine sound apparatus picked up the noise of the throbbing engines in the depths below. When the instruments showed that the submarine was directly beneath, a quick command was snapped to the waiting gunnery crew.

Five cylindrical depth charges were dropped overboard. The Destroyer was rocked along its length by the explosions many feet down in the inky sea. The men at the sound controls reported that the noise of the submarines engines had ceased. By daybreak several other British warships were on the scene following the Havock's radio message, and a seaplane was

launched from the Cruiser Galatea to follow a mile-long streak of oil across the sea.
The search yielded nothing, and the opinion among the Havock's crew is that there is nothing to find, for they say that the raider was sent to the bottom.

The matter of 'pirate submarine' attacks came to a head, when, on 1 September, the British tanker *Woodford* was torpedoed and sunk by the Italian submarine *Diaspro* off the Columbretes Islands while en route to Valencia. These two incidents resulted in a conference of nine European nations held at Nyon from 10 September. The countries agreed to provide warships, with orders to sink any submarine attacking a non-Spanish ship, to patrol the Mediterranean. An agreement was signed at Nyon on 14 September and there were no further acts of piracy in the Mediterranean thereafter.

After this excitement, it was back to the inevitable patrolling and *Havock* arrived in Gibraltar again on 8 September, left on the 10th, arrived in Valencia on the 11th, Barcelona 12th and Palma on the 14th. The torpedo incident passed into history and the DF2 assembled in Palma on the 15th, short of food, an event that was to become commonplace in the years of war ahead. But by 20 September, *Havock* and *Hotspur* were back at Malta to enjoy the pleasures of 'Blues and Gut' with the result-ant hangovers. For the remainder of 1937 and all of 1938 mun-dane and monotonous patrolling, exercises and practices filled the time.[12]

On 29 September 1938, Stoker Albert Goodey, the lead author's father, joined the ship's company and stayed with her for just over three years, covering her most active period. Like many oth-ers 'he saw too much action' and suffered nightmares after the war and into the 1950s.

On February 10th 1939 Sub-Lieutenant John Burfield joined *Havock*. As a key figure and eventually First Lieutenant during the rest of her life, John provided the lead author, in the 1980s, with an authoritative personal history[13] of his experiences on board, much of which is included in the remainder of this vol-ume. Here is the story of his journey to join *Havock*:

At 11.00 on Thursday 9 February, 1939 I boarded a train at London, Victoria station to join *Havock* in the Mediterranean. Little did I know that I would be with her for the rest of her days, a little over three years. I settled into my first class seat and the train headed for

Dover and the cross channel steamer. From Calais to
Paris I took an eight-hour Pullman, the lights of which
packed up at sunset and candles in ashtrays provided
the light for the remainder of the journey.

At 20.00 the train left the station pulled by a huge
steam engine, much bigger than English engines. I was
in a luxurious first class cabin – the standard level of
travel for British naval officers. I discovered that what
I thought was a cupboard door was in fact a connecting
door to the next cabin, which belonged to a young lady.
The door remained securely locked on both sides during
the journey although not necessarily by my choice!

At 08.00 on Friday 10 February the train arrived at
Marseilles. The climate was completely different with
the sun shining and the mimosa out everywhere. I took a
taxi to the docks to find *Havock*. On arrival, I was greeted
by Gunner Leslie Millns, later Captain Millns CBE, who
was officer of the day. Millns helped get the luggage
aboard and was most helpful. But there was nobody else
around. Apparently, they had all gone ashore to give a
departing member of the crew a good send off.

On Havock I replaced Sub-lieutenant Alistair Bruce
who moved up to navigational duties. Sadly, he was to
be lost later in the war. As the new 'subbie' I took over
the duties of torpedo control officer on the bridge, officer
of the watch when in action and anti-submarine officer;
all of these activities were served from the bridge. Other
duties included correspondence (Captain's Secretary),
keeping of the confidential books, on the foc'sle when
weighing anchor and also quarter deck division to look
after. Finally, the tobacco and stationery accounts for the
ward room.

Britain supported the Republican Government during the bitter
Spanish Civil War against Franco's Nationalists. Many nations
participated in the 'Nyon Patrols' between Marseilles and
Barcelona designed to stop overt interference from Nazi Germany
and Fascist Italy. By the beginning of 1939, it was clear that it was
only a matter of time before the Nationalist forces achieved total
victory which was due in part to the highly effective blockade of
Government ports by the Nationalist Navy.

Havock arrived in Barcelona in the forenoon of 12 February
1939. The harbour had suffered significant damage from bombing
and some thirty ships had been gutted or sunk, including a prison

ship. The next day she arrived at Palma and stayed until the 20th. The cruiser *Devonshire* was there having just negotiated the handing over of Menorca to the victorious Nationalists. Unusually, on 22 February, General Franco took the opportunity to review his fleet at Palma – thirty-eight days before the war ended.

On the 21st while at Gandia, *Havock* took on a prisoner in exchange for another returning to Marseilles on the 22nd, *Havock* discharged her prisoner as well as twelve men from SS *Locky* which had been bombed in Gandia. *Havock* sailed for Palma at 16.30 on the 23rd but the passage was very rough and sleep was well-nigh impossible. PO Gunner Freddie Kemp was unceremoniously thrown out of his bunk by the rolling action. John Burfield tied his own wrist to the bunk rail or got a scarf and wove it across him to stop the rolling motion. At meal times the chairs slid all over the room whether in use or not. Food, personal effects and other detritus was everywhere.[14] Arriving at Palma on the 24th *Havock* then sailed on to Gibraltar arriving on the 26th. From 28 February to 10 March, she participated in combined Home Fleet / Mediterranean Fleet exercises out of Gibraltar.

A typical officer's day at this time was described by John Burfield:[15]

24.00 - 04.30	Bridge
08.00 - 12.00	Bridge
12.30 - 16.00	Bridge
18.00 - 20.00	Bridge
04.00 - 08.00	Bridge

Time on the bridge was spent undertaking various duties with two officers being constantly employed, one conning the ship and the other responsible for navigating, guns, torpedoes and asdic. As Burfield observed, 'If you relaxed, you got caught out'.

The Spanish Civil War ended on 31 March 1939 and *Havock*'s crew had gained valuable experience during this stressful time, growing from a very green ship to a proficient and capable unit. The attempted bombing and torpedoing of *Havock* had been an early learning experience which would serve them well during the coming years. During every day spent in Palma the destroyer's crew had seen mainly Italian bombers heading off to bomb Madrid or Valencia. Clearly, both the Germans and Italians had gained invaluable war practice during this period. However, the Italians had sent so much war material to the Nationalists that their Army and Air Force suffered from severe equipment shortages during the first two years of the Mediterranean war.

Chapter 3

Run up to War
(March 1939 – March 1940)

Rumblings in Europe had suggested for some time that war may be coming. However, for now it was business as usual on board, and on 20 March 1939, *Havock* left Gibraltar, with *Hardy*, and arrived in Ajaccio, Corsica, three days later. The French island of Corsica was claimed by Mussolini as part of his general expansionist sabre-rattling and *Havock* was present as part of a show of defensive strength to demonstrate solidarity with the French at a time when the Italians might have been contemplating another foreign adventure as conflict in Spain drew to a close.

Havock's John Burfield, Alistair Bruce, 'Lofty' Isden, Jim Hoad, 'Choppin', Marshall, Carter, Pearson, Stokes, Griff Gleed-Owen and Hales all went off on a bus with the roof off, singing all the way. They left at 07.30 stopping in the hills to snowball on two occasions when above the snowline. On seeing a little old lady on a donkey, choruses of 'Donkey Serenade' went up for ten minutes. The bus stopped for lunch at a snow-clad village and Inn. Leading Seaman Marshall played his accordion attracting a large crowd of locals who applauded. They were delighted when the crew sang the French national anthem and soon insisted that the British also sang *God Save the King*. Everybody bundled back on the bus repeating the whole affair at the next village. They arrived back to the ship at 18.00 after a thoroughly good day out for ten shillings a head plus extras.[1]

Suspicions concerning Italy's territorial ambitions were well founded because Mussolini invaded Albania on 31 March, the very day that the Spanish Civil War ended. As far as *Havock* was concerned this could not have come at a worse time because the previous day she, and others of the 2nd DF had arrived at Sorrento in the Bay of Naples. The latter meant, of course, a visit to Vesuvius and Pompeii which boasted the oldest whore-house in the West – un-staffed – but still showing ample evidence of its vigorous heyday almost two millennia earlier.[2]

A packed Easter social programme had been arranged, start-ing with a party at the Hotel Vittoria on the cliffs overlooking Sorrento Bay – an event enthusiastically supported by a nearby girls' finishing school and where promises were exchanged to meet at the Blue Grotto the next day. It was not to be, however, as no sooner had they got back to the ship than they heard of Mussolini's invasion of Albania.

As a result, the ship darkened at midnight and, with the flo-tilla, slipped into the night on patrol to Malta. The Mediterranean Fleet immediately went to four hours 'Notice of Readiness for Steam'. On passage, live HE (High Explosive) shells were fused. God knows what the girls thought when they woke the next morning for the Grotto, only to find the five destroyers gone.[3]

Despite leadership and training problems Italy possessed a formidable navy and the possibility of meeting it as sea was very real. However, it had long been the practice of the Home and Mediterranean Fleets to hold joint exercises at least once a year and an attack by light forces on a well-protected Battle Fleet was always part of these manoeuvres.[4] This demonstration of Britain's sea power must have caused some concern for even the most modern of world navies.

The Italian annexation of Abyssinia in 1936 still cast long shad-ows. It had triggered massive reinforcement of the Mediterranean Fleet which in turn exposed the extreme vulnerability of Malta to air attack from nearby Italian bases. The threat posed by Italian air power was such that it was decided to base the Mediterranean Fleet at Alexandria which was a much safer place. However, Mediterranean Fleet was now so large that a satellite harbour had to be found in the Eastern Mediterranean and Haifa was an obvi-ous choice – although one which was not without its drawbacks.

Unhappily, Haifa had its attractions for others besides the Navy. Palestine, as the Jewish homeland, was targeted by Jewish refugees looking for a better life in a new land. Palestine was a British Protectorate and Jewish settlement had been banned by international agreement. Unfortunately, the Navy inherited the task of enforcing the ban that made them unpopular with Jewish refugees as well as Palestinian-born Jews. The latter resented the enforcement activity of the colonial power while Palestinian Arabs were angered by the continuing influx of Jewish immi-grants triggered by growing anti-Jewish sentiment in Germany.

In April 1939 *Havock* and *Hotspur* were sent to Haifa to support the Army and the Palestine Police by attempting to intercept the refugee ships running the blockade. The ships employed in this trade were potential, if not actual, death traps being overcrowded,

insanitary, in danger of foundering and prone to ditch their chol-
era victims over the side. Clearly, they were a menace to themselves and anyone who came in contact with them and those taking passage in such ships were desperate indeed. Shore leave for
Havock's crew was problematic as noted by Stoker John Burt who
recorded that:

> I can't really say that a run ashore amounted to very
> much. Most places were out of bounds and then only for
> men who had at least one good conduct badge I seem to
> remember. I suppose in the event of any misbehaviour it
> was thought they had more to lose![5]

Telegraphist John Thomson remembered that shore runs in Haifa
were potentially hazardous because of the terrorist activity in the
protectorate:

> I recall riding out to the Radio Station in an armoured
> truck. We had to travel at exactly 40 mph as someone
> had worked out that if we ran over a home-made mine
> it would just about lift the rear end and nothing more![6]

Havock left Malta on 26 April to resume anti-immigration patrols
off Palestine and arrived at Haifa three days later. Joy abounded
when *Havock* and *Hotspur* sailed from Haifa on 13 May as DF2
assembled at Alexandria where most of the Flotilla was preparing
to sail for home at the end of the commission. *Havock* was unlucky
and stayed for yet another three months in the Mediterranean. In
the five years of her very active life *Havock* saw little of England.

Havock and *Hotspur*, therefore, remained in Alexandria to
welcome Admiral Sir Andrew Browne Cunningham (ABC)
who had arrived to relieve Admiral Sir Dudley Pound as
C-in-C Mediterranean Fleet. As was usual in such changes the
Fleet Flagship, in this case the battleship *Warspite*, steamed
slowly between two columns of ships comprising most of the
Mediterranean Fleet.

In recognition of this tour of duty the ship's companies of both
Havock and *Hotspur* received the Naval General Service Medal,
with the Palestine Clasp. Added to her Spanish intervention
duties on the Nyon patrol *Havock* had laid the foundation of her
illustrious career.

At last, after nearly three years away, *Havock* headed out of
Gibraltar on 10 August 1939, for Chatham and seven weeks well-
earned leave – or so they thought. Havock arrived at Sheerness
for Chatham on 13 August and immediately docked for a

much-needed refit and repairs to defects. Unbelievably, less than three weeks later, *Havock*'s luckless crew was recalled from leave as news came in of Hitler's threatened invasion of Poland. This seemed unbearably unfair as the crew all wanted to see relatives and friends; but war waits for no man. For Telegraphist John Thomson, it was particularly poignant:

> On arrival at Chatham on 13 August, I was in the first watch for leave. I got married on the 19th, was recalled on the 26th, and we sailed the same day.[7]

In the meantime, the refit had got under way. Some gear had been replaced while some equipment that had been landed was hastily taken back on board. At Sheerness, arctic clothing was piled into the clothing store only to have tropical kit stowed on top of it, thus scotching rumours as to her destination. The tedious business of de-ammunitioning was reversed. Fuelled and stored *Havock* left for Gibraltar on 26 August, only thirteen days after arriving in England.

A war-ready *Havock* arrived at Gibraltar in company with *Hotspur, Hunter* and *Hyperion* on the 29th and, after refuelling and taking on stores, she left the next day for Freetown, Sierra Leone on the West Coast of Africa.

It was on Sunday 3 September 1939 at the morning service on board that Lieutenant Commander 'Nutty' Courage[8] announced the declaration of war with Germany. The crew, although half expecting the announcement, were still stunned that it had actually happened. They were now participants in a real war. Frank Hall[9] (Signals) recalled the actual signal read:

> Date: 3.9.39
> MOST IMMEDIATE
> FROM Admiralty
> Special Telegram TOTAL GERMANY repetition
> TOTAL GERMANY
> 1117/3

The following day at Freetown the ship fuelled and stored before leaving for patrol to Rio de Janeiro and the River Plate in South America with her chummy ship *Hotspur* on the 5th. On 7 September *Havock* stopped engines on the equator out of respect for King Neptune, so that he and his Court could come aboard over the bows, as was decent and traditional, to welcome *Havock* and her crew to his Kingdom. He superintended the anointing of the hitherto uninitiated (i.e. those who had not had the pleasure before) with a mixture of engine room gunge, flour and paint store bin ends, before making sure that his new subjects were properly shaved and bathed, his comely and voluptuous Queen at his side drawing attention to those pieces of the ceremonial which had been hastily or inadequately performed and which should therefore be repeated. Naturally the Court Doctor was in attendance throughout, with his syringe, willing and anxious to inject anyone whose behaviour suggested to the Queen that they were even a little below par. Certificates were duly awarded saving the crew from such experiences again in the future. Having completed ceremonies, the two vessels sailed on to rendezvous with the heavy cruiser *Exeter*.

Chief Petty Officer Freddie Kemp recalled that on the way to South America *Havock* and *Hotspur* visited the tiny remote island of Trinidade 600 miles to the east of Rio. In the Great War this had been used as a fuelling and victualling station by the Germans but on this occasion, the island was found to contain no such supplies.

On Wednesday 13 September, *Havock* arrived at Rio de Janeiro, Brazil, for fuel. Being a neutral port, Rio only allowed ships to stay for twenty-four hours but everyone managed to get ashore. As usual, luck was not with them as they were recalled before the time was up to sail on its South American patrol. John Thomson recalled:

> Whilst in Rio, two of our chaps were arrested and jailed for hauling down the German ensign outside their consulate. We got them back only just in time before we sailed.[10]

On 15 September *Havock* helped provide anti-submarine escort for the fast convoy (KJF1) from Kingston, Jamaica, to the UK via Freetown. A convoy system from Santos, Brazil, to Freetown had been arranged and the cruiser *Cumberland* was kept in distant support. The next day, after a short call, *Havock* left Rio at 09.00 to search for the German blockade runner *Monte Olivia*[11] which was reported to have sailed from Santos.

Between 21 and 23 September *Havock* and *Hotspur* were in the South Atlantic with the cruisers *Cumberland* and *Ajax* while from 1 October *Havock* was kept in the River Plate to cover convoys. Her planned visit to Montevideo, Uruguay, was postponed and *Havock* returned to Rio on 4th to refuel and continue patrols with *Hotspur*.

Eventually, however, on 12 to 14 October *Havock* arrived in Montevideo to refuel and the opportunity was taken for afternoon shore.[12] By John Thomson's estimate[13] *Havock* and *Hotspur* spent sixty-three days at sea with only ninety-six hours in harbour whilst attached to Captain Henry Harwood's South American Squadron.

The next port of call was Buenos Aires, Argentina. By now, *Havock* was overdue a refit and was ordered to Bermuda for a three-week docking period. However, on 31 October, whilst entering Pernambuco harbour, Brazil, for fuel, a sudden change in revolutions from half ahead to half astern stripped a turbine and on one engine only the ship became extremely difficult to manoeuvre in a confined space. To bring the ship's bows up into the wind the quarter deck awning was rigged on the main mast as a sail. This ingenious and seamanlike solution could not disguise increasing concerns over the reliability of *Havock*'s main engines. Their repair would require a 'heavy machine shop' dock which meant, to the delight of her crew, that she was ordered home to Chatham via Freetown and Gibraltar.

Despite many repairs, the vacuum to the starboard engine was unreliable at low revolutions causing a power loss to the starboard screw. This meant that the port screw pushed the ship to starboard and she was, therefore, always running with port rudder to prevent her going round in a circle. The result of this was that she 'crabbed' by a few degrees through the remainder of her life. The command on the bridge of 'all ahead both' followed by 'half port' was standard practice. The problem tended to go away at high revolutions.[14]

On 9 November, the ship finally arrived at Freetown on the one remaining good engine. Convoy duty followed on the 16th, protecting another convoy (SL9) to Sierra Leone. *Havock* eventually arrived in Gibraltar on the 27th remaining there until 12 December undergoing repairs to one of her engines and other defects. The repairs were apparently completed successfully and from 12 to 16 of that month *Havock* escorted a sixty-four-ship convoy from Gibraltar to Chatham in company with the coal burning minesweeper *Saltash*. Having spent a great deal of time on South American patrol *Havock* had only narrowly missed involvement in the action against, and scuttling of, the German heavy cruiser *Admiral Graf Spee* between 12 and 17 December.

On 8 December 1939, to the jubilation of the crew, *Havock* arrived in Chatham to refit at Sheerness and was also put under immediate command of the Commander-in-Chief Nore. The Phoney War was at its height and *Havock* was able to remain in Chatham under refit until 23 March 1940. Following a long period at sea a ship is empty and needs to suck in stores, meat, fuel, oil, water and ammunition. She also needs boats from the Boat Pool, chart folios and chronometers from the Hydrographic Department, crates of manuals and Confidential Books, ropes and wire coils, signal flags in bundles, cutlery, cotton waste and cordite. Watch and Quarterly Bills must be made out, messes and lockers must be allocated as the drafts from barracks are absorbed. All this would help to make *Havock* fit and ready for what was to be more or less two continuous years of war before her loss in April 1942. While under refit in Chatham the TSDS sweeps and davits on the quarterdeck were removed and two extra depth charge racks fitted, making a total of three. Two extra depth charge throwers were installed to give a total of four. For those staying with *Havock* until her loss, this home leave was their last, with the exception of three days in April, that they would have in nearly three years before their liberation from the Vichy internment camp at Laghouat in Algeria in November 1942.

On 23 March 1940, *Havock* sailed down the channel to Plymouth, Lands' End and then north through the Irish Sea to Scapa Flow where she joined the re-formed DF 2 for service with the Home Fleet. Ordinary Seaman J.A. 'Buster' Brown recalled:

> We left Plymouth escorting the old aircraft carrier *Furious* and the passage through the Irish Sea was very rough. For quite a few of the ship's company, myself included, this was our first taste of rough weather as we had just been called up from Civvy Street. It was very uncomfortable, but most of us eventually got used to the antics of a destroyer at sea. I was very sick. There is no heating on the ship and no hammocks. We slept on the mess deck benches and developed the ability not to fall off when asleep. We took a lot of water on board in the mess deck in bad weather and there would be about two feet slopping around with personal belongings, potatoes, vomit, boxes and boots bobbing around.[15]

Chapter 4

The Battle for Narvik
(April 1940)

An important supply of iron ore to Germany was sourced from the Gällivare ore fields in Sweden through the Baltic port of Lulea. However, this area of the Baltic froze during the winter months preventing shipping movements. As a result, ore was shipped by single track railway to the port of Narvik in Norway, which was ice-free throughout the year. Winston Churchill worked long and hard to persuade his government to force this traffic out of neutral Norwegian waters and into international waters where it could be stopped, searched, released, arrested, or sunk. The French, who feared an imminent invasion of their own country, were looking for any opportunity to open other fronts against Germany to deflect or delay them from this path. Churchill had his way as we shall see.

Alex 'Bugs' Levene joined *Havock* in March 1940 as Gunner's Mate to Freddie Kemp. During daytime he was responsible for the four-barrelled 0.5-inch anti-aircraft guns, mounted to port and starboard, on a gun platform between the funnels. At night, his post was on the bridge as star shell control and lookout. He therefore spent most of his time on the upper deck and consequently was able to provide detailed information before his death in 1987. He had a staggering memory for detail of names, places, times and events most of which have been easily verifiable. He was a popular man on board always doing something for someone. His fondest memories were of *Havock* and his greatest fear was capture, as he was Jewish[1].

Soon after at Scapa Flow in late March, *Havock* slipped her wires again and went on North Sea Patrol. Not long out of Scapa she suffered her first air raid since the Spanish Civil War but, thankfully, this was a half-hearted attack there were no adverse results on either side.

Operation *Wilfred*

Significant historical events were about to unfold as on 2 April, the DF2, consisting of *Hardy* (Captain. D2), *Hunter*, *Havock* and

Hotspur left Scapa Flow at 20.00 to take part in the plan, known as *Wilfred*, to lay mines off the neutral Norwegian coast. Freddie Kemp noted that:

> We didn't have enough crew to act as prize crew so we took on board ten extra crew from *Renown*, including three Marines. Two of the Marines crewed the twin-barrelled Lewis guns on each side of the ship. These proved invaluable. We changed the 4.7-inch ammunition to Direct Impact Percussion (DIP) and Semi-Armour Piercing (SAP) from High-Angle Timed Fuse (HATF). This took four hours. We were ready for surface action.[2]

The flotilla dropped in at Sullom Voe in the Shetland Islands at 07.00 on 3 April to take on fuel. Unfortunately, the minelaying operation was then delayed seventy-two hours and the 2nd DF finally sailed on Saturday 6 April at 04.30, to win the first-awarded VC of the war and to lose two of their number with much loss of life. The date and time was almost exactly two years to the hour before *Havock* would be lost.

On 7 April rendezvous was made, according to instructions, with the battle-cruiser *Renown* and the minelaying destroyers *Esk*, *Ivanhoe*, *Icarus* and *Impulsive* which had been ordered to lay minefields off the mouth of Vestfjord leading to Narvik. Warburton-Lee's DF2 was sent to cover the minelayers as they deposited their explosive cargo that evening. The eight destroyers entered Vestfjord without incident and by dawn on Monday, 8th, 234 mines had been laid.[3] Unbeknown to the British, the German invasion forces which were to land all along the coast of Norway, were already at sea and surprisingly close at hand.

All the destroyers were now ordered to re-joined *Renown* and act as an anti-submarine screen. However, on joining the battlecruiser the weather was so severe as to preclude screening and consequently the ships reformed in the sequence of *Renown*, DF2 and DF20. Suddenly, in the darkness at about 22.00 *Havock's* starboard engine developed a malfunction. Quite a few anxious moments followed as the minelaying destroyers of the DF20 and the other ships of the DF2 passed either side in the stormy seas whilst the defect was repaired. In this moment of weakness whilst the engine was repaired *Havock* could have become another victim of accidentally running into enemy forces as had happened to *Glowworm* which had been delayed while searching for a man overboard. The unfortunate destroyer ran into the *Admiral Hipper* and was overwhelmed in a one-sided encounter on 8 April.[4] This action, during which the sinking *Glowworm* succeeded in ramming the German heavy cruiser's starboard side forward, would result eventually in Lieutenant Commander Roope, the destroyer's captain, being awarded a posthumous VC after the war when the Germans provided details of the action.

Stoker Albert Goodey recalled the sea conditions were atrocious and the worst he had seen in eighteen months at sea.[5] Jim 'Buster' Brown added:

> When trying to keep up with *Renown* in the heavy seas, the ship, as always, managed to take a lot of water on the fore mess deck through the forward companion way. This usually meant a foot or so of water sloshing from side to side with a mixture of books, clothing, mess vegetables and other gear as the boat rolled (this problem was later corrected). The fore mess deck stanchions were bent by the weight of the water on the fore deck and had to be straightened.[6]

At 04.19 the following morning 9 April, action stations were suddenly sounded on board *Havock*. *Renown* had sighted the German battlecruisers *Scharnhorst* and *Gneisenau* which were covering the invasion force which was entering Narvik at that very moment. Aboard *Renown* the two ships, which were barely visible on the horizon in the appalling weather conditions then prevailing, were identified as *Scharnhorst* and the heavy cruiser *Admiral Hipper*. During a short, long-range engagement, *Renown* was hit by two 11-inch shells which did little damage while *Gneisenau's* main gunnery control position was put out of action at 04.17 by a 15-inch shell after which both German ships withdrew suffering some damage from the mountainous seas in the process. The weather conditions were far too severe for the destroyers to keep pace with the much larger 29-knot *Renown* and they were reduced to mere spectators.[7]

German destroyers at Narvik

Information from the Norwegians and other sources gave the clear indication that the invasion of Norway was well under way. Just before 10.00 on the morning of 9 April, Captain D2 Bernard Warburton-Lee, who had been patrolling the entrance to Vestfjorden, received an order directly from the C-in-C Home Fleet Admiral Forbes instructing him to 'send some destroyers up to Narvik to make certain that no enemy troops land there'.[8]

At noon the Admiralty also advised Warburton-Lee that: 'Press reports one German ship arrived Narvik and landed small force. Proceed to Narvik and sink or capture enemy ship. It is at your discretion to land forces if you think you can recapture Narvik from number of enemy present. Try to get possession of battery, if not already in enemy hands. Details of battery to follow.[9]

Warburton-Lee decided the best manner to comply with his orders would be to take only the ships of his 2nd Destroyer Flotilla, *Hardy*, *Havock* (Lieutenant Commander Rafe Courage), *Hotspur* (Commander Herbert F.H. Layman) and *Hunter* (Lieutenant Commander Lindsay de Villiers) into Narvik to gather information and leave the minelaying destroyers of DF20 in Vestfjorden. At 16.00, the four ships stopped at the Tranøy Pilot Station in the inner Vestfjorden and Warburton-Lee sent lieutenants Stanning and Heppel, to see if the local pilots could inform them of any German ship arrivals in Narvik. While this was happening, *Hostile* joined the flotilla. The pilots informed the officers that they had seen six large German destroyers and a U-Boat sailing toward Narvik. After the two officers returned to *Hardy* with their information Warburton-Lee sought some time alone to ponder his course of action, made all the more difficult as he had received a direct order from the Admiralty to go to investigate. About half an hour his mind was made up and at 17.51, he sent a laconic signal in the finest naval tradition:

> Most Immediate signal to the Admiralty repeated to Forbes and Whitworth: Norwegians report Germans holding Narvik in force, also six repetition six destroyers and one submarine are there and channel is possibly mined. Intend attacking at dawn, high water.[10]

At 20.00, the German submarine *U51*, which was positioned to intercept any enemy forces attempting to interfere with the invasion, reported five British destroyers at moderate speed on a south-westerly course, away from Narvik. Commodore Bonte, German commander of the naval forces in Narvik, concluded it was a routine patrol heading away from the fjord. Fortunately, when Warburton-Lee reversed his course half an hour later, *U51* had already dived and vacated the area.[11]

After midnight, the flotilla passed Barøy in continuous snowstorms with visibility seldom greater than 300 to 400 yards. They were all alert and at Action Stations. Navigation was by dead reckoning, Asdic and echo sounding, as neither side of the fjord could be seen, except when on one occasion they nearly collided with it. *Havock* was fourth in line and like the others struggled to keep contact with the ship ahead without actually running into it. Speed was reduced to twelve knots when the width of the fjord was down to about two miles. A frantic turn to starboard to avoid 'something' threw the ships out of line, recovering through USW radio and Asdic. A ferry festooned with lights lumbered out of the darkness causing *Hostile* a merry dance, losing the others again and finally making her own way to Narvik. All boats were now through the narrows and unseen by the 'sentries' *U25* and *U46*.[12]

The German invasion force was actually far stronger than any report had indicated and consisted of ten large modern destroyers each armed with five 5-inch guns per ship and displacing 2,000 tons. Clearly, there was the potential for a distinctly uneven contest. The Germans had posted a picket ship outside the harbour, but fortune favoured the five 'H' class boats. Thus, when the German destroyer *Diether von Roeder* relieved her sister *Anton Schmitt* no replacement had been nominated to take her place. Consequently, when at about 04.20 *Roeder* returned to harbour and anchored off the Post Pier no lookout then existed outside Narvik harbour, a situation which was to prove catastrophic for her flotilla friends. Possibly as little as a mile behind *Roeder* the five destroyers of the DF2 were sliding past the mountain of Ankenes just outside the harbour.

First Battle of Narvik

Also at 04.20 hours, as *Roeder* turned for harbour, Warburton-Lee ordered *Hotspur* and *Hostile* to eliminate the shore batteries on Framnes if fired upon. The reality was that these batteries did not exist. The morning light grew, the snow reduced and visibility temporarily improved. At 04.30 *Hardy*, *Hunter* (the junior boat) and *Havock* slid passed the Ankenes shoreline deep into the right-hand side of the harbour, eyes straining for warship targets amongst the mass of merchant ships.

Suddenly *Hardy*'s lookouts spotted a German destroyer between the many merchantmen. Turning slowly to port to present her torpedo tubes *Hardy* fired three torpedoes to starboard from the forward tubes and increased speed. Surprise had been complete. Four more torpedoes were fired at two more destroyer targets as they appeared and the order immediately given to open fire with the main 4.7-inch armament. The second salvo of torpedoes missed but devastated the ore quays.

The first torpedo, from the forward tubes, struck the stern of a freighter but the second torpedo scored a direct hit on the German

Flotilla Leader *Wilhelm Heidkamp* causing the aft magazine to
erupt in spectacular fashion destroying the silence of the arctic
dawn. Over eighty men were killed including Commodore Bonte
the naval leader of the expedition, who was in his bunk when the
British attacked. Captain Erdmenger of *Wilhelm Heidkamp* managed to tie the remains of his foreship to a merchant ship.[13]

Hunter followed *Hardy* firing salvoes of shells and torpedoes
at what appeared to be a destroyer and into the wall of other of
ships in the harbour. Merchant ships were sinking all around and
Anton Schmitt was hit by a shell and a torpedo.

There were five German destroyers in the harbour, soldiers
ashore and armed men on some of the freighters. These defenders were waking fast and consequently accurate fire was being
returned against their attackers as *Havock* followed *Hunter* into the
attack. *Havock* found herself in a short gun battle with *Hermann
Künne* oiling from the *Jan Wellem* before *Künne* got under way,
backing off the tanker, ripping off moorings and hoses as she went.
Quite suddenly *Anton Schmitt* came into view and *Havock* put a second torpedo into her, sinking her. *Künne* was only some forty yards
away and shockwaves from the underwater explosion seized her
engines and she became immobile, life becoming all the more difficult as the sinking *Anton Schmitt* rolled over onto her before sinking forty minutes later, taking sixty-three lives with her. *Havock*'s
torpedoes also struck two merchant ships and salvoes of shells hit
two more as she continued her tour of the harbour. *Havock* was
completely untouched by return fire until a lone German sentry
dared to fire a hand gun at her from the captured British merchant
ship *North Cornwall*. A long burst of Lewis Gun fire from one of
Havock's borrowed *Renown* marines eliminated the threat.[14]

Roeder, unable to see much but occasional gun flashes, fired
all eight torpedoes at the harbour entrance. Had these functioned
correctly the outcome of the battle would have been very different, but the faulty magnetic pistols of German torpedoes meant
that one or two passed under *Hardy*, two under *Hunter* and
one under *Havock* without exploding. Petty Officer Alex 'Bugs'
Levene on *Havock* related:

> Whilst we were in Narvik harbour my 0.5-inch gun
> crews, three each side and myself, saw a torpedo coming
> straight at us. We passed the bearing up to the bridge and
> then threw ourselves flat on the deck, holding hands.[15]

The torpedo which passed right under *Havock* without detonat-
ing was witnessed by many. 'Bugs' continued:

As my point five crews couldn't use their guns, which were frozen, we were used for anything that needed doing. In fact, when we were withdrawing from Narvik it was us who carried the 4.7-ammunition from the forward guns to the after guns, running down the length of the ship, because the after magazines were empty.[16]

As she withdrew, *Havock* was fired upon by *Roeder* and *Lüdemann*. *Havock*'s after guns returned fire hitting *Lüdemann* twice, knocking out her forward guns, starting fires, severing the rudder control and flooding her aft magazine causing the German destroyer to withdraw from the action.[17]

Able Seaman John Dodds was a loading number on *Havock*'s 'X' Gun and remembered that:

A lot of the gunfire was in local control. Fred 'Blood' Reid, the Captain of 'X' Gun was a 3 badge Seaman and a much respected 'old man' of 40 years. He would stand at the back of 'X' gun with his hand on the interceptor, which fired the gun, and just look and sum up the range, give the range to the setter and nine times out of ten he would hit the target. He was finally killed at the Second Battle of Sirte.[18]

Able Seaman Harry Jenkins recalled that:

My memory of *Havock* was of a very happy ship. At Narvik I was responsible for the aft magazine passing shells and cordite up on the lift to 'X' and 'Y' guns. By the time the action had finished we had cleared out the magazine and only had star shell and wooden practice rounds left.[19]

Hotspur and *Hostile* found no shore batteries or opposition of any kind and so hurried back to take part in the main event. Seeing the withdrawal of their three flotilla colleagues they laid a smokescreen to cover their escape. *Hotspur* fired four torpedoes into the packed mass of shipping, sinking at least two more freighters while *Hostile* entered the harbour taking *Havock*'s place as she left and putting at least five shells into *Roeder* which was fast becoming a floating wreck. Dragging her anchor *Roeder* was able to tie her stern to the Post Pier by a hawser with her bow still being held by the anchor. *Roeder* was out of the fight and had been mostly abandoned by her crew as being no longer battle-worthy.

An hour after the commencement of the fight it was full day-light but misty with snow flurries. No significant damage had been inflicted upon any of the five British destroyers but not having accounted for all of the expected six enemy destroyers, the DF2 boats returned into the maelstrom for another sweep. By this time, more than half of the DF2's torpedoes had been fired with *Hostile* having all eight left, *Havock* five (although errone-ously reported as three), *Hotspur* four and *Hardy* one. Assuming all merchant ships to be under German control, all were thus con-sidered legitimate targets.[20]

A signal was belatedly sent by *Lüdemann*, 'Alarm, attack on Narvik' which alerted the five other German destroyers in the vicinity for there were ten in all not the six Warburton-Lee had been advised. Unbeknown to Warburton-Lee, the egress of his 2nd DF would be fiercely contested.

The British returned, but not wishing to get too deep into the harbour they crossed the entrance at fifteen knots. Few targets could be seen through the smoke and snow and they were soon surprised by *Lüdemann* which fired four torpedoes at intervals towards the gun flashes but again without effect. *Hostile* suffered slight damage from a shell-hit forward in this attack. Suddenly, three enemy ships were reported coming at speed from the direc-tion of Herjangsfjord and a gun engagement ensued at relatively long range. Warburton-Lee ordered a withdrawal at thirty knots and sent and erroneous signal to *Renown* reporting 'One cruiser, two destroyers off Narvik. Am withdrawing to westward.' In fact, the enemy consisted of three destroyers.[21]

Anchored in Herjangsfjord, *Wolfgang Zenker*, *Erich Giese* and *Erich Koellner* had been alerted by the alarm from *Lüdemann*. Captain Erich Bey with his destroyers raced to the scene as soon as steam was raised but with one major concern on his mind – that his ships had not refuelled since the long journey from Germany and this would necessarily limit his involvement if the alarm was a lengthy one.

Firing their aft guns at the pursuing Germans the British began to make their escape. However, the fire from both sides produced no results at such range. Sadly for the British their worst nightmare was about to befall them because in Ballangen Bay, just down the fjord to port, the German destroyers *Georg Thiele* and *Bernd von Arnim*, which had been anchored, had also received *Lüdemann's* warning signal. They departed their moorings and at 05.50, and five British destroyers were sighted ahead laying a smokescreen as they advanced down the fjord. Now the Germans had the British trapped between two forces, one ahead and one astern. Crossing the bows of the DF2, the two German destroyers opened fire from all ten of their five-inch guns, concentrating their fire on the lead ship which was *Hardy* only 4,500 yards away. The latter had only two guns bearing and her consorts were unsighted by smoke. *Havock* was the only other ship other than *Hardy* which could see to fire from her forward guns.

Loss of HMS *Hardy*

Hardy steered to port to open the arcs for her aft guns but received devastating hits from the two Germans and Warburton-Lee's last signal at 05.55 leaves little doubt that he knew the game was up: 'Keep on engaging enemy'. *Hardy* was hit time and time again putting both forward guns out of action and then a direct hit on the bridge killed or wounded almost everyone including Warburton-Lee, who was mortally wounded. Desperate and brave acts followed as *Hardy*, having lost all power, was steered for the side of the fjord to ground and save the remainder of the crew, her last surviving gun aft still firing defiantly.[22]

Havock was now in the van and became the new target for the enemy to focus on as the other DF2 destroyers were behind the smoke. Range was down to less than two miles and she was regularly straddled, but this lucky ship escaped all but slight splinter damage. An incendiary shell lodged near an ammunition locker setting the cordite alight but failing to explode. J. McDonald, one of *Renown's* marines, grabbed the hot shell and threw it over the side earning himself a Distinguished Service Medal (DSM). Freddie Kemp, CPO Guns, ordered the out of action 'Y' Gun crew to run along the iron deck to 'A' Gun and throw all the burning cordite over the side and get the gun back in action.[23] Torpedoes were exchanged between the protagonists but to no effect.

Freddie Kemp tells of one of *Havock's* casualties:

> When we got to within 2,500 yards of the enemy they started spraying us with machine and anti-aircraft guns. One man on the torpedo tubes was badly hit in the leg.[24]

The wounded man was Chief Petty Officer Torpedo Instructor George William Clarke Carter who had to be taken to the Captain's Cabin where a First Aid Centre had been set up. He was a cot case and had to be transferred to *Penelope* the next day in Skjelfjord and subsequently to Gravdal Hospital in the Lofotens, where he was well cared for before managing to get home via Harstad much later. His mother's diary for April 27th 1940 records a letter from George in Hospital saying 'got shrapnel in leg – on way home'.[25]

Freddie Kemp continued:

> Lt Commander Courage cleverly steered *Havock* towards the shell splashes from the enemy fire, knowing that they were correcting their aim and would therefore miss again. We had no injury from their full calibre guns but we had perforations in the funnel and along the ship's side. By the end of the action we had fired two thirds of our ammunition.[26]

John Dodds on 'X' Gun remembered:

> We were very busy with the occasional misfire. We had to extract the round, throw it over the side and put another one in. In training before the war we were supposed to leave it in for half an hour. This was never going to happen in action. When you hit a target at close range you can see the target and you can see the shells hitting. The Gun Captain told us when we hit. They were firing at us as well and we were near missed with shrapnel coming inboard. One or two were wounded in the unprotected range finder. [27]

Jim 'Buster' Brown also on 'X' Gun added:

> The ship's company behaved impeccably except one chap who ran up and down on the iron deck shouting and waving his arms about. He had lost it. The M.O. and a medical 'Tiffy' quietened him down.[28]

Havock's 'Bugs' Levene reported that his 0.5-inch quad's water jackets were frozen and unable to be used.[29] This malaise did not seem to affect the German short range weapons. Many of the surviving British officers later commented that the short range of the encounter with multiple, swiftly moving targets was very different from anything they had practiced for in peacetime.

Having 'crossed-the-T' of the British ships, the German destroyers turned west, running parallel to and north of them, slightly ahead. The Germans believed that Captain Bey was still pursuing from behind and they could now corner the British. Unfortunately for them, Bey had stayed back from the British smokescreen showing little appetite for the fight and no doubt concerned about his ships' fuel situation. *Havock's* Rafe Courage turned back to fight off the pursuing group lost in the smoke but *Havock's* forward guns momentarily failed and he had to reverse his course again so that his after group could continue the engagement along with *Hostile* which was bringing up the rear at this point. Their action seems to have discouraged Bey and the German pursuit slowed even further.

The sinking of HMS *Hunter*

Hunter was now the lead ship and was taking hits from *Georg Thiele* and *Bernd von Arnim* which were now on a parallel course. However, the damage was far from one-sided with both German destroyers taking punishment from the DF2 vessels. On *Thiele*, a shell hit her port side, starting a boiler-room fire, a second hit aft starting a fire, prompting the aft magazine to be flooded, a third shell struck a forward gun killing nine men and setting fire to the ammunition hoist and finally two more shells caused further significant damage and started further fires. Many were killed or wounded and the remaining four guns had to go to local control.[30]

Unfortunately, *Hunter* suffered the same fate as *Hardy* being hit many times in quick succession by German 5-inch and 37mm shells which caused huge damage and fires. Explosions destroyed *Hunter's* engines and boilers and it is possible, but not confirmed, that she was hit by a torpedo from *Thiele*. The doomed destroyer's speed fell away and she appeared out of control. By now, *Hotspur* was getting the same treatment and her steering was soon put out of action. Unable to avoid the slewing *Hunter* she ploughed into her locking the two ships together in a deathly grip which made them an easy target for *Arnim* and *Thiele* who poured fire into them. With the bridge steering position out of service *Hotspur's* Commander Herbert Layman was reduced to shouting orders from the 'X' gun-deck to the engine room and tiller flat. As soon as *Hotspur* released herself *Hunter* rolled over and sank with heavy loss of life. *Hotspur*, having been hit seven times and substantially splintered from large and small calibre fire, was isolated between five enemy destroyers for a tense period.[31]

John Dodds on *Havock* saw the loss of *Hunter* from his position on 'X' Gun:

> *Hunter* was rammed and was under fire from all enemy destroyers. *Havock* and *Hostile* turned back to lay a smoke screen round *Hunter* and *Hotspur*. I saw *Hotspur* withdraw. *Hunter* was on fire from stem to stern. She just dipped and sank. I got scratched by shrapnel on my right shoulder but was unaware until afterwards when I

saw my oilskin was ripped at the shoulder. Before action
stations we were always told to put on clean clothing
because of the risk of infection when wounded. We were
in action for three hours.[32]

As indicated by John Dodds, *Havock* and *Hostile* boldly turned
back, *Havock* for the second time, fighting the German destroyers
off *Hotspur*. Behind a smokescreen laid by *Hostile* all three made
their escape from the also heavily mauled *Arnim* and *Thiele*, at
Hotspur's best speed. Stoker Albert Goodey on *Havock* always
held that his ship achieved thirty-six knots at times while withdrawing, 'being very low on fuel, shells and torpedoes and very
high on adrenaline'. He also claimed only seventy-six rounds of
SAP remained plus some star shell and practice rounds out of the
initial outfit of 1,000 4.7-inch shells.[33]

At 06.45, Commander Wright of *Hostile* sent a 'business like'
post-battle signal to *Penelope* and *Renown* 'Returning with *Hotspur*
and *Havock*. *Hunter* sunk in Vestfjord. *Hardy* ashore. 5 or 6 large
German destroyers in Narvik.' The Germans rescued just fif-
ty-one survivors from *Hunter* five of whom later died, 108 men
including Lieutenant Commander de Villiers were killed. In 2003,
eighty-five-year-old Albert Goodey of *Havock* and Colin Orton of
Warspite (from the Second battle of Narvik) unveiled a memorial
at the spot where *Hardy* finally rested, in memory of all those that
fell in the Narvik battles.[34]

Destruction of the supply ship *Rauenfels*

Further down the fjord the trio sighted the German supply vessel
Rauenfels (8,450 tons). Her holds crammed with AA and artillery
guns and ammunition, 5-inch shells for the German destroyers,
torpedoes and much more. *Hostile* fired a shot across her bows to
stop her. *Havock* remained, firing a second round into her bows
while the other two continued down the fjord. An inspection to
verify her identity found the transport on fire and Lieutenant
Commander Courage ordered his boarding party, led by First
Lieutenant John Burfield, off the burning vessel. Further shells
fired by *Havock* hit some of the ammunition and *Rauenfels* blew
up with a gigantic explosion and a column of smoke, reportedly
3,000 feet high, which could be seen by the destroyers returning
to Narvik. One German sailor from *Rauenfels* was killed and some
were arrested by Norwegian forces, while sixteen, including the
captain, were taken prisoner on board *Havock*. When *Rauenfels*
exploded at 07.45, *Havock* was so close that she avoided most

of the debris which was blasted right over the destroyer. It was later established from the prisoners that *Rauenfels* had been carrying mines, torpedoes and other ammunition which would have replenished the German naval units in Narvik. The supply ship's crew had also been congratulating themselves on evading the British blockade when the remnants of DF2 put in an unwelcome appearance.

Freddie Kemp recorded:

> When the men were safely back on board, with the Master of the *Rauenfels*, who was questioned and locked in a cabin aft, two 4.7 inch D.I.P. rounds were fired from 'B' gun to hasten *Rauenfels* destruction. *Havock* was only lying off *Rauenfels* by 300-400 yards, which turned out to be too close. The ship was showered with metal and a piece of heavy angle iron went straight through the gun shield of 'X' Gun.[35]

Leslie Millns Warrant Gunner (T) described the explosive destruction of *Rauenfels*:

> We saw a bright flash in the centre of the ship which expanded until she shone from end to end: it seemed that it was not just the cargo which had detonated, but the whole ship. I shouted to those around me to take cover because what goes up must come down, and the air was full of ironmongery and a great deal of it came down on *Havock*.[36]

ERA Maurice Cutler provided more detail regarding the damage suffered by *Havock*:

> There was a square yard of plating missing from the funnel and perforations along the port side. When we got into Skjelfjord I filled in a hole in the quarter deck. Shrapnel had also damaged the port siren.[37]

Havock's commanding officer, Lieutenant Commander Courage, compiled a detailed account of his ship's involvement in the first Battle of Narvik which can be found in Appendix II.

After the battle

Although the British had lost two destroyers, losses to the numerically much smaller German destroyer fleet were little short of catastrophic. Thus, in Narvik, *Schmitt* had sunk with fifty dead, *Heidkamp* sunk with eighty-one men dead, *Roeder* with five hits had been abandoned, apart from her gun crews, and had thirteen dead. Furthermore, *Arnim*, which had also suffered five hits, was out of action, *Thiele* had taken seven hits killing two men, *Lüdemann* hit twice had thirteen dead, *Künne* had nine dead while the remaining three of Bey's group from Herjangsfjord had no damage or casualties but were low on fuel and ammunition. Eight merchant ships had been sunk along with the ammunition ship *Rauenfels* and many others damaged. Low on fuel and ammunition and trapped in the fjord a long way from home, the remaining German destroyers were doomed. An attempt to escape later by some that had refuelled was cancelled when British warships were spotted further down the fjord.

Leading Signalman Frank E Hall, who made copious notes and copied *Havock*'s Signal Log from just after 00.00 on the 10th to 05.59 that morning (see Appendix III) made an untimed record of the congratulatory messages that were sent after the First Battle of Narvik:

> To: Second Destroyer Flotilla from Admiralty: Their Lordships congratulate all concerned on your determined action against superior forces and on successful result you achieved despite severe losses.
>
> To: *Havock, Hostile* from *Hotspur*: The gallant manner in which *Havock and Hostile* returned and covered their sister Chatham ship out of Narvik resulted in the saving of the ship and many lives and is highly appreciated.
>
> To: *Hotspur* from *Havock*: Many thanks for your kind message, after three years together even the Germans cannot part us.
>
> To: All Concerned from Admiralty: Following has been received from the Governor, Government and people of Malta. Deepest respect and admiration on the successful operation just completed especially to ships of the Mediterranean Fleet.
>
> To: All Concerned from Admiralty: Their Lordships congratulate all officers and men who took part in planning and execution of vigorous, daring and skilfully conducted action in Narvik and Rombaks Fjord the valour of which resulted in the destruction of all the enemy ships and may well tend to clarify the situation on this part of the Norwegian Coast. This operation completed the effect of the courageous, determined and damaging attack of

the Second Destroyers Flotilla so ably led by *Hardy* to the discretion of whose late Commanding Officer it was left to go into action against odds.

To: *Havock, Hostile & Hero* from Admiral Whitworth: Having once been 'D' it has been a special pleasure to me to have had ships of the Second Destroyer Flotilla in company during these past few days. I share with you to the full the loss of your Gallant Captain D, an old friend and Second Flotilla mate of mine.

To: Admiral Whitworth from *Hostile*: Very many thanks for your signal, we hope to see action with you again.

To: *Hostile* and *Havock* from Rear Admiral Destroyers: Welcome home after your gallant achievement.

To: Rear Admiral Destroyers from *Hostile*: Very many thanks for your kind signal.[38]

Off Tranøy at 09.30 on 10 April the surviving British destroyers *Havock, Hostile* and *Hotspur* proceeding down the fjord were met by the destroyer *Greyhound* and were joined by the cruiser *Penelope* about two hours later. *Havock, Hostile* and *Hotspur* were told to form line ahead astern of the cruiser after which the whole force proceeded down Vestfjord. The commanding officers of *Havock* and *Hostile* wanted to re-enter Narvik as soon as possible in company with *Penelope* and her accompanying destroyers to finish off the remaining German ships. Unfortunately, Captain Yates in *Penelope* felt that would exceed his orders and a patrol was instituted to close the Vestfjord so as to prevent any chance of escape by the remaining German destroyers and the many U-boats believed to be in the vicinity, although, in fact only *U64* remained.

Hotspur had a lot of damage and over twenty casualties and to buy time for repairs and to transfer the wounded, *Hotspur* escorted by *Hostile*, went into the secluded Skjelfjord. The latter was to become a substantial, remote repair and refuelling base for a month before it was discovered by the Germans and had to be abandoned. The Norwegian locals were of enormous help and their skilled craftsmanship helped to secure many of the ships. Those that were too badly wounded to be transferred to *Penelope* were sent to Gravdal Hospital where they were wonderfully cared for.

John Dodds wrote that:

After the action we withdrew to Cripples Creek (Skjelfjord) where all damaged ships went subsequently.

All we had left were practice shells and no torpedoes.
But we were kept in Norway doing anti-submarine
patrols as we had depth charges.[39]

Meanwhile, *Greyhound* and the superficially damaged *Havock*,
which had refuelled at Skjelfjord, patrolled outer Vestfjorden,
between Skjelfjord and the British minefield. At 15.25 on 10 April
they obtained a sonar contact and shortly after, in mid-afternoon,
they sighted a submarine. Depth charges were dropped liberally
and an oil slick appeared on the surface but *U64* (Captain Schulz),
which was on her first patrol and en route to Narvik, escaped
with minor damage having dived to 400 feet to avoid destruction. However, she did not survive long thereafter being bombed
and sunk on 13 April at Bjerkvik by a Fairey Swordfish floatplane
launched from the battleship *Warspite* during the Second Battle of
Narvik. Eight of *U64*'s crew went down with her but the remaining thirty-eight were rescued by German mountain troops stationed ashore.[40] The story of the Second Battle of Narvik on 13
April, which resulted in the destruction of all of the remaining
German destroyers as well as *U64* and further merchantmen, is
beyond the remit of this history but can be found in Geirr Haarr's
definitive histories of the Norwegian campaign.[41]

On the morning of the 13th, *Havock* was patrolling off Skjelfjord
when she sighted the approaching British force coming in for
the second battle. Admiral Whitworth in *Warspite* commanded
Havock to lead the fleet into the fjord, which she proudly did,
the fleet eventually passing to starboard. *Havock* subsequently
maintained asdic duty to port of the fleet off Narvik harbour and
therefore had a little involvement in the follow up battle.

After the battles of the 10th and 13th Narvik harbour was
a marine graveyard covered with oil and floating debris and
was also the final resting place of 282 Norwegian sailors killed
on the two defence ships *Norge* and *Eidsvold* sunk on 9 April.
Bows, masts and funnels stuck out of the water, often at crazy
angles, as deathly memorials to the carnage that had taken place.
Revenge had been exacted and, in May, Narvik was recaptured by
Norwegian, Polish and French forces which were then withdrawn
after the German invasion of the Low Countries and France.

During 13 and 14 April *Havock* was kept very busy because
Captain Gunnar Brekke and his First Officer Lieutenant Haug had
taken their Norwegian submarine *B3* from Narvik to Oksfjord,
outside of the narrows, but east of Skjelfjord. He then sent some
of his men on two puffers[42] to contact one or more of the British
destroyers operating in the fjord. Contact was made, on the

morning of the 13th when First Officer Haug was picked up by *Havock* south of Balstad Lighthouse. The destroyer then sailed west on the Vestfjord to meet the C-in-C Home Fleet, Admiral Sir Charles Forbes, off Moskenes Island at 20.00. The sea was too rough for Haug to be taken on board the flagship *Rodney*, but communication was established between Haug and Admiral Forbes using signal lamps. The Home Fleet Diaries[43] for 13 April record that at '20.00 *Havock* joined screen with Norwegian Lieutenant Haug on board. Latter gave C-in-C replies by signal to questionnaire on enemy forces, local conditions and facilities, etc. *Havock* left at 23.30 and returned to Vestfjord'.

Forbes had many questions and Haug answered as best he could but there were some he could not answer and it was agreed that Brekke should visit Skjelfjord to talk to the staff on board the crippled cruiser *Penelope*. *Havock* then returned Haug to Oksfjord, embarking Brekke in his stead in the afternoon of 14 April, after which a course was set for Skjelfjord. They arrived there at 18.00 on the 14th. In Skjelfjord, Brekke had discussions with the officers of *Penelope* who had received a series of questions by radio from Forbes. While there, Lord Cork arrived on board *Aurora* and Brekke subsequently went on board her for discussions with him as well. The final conclusion, other than much information provided for further British involvement, was that B3 should not operate in Vestfjorden and the Norwegian submarine eventually went to Tromsø with the intention to operate off the Finmark district.

Morale was raised briefly aboard *Havock* on Sunday 14th when the ship received the good news that she was to head for home. Thus, the destroyers Esk, *Ivanhoe*, *Icarus*, *Punjabi*, *Havock*, *Hostile* and *Hero* were ordered to take on no more oil fuel than required to reach Scapa Flow and then rendezvous with the C-in-C Home Fleet in the Narvik area early on the afternoon of 15 April. Unfortunately, it turned out to be a false hope because at 16.15 the battleship *Warspite* and the destroyers *Hostile*, *Hero*, *Havock*, *Foxhound*, *Encounter* and *Grenade* were detached from the main body of the Home Fleet to patrol west of Skomvær Light.[44] *Havock* would be the last 'H' boat to get home, sadly when all the fuss and media coverage had died down.

As the fight for Norway developed, more ships were slowly gathering in Skjelfjord to rest, repair and refuel. Lieutenant John Burfield of *Havock* described the activity in his unpublished memoirs:

The refuge at Skjelfjord was desolate, bare, and apart from a handful of cottages, deserted. One of the cottages, however, belonged to the local policeman and had a telephone – but otherwise the world outside was far away. Nevertheless, it was secluded, peaceful, and German air reconnaissance had not yet got off the ground. The repairs to *Hotspur* and *Hostile* could begin, without interference but from within their own resources. The scale of the operation was dramatically increased by the arrival of *Penelope* on the morning of 12 April. The day before she had run aground and had suffered such severe bottom damage that she was in imminent danger of sinking. She was anchored in the shallowest possible safe water. Then, the next day, arrived the casualties from the second battle – *Eskimo* with her bows blown off, *Punjabi* who had been hit in the engine room and *Cossack* who had fouled one of the many wrecks in Narvik harbour.

Luckily facilities within the anchorage gradually improved. Local initiatives had produced a very small, but very welcome, salvage vessel, a fleet of Clyde-type 'puffers', also locally raised, was mobilised to bring provisions such as casks of drinking water and, amongst other things, fifteen thousand eggs. Then, the fourth German supply ship *Alster* had been intercepted, boarded and brought into Skjelfjord. She carried a general cargo which included clothing, tinned food, butter – all most useful. But even more useful was her cargo handling gear: her derricks were able to pluck *Eskimo's* twin gun mounting off her twisted forecastle and so relieve the pressure on the internal bulkheads. The base remained operational for about a month, until *Penelope* was capable of crossing the North Sea and until air raids made the fjord untenable. During this time *Havock* was one of the few ships which had come through the past few weeks virtually unscathed. Accordingly, she fetched and carried, she escorted heavy ships, she patrolled, she watched, she worked.[45]

During this period four wounded men were transferred from *Havock* to the local hospital at Gravdal. They were CPO Torpedo Instructor George W. C. Carter who had shrapnel wounds from the running battle on the 10th, Robert Dulieu, Ronald Goddard and Lieutenant Hugh Aldridge Smith, who earned a Mention in Despatches for his work during the first battle. All were repatriated from Harstad to England some weeks later, some aboard the Hospital Ship *Atlantis* which had been a luxury cruise ship during the inter-war period.

By 24 April dreams of home leave and a welcome fit for heroes, similar to the reception *Hardy's* survivors were getting, soon faded as *Havock* and *Hostile* were kept on station to support the attack on Narvik. Pressure was maintained on the German troops ashore as Admiral of the Fleet Lord Cork shelled Narvik with *Warspite, Effingham, Aurora, Enterprise* and *Zulu; Havock* being part of the defensive screen. The attacking British force was screened against U-boats in Vestfjord and Ofotfjord by the destroyers *Faulkner, Encounter, Escort, Foxhound, Hero, Hostile*, the overworked *Havock* and the Polish *Grom* and *Blyskawica*. Eventually, on 29 April, nearly three weeks after the first battle of Narvik, *Havock* finally was given permission to return to Rosyth to have splinter and other damage repaired. On arrival half of her crew was given seventy-two hours leave and took the train to London, the other half taking its turn upon return of the first group. Meanwhile, *Havock* sailed on to Leith, a few miles further up the Forth estuary, for repairs which lasted until 3 May 1940. Petty Officer Alex 'Bugs' Levene noted:

> Back to Rosyth after Narvik and looking after everyone in Cripples Creek. Still having engine room trouble – kept losing vacuum on the starboard engine condenser. Couldn't get steam pressure up. We went into Leith for about ten days to correct this problem and to repair some splinter damage, mostly caused by the *Rauenfels* explosion. Also something had happened to the capstan motor, which meant we had to raise the anchor by hand. Anyway, we got 72 hours leave each watch.[46]

Many lives had been lost at Narvik and many friends were mourned. However, the saddest loss for Lieutenant Commander Rafe Courage of *Havock* was the shocking and unexpected loss of his wife. The *Daily Mirror* of 6 May 1940, reported:

Naval Hero Home, Finds His Wife is Dead
After saving his ship in the Narvik engagement, Lieutenant Commander R.E. Courage, of the *Havock*, set a triumphant course for home and leave. Reaching port, he found that his young wife, Irene, had died suddenly. Instead of the happy reunion he had planned with her, there was a funeral. 'I understand Mrs Courage worried greatly about his safety' the *Daily Mirror* was told. 'It was that which made her so ill'.

The whole crew were mortified at this loss as they knew Mrs Courage well. The sympathy and tears poured out of them for their gallant captain. Rafe Courage, who was a nephew of Admiral of the Fleet Lord Beatty, remarried over two years later after he had left *Havock*.[47]

Thus, ended *Havock*'s furious baptism of fire in a memorably historic battle. She had performed superbly and begun to build her reputation as a hard-working fighting ship. A reputation which would grow and grow over the next two years.

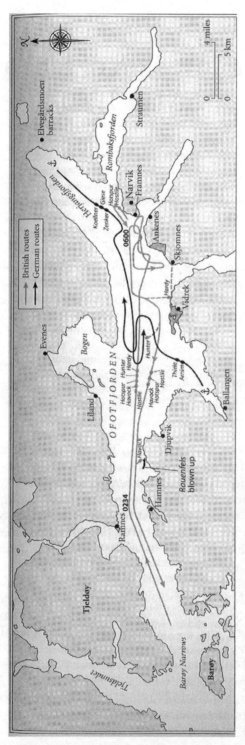

Map 1. The fighting at Narvik, 10 April 1940.

Chapter 5

The Invasion of Holland
(May 1940)

The start of the German Blitzkrieg on the Low Countries and France on 10 May 1940, created much confusion by its unexpectedly early timing as well as bewilderment in the minds of the disparate Staffs as to how to contain this unique assault based, as it was, on the twin principles of mobility and the use of air power as a form of artillery. Essentially a land battle, the Navy's role was, of necessity, to patrol the boundary. Only at the end of the campaign, when defeat was certain and imminent, was the Navy needed to hold the back door open – often by risky and determined rear-guard actions carried out by individual ships, whilst the armies and the governments were evacuated.

Having returned to Leith on 29 April, the first seventy-two hours of leave soon expired and the second group of liberty men returned by Sunday 5 May 1940. All repairs to *Havock* were completed on the same day and the following day she departed for engine trials off Bass Island on the east coast of Scotland and anti-submarine patrols for the cruiser *Birmingham*, which had also just come out of dock after having had damage repaired from a bomb hit on the bridge. If the crew of *Havock* thought April had been a busy month, then May was soon to be just as active and furthermore add a second battle honour to her mast. The relatively short and leisurely life of trials soon ended when ominous new signals and orders were received on the 7th:

> Orders 1. '8 modern destroyers, including one leader, to be sent to Harwich as soon as possible. To come under orders of C-in-C Nore. (1st SL 2249/7 to C-in-C HF).'
> Orders 2. '8 destroyers to be concentrated under a Captain (D) at Rosyth for service as a flotilla on east coast as ordered by Admiralty. (C-in-C HF 2335/7 to RA (D)).'
> Orders 3. 'Yours 2335/7. D5 in *Kelly, Kimberley, Kandahar, Janus, Hyperion, Hereward, Hostile, Havock* are detailed. (RA (D) HF 0125/8).'

Message to *Havock:* 'To Harwich with other destroyers to form a flotilla for the defence of the east coast under the orders of C-in-C Nore.'[1]

Just ten days after returning from Norway to Leith *Havock* had been repaired, fuelled, stored and ammunitioned and hurried south from Rosyth on 9 May in company with *Hostile, Hereward* and *Janus* acting as an anti-submarine screen for the *Birmingham.*[2] They joined the new command and were immediately ordered to participate in an operation to prevent the Germans laying mines in the Skagerrak as the following signal to *Havock* indicates:

With *Birmingham* and destroyers steer north to meet enemy force 1 torpedo boat, 4 minelayers, 3 destroyers.[3]

The group cruised in the Skagerrak area in darkness keenly watching out for the enemy minelayers and their escort when out of the blue the enemy found them first, as announced by a huge explosion. In the darkness *Kelly* had been torpedoed by an E-Boat. Very significant damage had been caused and *Kelly* was in a borderline sinking condition. Other ships in the group were quickly ordered to cover her retirement as she was taken in tow by the destroyer *Bulldog*. The official documentation describes *Havock*'s contribution succinctly:

During the night *Havock* engaged MTB at 3,000 yards. Enemy made smoke. *Havock* went through smoke. After seven salvoes, may have hit. Saw reddish smoke. No torpedoes fired.[4]

The message, 'Proceed to *Kelly's* assistance', was received from *Birmingham* by *Gallant, Mohawk, Janus, Fury* and *Hyperion*. It was followed immediately by 'What is state of *Kelly*?' Soon afterwards Birmingham received answering signal '*Kelly* in tow by *Bulldog* having been torpedoed'.[5]

Havock soon found herself in the unenviable position of lone rearguard, eventually losing touch with her own squadron as she covered the retreating group in the Skagerrak. After searching for some time and finding nothing, Lieutenant Commander Courage decided there was nothing more to be done and eventually turned for home feeling a trifle lonely. *Kelly* had a very eventful journey home under tow at a snail's pace. On arriving back in Britain on 10 May the news was received advising that the Germans had invaded Holland and Belgium.

The following day, Saturday 11 May, *Birmingham* and her three destroyers had returned to the Humber from the Dutch coast.

However, there was no respite for *Havock* and *Hyperion* which were hurriedly refuelled and sailed for the Hook of Holland. At 13.30 hours that day they received a request from the Dutch authorities for the pair to shoot down German Junkers Ju 52 three-engine troop carriers which were supporting and reinforcing land-based troops. These were spotted at 10,000 yards' distance and were in company with three Junkers Ju 88 bombers. At 14.25 these dived on *Havock* which was subjected to a succession of bombing attacks. Fortunately, the bombs were skilfully avoided by Rafe Courage using high speed and rudder. However, all explosions were within fifty yards and *Havock* was liberally sprayed with shrapnel with one near miss bodily lifting her stern. At 16.50 another aircraft came in from astern, bombing her and raking the ship with her rear gun while retiring.[6]

The air was full of signals as the hard-pressed naval units tried to grasp the enormity of the situation and what part they should play in it. A selection of signals from 11 May gives a sense of the chaos and confusion engendered by the German Blitzkrieg:

Wild Swan to V/A, Dover 1324/11: 'Your 12.28. *Hyperion* and *Havock* alongside. Placing the parcel charged for local demolition should be completed by 1600. Little air activity. Local isolated groups of German troops in the vicinity. No details of Rotterdam party available. Am proceeding to bombard the wood to eastward of town at the request of the Dutch authorities.'

(Street fighting) 'Give all support practicable but the moment for your withdrawal must be entirely at your own discretion.' (C-in-C Nore to *Hyperion* and *Havock*). '*Havock* will patrol off Hook entrance during night.' (During Royal Marine landings).

'*Valorous* and *Hereward* to relieve *Hyperion* and *Havock*.'

'*Havock* bombed by three aircraft.' (*Havock* 1430/11).

'*Havock* patrolling between Hook and Ymuiden endeavouring to destroy German troops seen to land by parachute flares and to deal with further landings. *Wild Swan* completed bombardment of wood close to eastward of Hook. Both at request of local authorities.' (*Hyperion* 1440/11).

'My 1430. No hits.' (*Havock* 1451/11).

'Withdraw if air attacks too heavy.' (C-in-C Nore 1930/11 to D1).

Fifteen destroyers were operating off the Hook at this time and the situation became quite chaotic due to fast changing events.

The next four days produced a flurry of hastily-planned reactive activity, the outcome of which was never in doubt because of the overwhelming strength of the well-planned and efficiently executed land invasion. The Royal Navy contributed all that it could along the coast but the poorly led and demoralised French and Dutch armies were no match for the Wehrmacht. During this hectic period, Lieutenant Commander Rafe Courage received notification that he had been awarded a well-earned promotion to Commander, but for some reason did not wear the stripe.

The very next day *Codrington, Havock, Hereward, Mohawk, Vivacious* and other ships were attacked almost continuously by dive-bombers from 07.00 onwards in various positions off the Dutch coast. Overnight *Havock* had patrolled off the Hook and further north. At 07.00 on the 12th there was an air attack across the ship, followed by one high-level bombing and three dive-bombing attacks before 10.00.[7] There were fortunately no reports of ships being hit but plenty of near misses and minor shrapnel damage. The Royal Navy was once again being taught a lesson about the woefully inadequate nature of the anti-aircraft capability of even its most modern destroyers. The dive-bombing was a new and highly unpleasant experience for the crew of *Havock* not least because their 4.7-inch guns were unable to elevate beyond 40 degrees while the 0.5-inch machine-guns lacked the range and punch to bring down a dive-bomber before it could do serious damage.

Able Seaman A. J. Brown, not to be confused with J. A. 'Buster' Brown, was wounded on 'X' Gun by an aircraft tracer bullet, and a pipe on the torpedo tubes was severed. In total five or six crew were wounded. All other damage was largely superficial.

Jim 'Buster' Brown ('X' gun) recollected:

> Off the Hook of Holland when first bombed by Ju 88s we thought we had hit them when they came down in a steep dive, but thought differently when they pulled out of the dive and 'threw' their bombs at us. After one aircraft made its attack and was pulling out of its dive, the rear gunner raked the ship with machine gun fire. I looked at A.J. Brown (I'm J.A. Brown), standing beside me on 'X' gun. He had a vacant look on his face and I noticed blood dripping from his sleeve. We realised he had been hit on the upper arm.
>
> I also remember *Wild Swan*, one of the old V & W class destroyers tied up ahead of us at the Hook. She had a single Pom-Pom two-pounder which seemed to

jam after a couple of rounds, until given regular swipes with a hammer. I also remember hearing rifle shots ashore in the railway siding as the German parachutists that were dropping at the time, were being engaged by Allied troops. There was a story being told on our ship that when it entered Ymuiden to pick up our passengers someone ashore said to 'Nutty' Courage, 'I hope you remember which way you came in and be sure to go out the same way as the entrance is heavily mined'.[8]

At 13.08 *Hyperion* ordered *Havock* to salve confidential papers from sinking 2,908-ton *Prinses Juliana* which had been mined while carrying troops from Flushing to Ymuiden but was still afloat at 12.00. *Wild Swan* and *Havock* took survivors to Hook of Holland.[9]

In the second afternoon of an already action packed forty-eight hours, one of *Havock's* officers boarded the abandoned *Prinses Juliana* to retrieve confidential papers left behind by military passengers when the ship was given up as a total loss. As it transpired most turned out not to be very confidential. At 12.05 *Havock* was ordered to return to Harwich to refuel bit still reported as being under air attack at 1400.[10]

At 17.45 on the 12th the Dutch authorities asked for a gun attack on a wood near the Hook, reputed to contain 200 German paratroopers. *Havock* proceeded up the River Maas and fired ten salvoes of 4.7-inch High Explosive shells. Three houses were demolished and two cows killed! One 4.7-inch shell from 'B' gun on maximum depression had misfired gaining little height and exploded in a field killing the two animals. No enemy was observed and fire was not returned though the range was only 1,700 yards. Soon four enemy Ju 88 bombers were spotted heading towards the canal. To avoid being trapped in a narrow canal with no ability to manoeuvre, *Havock* beat a hasty retreat down the canal stern first. 'Nutty' Courage proving again what a fine captain he was with much skill and coolness.

In Alex 'Bugs' Levene's words:

We pulled alongside the wharf at Ymuiden, it was a banana store. They told us ashore that a party of German paratroopers had landed in the field further up the canal. So 'Nutty' Courage decided to go up after them. So up we went and started bombarding a farmhouse. As 'B' Gun fired, two cows dropped dead in the field, so Alf Ayling, the captain of 'B' Gun, chalked up two cows on his gun shield. Then these dive-bombers arrived. We couldn't turn round in the canal so 'Nutty' went out astern, at full speed, the quarterdeck practically under water.[11]

Havock eventually arrived at Parkeston Quay Harwich at 07.00 on 13 May, landed her wounded and took on fuel, ammunition fuel and water before sailing again the following morning to transport a demolition party to Ymuiden. Entering the harbour at noon with a detachment of the Grenadier Guards her activities are described in the following disparate signals:[12]

> Captain Davis (army) landed. Amsterdam being evacuated. Have arranged to close harbour for more removals tonight, Tuesday, in view of magnetic mining and immediate air attacks when ships enter harbour CO force XDA does not consider it justifiable to send destroyers in for evacuation and has made arrangements to evacuate eventually with Dutch force by local craft. (*Havock* 1505/14).
>
> Your 1812 have encountered *Havock* and have detached her to Ymuiden and HMS *Vivacious* to Helder to make all preparation.
>
> Your 1812/14 request destination for troops from Ymuiden. (*Havock* 2126/14).
>
> Reply Tilbury. (C-in-C Nore 2159/14).

During this period of bedlam *Havock* met an MTB which informed the destroyer that the Dutch had surrendered. This is the message John Thomson (Signals) was ordered to send confirming the surrender:

> Dutch army in Ymuiden has surrendered. Demolition programme completed. Am embarking what Dutch I can from fishing boats. Request *Hereward* and *Vendetta* join me off Ymuiden to assist. Understand situation is same all over Holland and suggest channel steamers be returned. Will proceed towards Harwich. (*Havock* 2339/14).[13]

At 01.30 on 15 May *Havock* went back into Ymuiden to prepare evacuation amidst large fires everywhere. C-in-C Nore ordered the destroyer to try to get in touch with the trawlers *Asama* and *Norse* proceeding from Flushing to Ymuiden and direct them to proceed to Den Helder to assist two Dutch submarines trying to escape. On completion trawlers to proceed to Zeebrugge.[14]

On the following day, Commander Courage reported that he was bringing back part of the naval and military demolition parties from Ymuiden, including Lieutenant Hermans, Captain Keeble R.E. and Captain Davis, having been heavily machine-gunned by Heinkel 111s in the harbour.

Alex Levene remembered:

> We picked up dignitaries, refugees and government people. We had orders to stream the grass astern (biggest rope we had). All the small boats latched on to it, 40-50 of them and we towed them back to Harwich.[15]

Towing these many small boats astern, they had arrived at Harwich at 06.00 on the 15th in an exhausted condition, and were not debriefed.

Thinking it was all over and now a breath could be taken the crew and Commander Courage were heartily disappointed to receive an immediate order to make the ship ready and slip as soon as possible for Plymouth. A signal had been passed from the Admiralty a day earlier whilst *Havock* was off the coast of Holland which was to see her urgently pass into yet another war arena. The signal sent from the Admiralty at 01.02 on 14 May to C-in-C Nore read:

> Four Tribal, four 'K' class and nine 'A' to 'I' class, one A/A cruiser with RDF and three Sloops with good A/A armament to assemble at Plymouth and sail for Mediterranean in one or more groups as soon as is practicable (Admiralty to C-in-C Nore in C HF 0102/14).

Havock and *Hostile* were included in this group and so would be returning to their peacetime Mediterranean station. After the hurried departure from Harwich, *Havock* arrived at Plymouth the next day 16 May to prepare for the Mediterranean. The pace of war seemed to be gathering momentum. It had become apparent that Mussolini, seeing the ease with which Hitler had quickly made massive gains across Europe, was likely to decide that now was a good time to enter the war and make the land grabs necessary to satisfy Italy's ambitions. Italy, which had a substantial, fast and very modern fleet, was expected to enter the war very soon and the time had come to reinforce Mediterranean Fleet to meet the challenge posed by the Duce's navy. Now, after what seemed like five weeks of madness with many near death experiences, *Havock*'s battle-weary crew were at least pleased to be going to warmer waters.

Chapter 6

Mediterranean Maelstrom (May 1940 – February 1941)

The day after arriving at Plymouth, Friday, 17 May, the programme for sailing to the Mediterranean had been planned to be in three groups with *Havock* being allotted to Group 3 along with the AA cruiser *Carlisle* and the destroyers *Kimberley, Mohawk, Hereward, Hero, Ilex, Janus, Juno* and *Imperial*. The group had been expected to leave Plymouth that afternoon or as soon as ready to sail. In the event, only *Carlisle, Hereward, Havock, Hero* and *Imperial* were ready to sail leaving Plymouth at about 21.00 en route to Alexandria via Gibraltar and Malta.

The ships arrived at Alexandria on 26 May and the four destroyers joined DF2. The latter was tasked with providing an anti-submarine screen to the fleet based at Alexandria and consequently the period from 26 May to 10 June was spent on tedious boom patrols. The tedium was however, relieved by some rest and relaxation in 'Alex'. Sadly, whilst this was occurring, over 366,000 troops were being evacuated from Dunkirk and all commanding officers of Royal Navy vessels in Alexandria were kept advised of the situation in the English Channel. These were dark days for Britain as the litany of defeats grew almost daily and Germany was now on the nation's 'doorstep'. The men serving in the Mediterranean were concerned for their friends and families back home but they knew they had a duty to protect Britain's position in the Mediterranean and the Middle East.

On 11 June, the much needed rest and relaxation was rudely interrupted when Italy declared war on France and Britain. At the time *Havock* was at sea with friendly French cruisers east of the Bay of Taranto. At 14.00 on 16 June, soon after returning to Alexandria, DF2 (*Hyperion* (Captain D2) *Havock, Hereward* and *Hasty*) sailed to carry out an anti-submarine sweep in the eastern Mediterranean returning the following day.[1] Admiral Cunningham's policy of aggressive patrolling continued when DF2 (*Hyperion, Havock, Hero, Hereward* and *Hostile*) sailed from Alexandria at 08.00 on 20 June to carry out Operation *MD3* which involved a sweep along the coast as far as Tobruk to destroy enemy installations at Bardia as well as hunting for Italian submarines. This high-speed sweep ended at 18.30 the following day when all five destroyers returned to harbour.[2]

When, on 22 June news was received of the French capitulation, *Havock* helped to escort the French warships back to Alexandria for fear these valuable ships would fall into German or Italian hands, which could not be allowed to happen under any circumstances. The French officers were very unhappy about this situation, but being hemmed in by British cruisers and destroyers they had no option other than to do as they were requested. They were now a fleet with no home and were effectively 'interned' in Alexandria and were steadily demilitarised over the next few weeks.

At 12.30 on 28 June, the battleships *Royal Sovereign* and *Ramillies*, the aircraft carrier *Eagle* and the destroyers *Hyperion*, *Havock*, *Hero*, *Hereward*, *Hasty*, *Janus* and *Juno* sailed to cover the passage of one thirteen-knot and one nine-knot convoy from Malta to Alexandria (Operation *MA3*) returning on 2 July.[3] Once back in port, *Havock* was taken in hand for repairs to defects which were not completed until 11 July, which meant that the destroyer was not present at the Battle of Calabria two days earlier.

On 11 July, she sailed as part of the escort for the fast convoy *MF1* (Malta Fast 1) from Alexandria to Malta arriving on 13 July. After releasing the convoy in Malta *Havock* immediately and uneventfully escorted a return convoy of empty ships back to Alexandria. This was to become a gruelling and well-trodden path. As soon as she was back at Alexandria *Havock* was off again on the 19th intending to assist in a raid on Italian shipping in the Gulf of Athens, off the Dodecanese. What could be a something or nothing adventure soon turned into an incident which added a further battle honour to her record.

Action off Cape Spada

It was Admiral Sir Andrew Cunningham's policy to use his light forces in periodic sweeps to counter the activities of Italian submarines in areas through which British convoys had to pass while at the same time attacking Italian shipping. On 17 July orders were issued for such an operation which was to consist of a submarine hunt towards the Kaso Strait and round the north coast of Crete by four destroyers, combined with a sweep by a cruiser and one destroyer into the Gulf of Athens for Italian shipping. The cruiser was to be prepared to support the destroyers in case of need. The signal read[4]:

(i)   To D (2): repeated to C.-in-C., C.S.3, R.A. (L), *Hero*, *Havock*, *Hasty*, *Ilex*, *Sydney*. IMPORTANT. Carry out following operation. Object destruction of U-boats. Leave Alexandria 0001 tomorrow, Thursday with *Hyperion*, *Ilex*, *Hero*, *Hasty*. Sweep to Kaso Strait to pass through about 2130, then along north coast Crete to pass through Antikithera Channel about 0060C, 19 July, then to Alexandria to arrive 0800C, 20 July. *Sydney* and *Havock* will support as in my 1451/17.

(ii)   To: *Sydney*, repeated to *Ilex*, *Havock*, R.A.(L), C.S.3, *Hero*, D(2), *Hasty*. IMPORTANT. My 1447. Carry out following operation. Objects support of force under D(2) and interception of Italian shipping in Gulf of Athens. Leave Alexandria with *Havock* at 0430, tomorrow Thursday. Pass through Kaso Strait at about 2200C thence to Gulf of Athens to search for enemy shipping, then pass through Antikithera Channel to arrive Alexandria 1400C, 20 July.[5]

Sydney and *Havock* sailed from Alexandria at 04.30 on the 18th, and after passing through the Kaso Strait at 23.45, steered a mean course 295 degrees at eighteen knots, zig-zagging on account of full moon and improving visibility. *Sydney's* Captain Collins seems to have found the double object given to him something of an embarrassment, for he subsequently wrote that in the morning of the 19th:

I was proceeding on a westerly course about 40 miles north of Crete in accordance with my instructions to afford support to D(2) and destroyers … My instructions included the second object of the destruction of enemy shipping in the Gulf of Athens. I decided however that it was my duty to remain in support of destroyers until 0800 by which time they should have cleared the Antikithera Strait, although this precluded the successful achievement of the second object.[6]

Meanwhile, unbeknownst to the British, the Italian light cruisers *Giovanni delle Bande Nere* (flag Vice-Admiral F. Casardi) and *Bartolomeo Colleoni* had sailed from Tripoli at 22.00 on the 17 July for the Aegean. During the 18th they steered eastward for a point thirty miles north of Derna, which they reached at 23.07 and then turned to the northward. At 07.00 the following day they were on course to enter the Aegean through the Antikithera Channel, just as Commander Nicholson's destroyers were approaching it from the east-north-east.

At 07.22 on 19 July the two Italian cruisers were sighted ahead by *Hero* but the Italians had sighted the British destroyers about five minutes earlier and turned to head them off. However, it appears that Admiral Casardi suspected that the destroyers were screening heavy ships and hauled round to port at about 07.23 thereby losing the opportunity of inflicting serious damage to the destroyers with his heavier armament.

On sighting the enemy at 07.22 Commander Nicholson at once turned his division to starboard together to course 060 degrees, and increased speed. He estimated that at 09.00 *Sydney* would be in position 010 degrees, fifty-five miles from Cape Spada, and while steering for this position he endeavoured to work round to the northward. Actually, thanks to Captain Collins' decision to give precedence to supporting the destroyers, *Sydney* was a good deal nearer, and when, at 07.33, she received Commander Nicholson's signal of the siting of the enemy (two enemy cruisers steering 160 degrees, bearing 255 degrees, distant ten miles) her position was 010 degrees, Cape Spada forty miles.[7]

Sydney, with *Havock*, altered course to 190 degrees and worked up to full speed so as to intercept the Italians while at the same maintaining radio silence so as not to alert them as to his presence nearby. The Italian cruisers opened fire at 07.26 well beyond the range of the destroyer's 4.7-inch guns but their shooting was erratic with their salvoes falling short, throwing up red, yellow and green splashes because of the use of identifiers. Commander Nicholson kept Collins informed while the latter continued to maintain wireless silence. At about 08.00 the destroyers were instructed by the C-in-C Mediterranean Fleet to join *Sydney* which was directed to support the destroyers.

At 08.29 *Sydney* opened fire at a range of 20,000 yards on *Giovanni delle Bande Nere* taking the Italians completely by surprise, the first intimation they had of her presence being the arrival of her salvoes. At 08.32 the Italians returned the fire concentrating on the *Sydney*'s gun flashes, which were all they could see in the low-lying mist, but their salvoes fell short at first, then over, with an occasional straddle. At about 08.35 *Giovanni delle Bande Nere* was hit by a 6-inch shell which passed through the fore funnel and exploded near the after part of the aircraft launching machinery, killing four ratings and wounding four more. The Italians made smoke and turned away. By 08.46 *Sydney*'s original target was so obscured by smoke that fire was shifted to *Bartolomeo Colleoni* the rear cruiser which was engaged by 'A' and 'B' turrets on bearing 203 degrees at a range of 18,000 yards.

There now ensued a chase in a south-westerly direction with *Sydney* firing on whichever Italian cruiser was visible through the smoke and mist. At 09.08 fire was shifted back again to *Bartolomeo Colleoni* then bearing 210 degrees at a range of 18,500 yards. At 09.15 *Sydney* altered course 30 degrees to starboard to open her 'A' arcs, and began to hit her faster adversary. At 09.19, with the range down to 17,500 yards, *Sydney* also came under an accurate fire receiving her only hit at 09.21 when a 6-inch shell burst on the fore funnel blowing a hole about three feet square in the casings but suffering only one minor casualty. Meanwhile, *Bartolomeo Colleoni*, the fastest cruiser in the world at the time, was being hit repeatedly by *Sydney* although the range was too great for *Havock* and the other destroyers to have any effect.[8]

'Buster' Brown (*Havock* 'X' gun) recollected:

> When pursuing the retreating *Colleoni*, she was still engaging with her aft guns until she was disabled. The shells could be heard passing overhead. It was a good job her ranging was poor; the shells could be seen dropping astern of *Havock*.[9]

At 09.23 *Bartolomeo Colleoni* was seen to be stopped and apparently out of action in a position about five miles east-north-east of Cape Spada. Survivors afterwards stated that she was brought to a standstill by a shell strike in the engine or boiler room which caused the complete loss of electrical power. All her lights went out and ratings stationed in the magazines groped their way out by means of matches and cigarette lighters. *Giovanni delle Bande Nere* made off at high speed to the southward, rounding Agria Grabusa Island with *Sydney* in hot pursuit, leaving the destroyers to finish off the doomed *Bartolomeo Colleoni*.

Commander Nicholson's destroyers altered course to 240 degrees and opened fire at a range of 14,500 yards. By 09.30 the range was down to about 5,000 yards. The Italian cruiser, which was drifting and silent, had been hit repeatedly below the bridge, her control had been put out of action and some HA ammunition set ablaze. The whole bridge structure was soon enveloped in flames but she was still afloat and consequently, at 09.33, *Sydney* signalled the one word 'Torpedo'. Ordering *Hero* to take charge of the other destroyers and follow *Sydney*. As Commander Nicholson in the *Hyperion* with *Ilex* approached *Bartolomeo Colleoni*, the latter was on fire amidships, her colours on the mainmast shot away and she had suffered a heavy explosion forward.

At 09.35 *Hyperion* fired four and the *Ilex* two torpedoes at a range of 1,400 yards. One torpedo from *Ilex* hit the *Bartolomeo Colleoni* forward, blowing away about 100 feet of her bows and her aircraft. *Hyperion's* torpedoes, because of too great a spread, passed two ahead and two astern, and ran on to explode ashore on Agria Grabusa Island. *Hyperion* then closed in, and Commander Nicholson decided as he passed down her starboard side to go alongside and see what could be salved. Barely two minutes elapsed, however, before a large fire broke out in the forward superstructure followed by an explosion which blew the whole bridge away in a cloud of smoke. *Hyperion* then fired another torpedo at short range which hit the doomed cruiser amidships at 09.52, and seven minutes later she heeled over and sank bottom up in position 029 degrees four and a half miles from Agria Grabusa Light.[10]

Hyperion and *Ilex* immediately began to rescue survivors being joined by *Havock* which had been too far off to read *Hero's* Commander Bigg's signal to join him. According to survivors' accounts, the crew of *Bartolomeo Colleoni* had started to jump overboard as soon as the ship stopped and many of them were in the sea before *Ilex's* torpedo struck the ship. The cruiser had suffered many casualties forward, on the upper deck and around the bridge, among them Captain Umberto Novaro who later died from his wounds on board the hospital ship *Maine* at Alexandria on 23 July. There seems to have been little or no attempt to launch any boats or rafts, but all the crew had life belts. During the rescue work several signals were received from Captain Collins directing the destroyers to join him as soon as possible, but it was not till 10.24 that the *Hyperion* and *Ilex* complied, leaving *Havock* to continue picking up survivors. [11]

At 09.50 *Sydney* hit *Giovanni delle Bande Nere*, with the shell penetrating the quarterdeck and exploding on a bulkhead killing four and wounding twelve ratings. At about 10.22 *Sydney* broke off the action because *Giovanni delle Bande Nere* was drawing ahead and almost out of range and because her 'A' gun turret was down to four rounds per gun and 'B' gun turret down to one round per gun of common shell.

At 12.37, after *Havock* had picked up some 260 survivors, six Savoia 79 bombers were sighted, approaching from the southward forcing her to abandon her humane task and proceed at full speed for Alexandria. Altogether, 525 survivors out of a complement of 630 had been picked up by the three destroyers. At 12.45 and 12.50 the bombers, in formations of three, attacked her without success, doing no more than deluge her with water from near misses.

At 13.28 *Havock* signalled:

> Have 250 survivors including 12 cot cases and 20 other wounded from the Italian cruiser *Bartolomeo Colleoni*. Am returning to Alexandria, expected time of arrival 0500. (*Havock* 1328/19).

At 14.55 nine more aircraft, in flights of three, attacked her off Gavdo Island. These attacks, made from levels between 3,000 and 4,000 feet, were countered with effective 4.7-inch gunfire, which in two instances broke up the formations. *Havock* fought off the various attacks exhausting her anti-aircraft ammunition in the process. This proved almost fatal when the last bomb of the raid near-missed amidships, badly holing her in the No. 2 boiler room which was flooded and caused severe damage. The bomb that caused the damage appeared to be one of 250lb, which burst six feet under water about ten feet from the ship's side.

After some urgent and swift damage control work *Havock* was eventually able to proceed at a pedestrian ten to twelve knots rising to twenty knots later but still in very exposed and dangerous waters. There were no casualties from the bombing among the crew, but some of the Italians survivors in exposed positions were badly wounded as shrapnel swept the upper works.[12]

Able Seaman 'Buster' Brown on *Havock's* 'X' Gun related:

> We picked up some 250 of the *Colleoni*'s crew. Then on the way back a load of S79s started high level bombing. There wasn't much we could do about this as we didn't have high angle guns. We would steer on a steady course until there were five or six bombs in the air and then someone would sing out 'Bombs gone!' and 'Nutty' would order Port or Starboard 30. This usually worked, but then the last bomb of the last pattern exploded on the port side abreast of the whaler and pushed the whole side in, flooding No. 1 Boiler Room. The only casualties were the Italian prisoners who were exposed on deck and who received some terrible blast and splinter injuries. The damage was from the keel right up to the waterline and it was only the starboard plates and the upper deck which prevented her from breaking in two. When we reached Alex they sent us down to Port Tewfik which is just south of Port Suez on the Canal where she was hand riveted by local labour.[13]

At about 15.00 Captain Collins, on receiving the *Havock*'s signal reporting her damage, turned back in *Sydney* in support, after ordering *Hero* and *Hasty* to continue on their course for Alexandria. Meanwhile, *Havock*'s plight had been picked up and rebroadcast by the Malta W/T station at 15.40 that day:

> H43 [*Havock*] 3 miles south of Gavdos [south of Crete] has been bombed by aircraft – his boiler room flooded – does not require assistance

Commander T.J.N. Hilken of HMAS *Sydney* commented:

> I must admit my heart sank at the prospect, but there was no alternative. *Havock* was alone and having no anti-aircraft ammunition would have been a sitter when the attack was renewed. We met *Havock* making about 20 knots and throwing up a huge column of spray from the rent in her side.

Sydney made contact with the *Havock* at about 16.40 and took station a mile astern of her and as she did so Commander Courage signalled:[14]

> Thank you. I hope your H.A. [gunnery] is as good as your L.A. [gunnery]

Havock finally struggled into Alexandria, unloaded the unfortunate Italians and was immediately committed for repair as this signal sent on 25 July indicates.

> Ship made seaworthy in Admiralty floating dock [in Alexandria] and proceeded to Suez 25/7 for permanent repairs. Estimated 5 weeks. Hull damaged, portion of bilge keel to be renewed, boiler seating port side to be repaired, boiler tubes require renewal, boiler feet distorted and require renewing. (C-in-C Med wire 1849/25.7.40)

Subsequently, the British Press extracted the maximum propaganda from the action with, for example, a headline in the *Daily Record* of 22 July proclaiming:

British Rescuers Bombed by Italians

The *Illustrated London News* of Saturday 27th July summed up the situation succinctly in a cleverly worded caption beneath a picture of the *Bartolomeo Colleoni*:

> *Colleoni* in which armour was vainly sacrificed to
> speed her gun-power being nominally exactly the same
> as the *Sydney*. The action was fought in waters which
> Italy claims to dominate with her naval and air forces.
> Colleoni, in which armour was vainly sacrificed to
> speed, her gun-power being nominally exactly the same
> as the *Sydney*'s.

By 27 July, having been patched up at Alexandria, *Havock* arrived at the Suez Canal Company's yard at Port Tewfik at the southern end of the Suez Canal for repair until 15 September. Once docked, the damage was seen to be serious as the bomb seems to have fallen about four feet short from the port side abreast No. 2 boiler room, causing damage to the hull structure and flooding the boiler room because of strained rivets. Minor damage was also caused to the boiler room and auxiliary machinery.[15] The hull plating over some twenty frames had to be removed, the frames themselves replaced, a portion of the bilge keel was twisted along with the plates, the boiler seating had to be repaired, and the boiler tubes renewed. Clearly, a fragile and unarmoured destroyer couldn't just 'walk away' undamaged from a near miss by a 250lb bomb. The repairs were originally estimated to last for five weeks, but in fact it was practically two months before the job was completed. However, the dockyard authorities at Malta were not prepared to accept that the work done in Port Tewfik by an Egyptian labour force was of sufficient quality and *Havock* was eventually sent to Malta where her repairs were completed.

At 10.36 on 5 August, while *Havock* was still under repair, Admiral Sir Andrew Cunningham sent a signal to the Admiralty informing them that all [Mediterranean Fleet] ships were going to be dazzle painted on the following principles:[16]

(a) A foundation of Mediterranean grey.
(b) Dazzles of darker colour, chosen by Commanding Officers, but not too strong a contrast.
(c) Decks not scrubbed white but stained or darkened.
(d) Turret tops to tone in with the rest of the scheme.
(e) All paint to have as dull a surface as possible.

Soon after her return to service, *Havock* would sport just such a dazzle camouflage scheme with dark bands radiating aft from her waterline just forward of 'A' gun.

By now it was clearly apparent to all that the Mediterranean Fleet was deficient in its close-range AA capability and at 19.14 on

14 August, Admiral Cunningham sent a signal to the Admiralty requesting that they ship modern light AA weapons, such as 20mm Oerlikon guns, to the Mediterranean. Fleet.[17] Such was the shortage of such weapons in the United Kingdom that it would be many months before these weapons would be made available outside Home waters. Consequently, ships of the Mediterranean Fleet had to make do with whatever they already had plus captured Italian 20mm Breda guns. In due course *Havock* would become one of the recipients of many 20mm guns captured during General O'Connor's advance across Cyrenaica which began in September 1940. On 13 September the Mediterranean Fleet received reports that the Germans had provided the Italians with 200 Stuka dive-bombers[18]; clearly Cunningham's request had come not a moment too soon.

Convoys and the sinking of the submarine *Berillo*

On 15 September, the C-in-C Mediterranean Fleet reported that *Havock* was making good her bomb damage at Suez.[19] Five days later, her repairs completed, she sailed for Port Said to escort a local convoy arriving on 21st of the month. Three days later, on 24 September *Havock* and *Hasty* sailed for Port Said as escort for convoy A.N.4 which was destined for Piraeus.[20] The two destroyers were ordered to return independently to Alexandria after finishing escorting the Piraeus-bound convoy.[21]

The passage of convoy A.N.4 coincided with Operation *MB5* which began on 29 September and involved the cruisers *Gloucester* and *Liverpool* which left Alexandria for Malta with 1,200 troop reinforcements. The escort for the operation was provided by Admiral Sir Andrew Cunningham with the battleships *Warspite* (flag C-in-C) and *Valiant*, the aircraft carrier *Illustrious*, the cruisers *Orion*, *Sydney*, *York* and eleven destroyers of DF2 and DF14.[22]

Italian air reconnaissance located the force and the Italian Fleet, consisting of the battleships *Littorio*, *Vittorio Veneto*, *Cavour*, *Cesare Dulio*, the heavy cruisers *Pola*, *Zara*, *Gorizia*, *Fiume*, *Bolzano*, *Trento*, and *Trieste*, the light cruisers *Duca d'Egli*, *Abruzzi*, *Garibaldi*, *Eugenio de Savoia*, *Duca d'Aosta* and twenty-three destroyers, put to sea from Taranto and Messina. Numerous high-level air attacks, involving twenty-eight Savoia S79s, caused no damage to Cunningham's Fleet. When *Illustrious'* reconnaissance aircraft reported spotting the Italian Fleet only nine Swordfish were available and these could not be used because of Italian air superiority.

Fortunately, despite their equally overwhelming naval superiority, the Italians inexplicably returned to their home ports on 30 September, having neither sought nor been brought to battle. This was to become an all too familiar pattern in the coming months.

Without further ado *Gloucester* and *Liverpool* were detached on 30 September and, after successfully disembarking their troops at Malta, re-joined the Fleet the following day. The return journey to Alexandria was uneventful, unlike that of *Havock* and *Hasty*.

Havock and *Hasty* with convoy A.N.4 had arrived safely in Piraeus on 1 October[23] and the two escorting destroyers set off for Alexandria. At 04.25 the following morning they surprised the Italian submarine *Berillo* on the surface in position 33°26′N, 26°12′E and immediately opened fire with their 4.7-inch guns forcing her to dive in an attempt to escape her tormentors. The very capable and battle-hardened pair of destroyers now used their Asdic sets to attack *Berillo* with depth charges. At 08.15 the successful conclusion of their action was signalled by *Havock* who reported that the submarine had surfaced at 06.15, surrendered and had been scuttled at 07.15 and that forty-five survivors had been rescued.[24] The story told was that the Italian Captain mounted *Havock*'s bridge to offer his congratulations but was swiftly removed following an altercation with 'Nutty' Courage who apparently wanted the uninvited Italian off his bridge. *Havock*'s First Officer Lieutenant John Burfield later related:

> Later on, I took the captain of the *Berillo* down to our captain's cabin. He told me that he'd had engine trouble and had tried to put matters right on the surface. He had sighted us and actually a fired a torpedo at us before submerging. This interested me, as some time previously I had consulted the army camouflage experts about how to disguise the fact that we were a two-funnelled destroyer – and therefore pre-war and not armed with pom-poms – and also how to create the illusion that we were going in the opposite direction. We fitted a triangular piece of canvas to the after funnel to make it look like a piece of the superstructure and 'dazzle' painted on the hull, together with a false bow wave. The Italian told me of his torpedo sighting calculations, from which it was apparent that the false bow wave wasn't particularly effective – so maybe it was our zig-zagging which saved us from a torpedo. He told me that after he had submerged he went into 'silent routine', but despite this *Havock* had been able to find him and he wondered how

we did it. He couldn't have known about Asdic and how it was operated on an echo system and not a hydrophone listening system. It surprised me that an enemy submarine captain didn't realise how Asdic worked, although it had been in operation since before the war. He was quite a charming man as a matter of fact and pleased for himself and his crew that we had rescued them.[25]

On hearing of the encounter with the enemy submarine, Admiral Cunningham detached the AA cruiser *Calcutta* from the returning Mediterranean Fleet with orders to join the two destroyers to provide them with AA cover.[26] However, before *Calcutta* arrived, *Havock* and *Hasty* were attacked by five Savoia 79s when thirty miles south of the Kithera Channel. Fifteen bombs were dropped but there were no hits.[27] Subsequently *Calcutta*, *Havock* and *Hasty* joined the Mediterranean Fleet at noon in position 32°40′N, 28°05′E.[28] Soon afterwards, Cunningham informed that Admiralty:

> *Havock* and *Hasty* sank a submarine after a three-hour hunt at 0730/2 in 32. 33 N, 26. 09 E, (C-in-C Med 1259/2).

A later signal on 6 October expanded on the C-in-C's earlier message:

> My 1259/2 *Havock* and *Hasty* in company sighted submarine on surface at 0425 and engaged with gunfire. U/B dived and was hunted by *Havock* and *Hasty* until 0615 when surfaced and crew surrendered. U/B scuttled herself. CO, 6 officers and 40 ratings picked up. (C-in-C Med 0955/6).

By coincidence the Italian submarine *Gondar* was sunk by the Australian destroyer *Stuart* the same day.

Operation *MB6* and the attack on Leros

By the afternoon of 8 October, this moment of glory and celebration had passed and *Havock* was back at sea yet again with the Mediterranean Fleet, consisting of the battleships *Warspite* (F), *Malaya*, *Ramillies*, the aircraft carrier *Illustrious*, the cruisers *Gloucester*, *York*, *Ajax*, *Orion*, *Sydney* and *Liverpool* and destroyers belonging to DF2, DF10 and DF14, to cover the passage of the fast convoy MF3 to Malta (Operation *MB6*).[29] The convoy arrived safely at Malta at 16.00 on 11 October. Just two hours later *Havock*,

Nubian and *Hero*, which had been sent to Malta to refuel re-joined the Mediterranean Fleet.[30] At 11.20 on 13 October, *Illustrious*, *Gloucester*, *Liverpool*, *Nubian*, *Havock*, *Hereward* and *Hero* were detached to carry out a night attack on the island of Leros. That night, fifteen Swordfish from *Illustrious* dropped ninety-two, 250lb bombs destroying hangars in Lepida Cove and a fuel oil tank in San Giorgio. The aircraft encountered ineffective AA fire and all returned safely to the aircraft carrier.[31] The Mediterranean Fleet returned safely to Alexandria at 01.00 on 16 October.[32]

On Thursday 24 October, she was involved in more convoy escort work this time covering Convoy AN5 (Operation *MAQ2*) to Piraeus along with her sister *Hero* and the AA cruiser *Calcutta*. The following day the considerably expanded force, including *Malaya*, *Eagle*, *Orion*, *Sydney*, *Coventry* and eight destroyers left Alexandria to provide heavy cover for AN5 which had left Egyptian ports the previous day.[33] The fleet returned during the 27th-28th with *Orion*, *Sydney*, *Jervis*, *Juno*, *Calcutta*, *Havock* and *Hero* passing southwards through the Doro channel at 00.01 on the 28th and thence through the Kaso Straits arriving at Alexandria that evening.

Some days later on 6 November, after taking on stores, fuel and ammunition, convoys AN6 and MW3 left Port Said and Alexandria for the Aegean and Malta respectively. These convoys were coordinated with that of *Ajax* and *Sydney* which left Alexandria on the 5th with supplies for Suda Bay in Crete and then joined the fleet the next day for Operation *MB8*, the passage of five supply ships (convoy MW3) Malta. These were further covered by *Warspite*, *Valiant*, *Malaya*, *Ramillies*, *Illustrious*, *Gloucester*, *York*, *Ajax* and *Sydney* and thirteen destroyers (*Nubian* (D14), *Mohawk*, *Jervis*, *Janus* and *Juno* of DF14 plus *Hyperion* (D2), *Hasty*, *Hereward*, *Ilex*, *Decoy* and *Defender* of DF2.[34] The passage of this convoy was used to cover one of the most famous operations of the Second World War, namely the attack on the Italian naval base of Taranto on 11 November 1940.

Taranto

Havock and *Hero* re-joined the Mediterranean Fleet at 07.15 on 10 November. At 18.00 hours the following day *Illustrious* (Rear Admiral Lyster), *Gloucester*, *York*, *Ajax*, *Sydney*, *Hyperion*, *Havock*, *Hasty* and *Ilex* were detached from the fleet to carry out Operation *Judgment* on the night of 11-12 November. *Havock*, with others, escorted the aircraft carrier *Illustrious* to a position from which her Swordfish aircraft were able to carry out the legendary attack

on the Italian fleet in Taranto harbour which left two of the six
Italian battleships in harbour beached or sinking and badly damaged a third. A shattering defeat had been inflicted on the Italians
for the loss of just two obsolescent Swordfish torpedo bombers.[35]
John Burfield remembered:

> I was Director Control Officer of *Havock* at Taranto. There
> were four of us destroyers as escort to *Illustrious*: we called
> ourselves the Iron Guard as our job was to ensure that none
> of the Italian fleet interfered with our aircraft carrier. In the
> Director I had the best pair of binoculars in the ship and I
> was supposed to keep a look-out away from the Carrier,
> but just occasionally I did take a look at her and in the dark-
> ness I could just make out some of the aircraft taking off
> from her flight deck. At one stage, *Illustrious* opened up an
> anti-aircraft barrage; this caused some of us concern as we
> wondered what she had seen; as it turned out this was one
> of her Swordfish returning early with engine trouble. Later
> on, as Officer of the Watch, I remember the difficulty we had
> keeping station on an aircraft carrier when one was only a
> mile away, on a dark night, and were pounding along at
> thirty knots or more.[36]

Illustrious and her consorts re-joined the fleet at 07.00 on 12
November. Rear Admiral Lyster had wanted to carry out a second attack that night but bad weather led to its cancellation.

The *Portsmouth Evening News* of 19 November carried a piece
in which it refuted Italian claims that their battleships had only
been damaged:

Italy's Crippled Battleships

Apropos of Mussolini's assertion yesterday that three
of the Italian battleships were damaged but not sunk, it
was pointed out by authoritative Naval quarters London
to-day that no such claim was made. The Admiralty
said that they had crippled three battleships, and later
reconnaissances proved that they were partially under
water. It is pointed out that the water in Taranto Harbour
is hardly deep enough entirely submerge a battleship
unless she lay on her side.

The outcome of the attack was very far reaching with the
Italian Battle Fleet being withdrawn to Naples, where it was
bombed by RAF Wellington aircraft from Malta. Clearly, the
balance of power had swung to the British Mediterranean

Fleet which now enjoyed more operational freedom in the eastern Mediterranean than hitherto, although the Italian battlefleet was prepared to sortie against British forces operating out of Gibraltar. Two of the three damaged battleships were repaired by mid-1941 and control of the Mediterranean continued to swing back and forth until the Italian armistice in September 1943 because Operation *Judgment* failed to deliver a knock-out blow which would have changed the context of the Mediterranean war. Furthermore, the Taranto attack had no effect on Italian shipping to Libya which actually increased over the next two months. The raid did, however, make the passage of slow convoys through to Malta a practical possibility once more, at least until mid-1941. In fact, the whole question of reinforcements for Malta, Greece and eventually Crete was made immeasurably easier until Italo-German air supremacy intervened. Lastly, for a few months, the Fleet Air Arm, with their tails up, pressed home a series of attacks on the airfields of the Dodecanese and the supply ports along the North African coast.

The excitement engendered by the raid on Taranto was followed the next day by a return to more mundane convoy duties, being deployed as Fleet screen for passage to Alexandria covering transit of Convoy ME3 from Malta and Greek convoy escort duty for the next month.

There was some minor excitement on the morning of 22 November when *Havock* and *Hasty* sailed from Alexandria to undertake an unfortunately fruitless search for a submarine reported to be in the approaches to Alexandria.[37]

On 25 November *Havock* was part of a destroyer screen for major units covering passage of reinforcements for the Mediterranean Fleet and Malta Convoys MW/ME4 (Operation *Collar*). Ironically, this latter operation led to the Battle of Spartivento on 27 November when Italian battleships put to sea to try to block the passage of a convoy from Gibraltar.

Collision with HMS *Valiant*

On 3 December[38] the battleships *Valiant* and *Barham* were returning to Alexandria after gunnery practice when the 1,350-ton *Havock* was in a somewhat violent collision with the 31,000-ton battleship *Valiant*. Substantial damage was sustained on *Havock* and she was holed below the water line in several places. Stoker Albert Goodey recalled being dangled over the side to bang wooden pegs into holes as the ship rolled to reveal them, getting a regular ducking for his efforts.[39] Frank 'Nobby' Hall (Signals) recollected:

> Valiant with four destroyers (Havock starboard wing screen position abeam of Valiant) was proceeding down Great Pass to enter Alexandria after exercise. The actual speed I'm not certain of but it was a filthy night. Valiant made the following signals 'speed 8 knots, Valiant in paravanes, destroyers enter harbour'. Captain D3 in Ilex signalled 'destroyers to form single line ahead at speed fifteen knots'. To conform, Havock increased speed and altered course 10 degrees to port to pass in front of Valiant. The next thing we knew was seeing the Valiant towering overhead. Havock hit the Valiant abreast the bridge bounced off and hit again amidships, which probably accounted for Albert's holes. The next day in harbour we received a correction to the Fleet Signal Book, it said 'On recovery of paravanes capital ships will increase to fifteen knots without signal'. It looks as though Valiant had that correction and had increased speed unknown to Havock. I think we tangled with the boom before getting tied up. The subsequent 'Court of Inquiry' was held on board Illustrious – as to the result, I never did find out.[40]

Hugh 'Bob' Langton was a Royal Australian Navy Asdic Operator who earned a DSM on Havock for his part in the sinking of the Italian submarine Berillo. He possibly would have received a second in the Malta bombing, but all Havock records were lost with her before the award could be made, to his everlasting chagrin. His asdic compartment was located low down near the hull of Havock and as close to the transducer as possible. The compartment was a watertight section and as such, like the magazines and shell rooms, the sailors inside were sealed in, in case a necessary decision to flood them was made. When Havock hit Valiant, Bob and his range recorder thought the ship had either been shelled or mined as she heeled over dramatically and they lost all power to the compartment. They were in total darkness and sealed in. The bridge did not contact them and they could get no response from anyone for over an hour. They both thought the ship was sinking and they were going down locked inside a steel coffin. Eventually someone contacted them and they were let out, but the effect on the men was very traumatic. Bob had terrible nightmares for twenty years after the war despite seeing many more horrific events.[41]

Such was the need for escort vessels that on 16 December, despite being still not properly repaired, *Havock*, with others, escorted convoy MW5B (*Volo, Rodi, Devis, Ulster Prince* and *Hoegh Hood*) to Malta during the combined Operation *MC2/Hide* which also involved the passage of the battleship *Malaya* to the Western Mediterranean. At this time, many ships operated in a sub-optimal condition because of the very high workload demands and the paucity of ships for escort work. On this occasion *Havock* was given the dubious responsibility of escorting the very slow tanker *Hoegh Hood* to Malta alone, finally arriving at Malta on 20 December. From all related stories, it seems that Christmas 1940 was a memorable one in Malta if not just for the hangovers.

Meanwhile, *Havock* was taken in hand in Malta Dockyard for repairs to damage sustained in collision with *Valiant* on 3 December and the signal sent on 16 January 1941 gives an idea as to the damage suffered by the destroyer:

> All frames distorted at forecastle deck level. Forecastle deck buckled and split from stations 8-14. No 6, 9 and 13 bulkheads buckled. Fuel tanks leaking. Ship side holed, etc. (NL 6908 C-in-C Med 16/1/41).

Whilst in Malta for repair over the next seven days she watched anxiously from her dry dock as the *Illustrious*, which was about 300 yards away and also in for repair, was bombed relentlessly. Escaping major damage *Illustrious* finally left Malta en route for Alexandria on 23 January before going through the Suez Canal for repairs in safer waters.

Large bombs were exploding near *Havock* and *Hotspur* on the dockside, covering them with rocks, debris and cement dust to half an inch thick. One bomb hit the caisson, the dam-gate that keeps the water out of the dry dock, fortunately not letting the sea in which could have been disastrous. Also, the merchant ship *Essex* was bombed in Malta with her cargo of ammunition that had not been fully unloaded because of air attacks. She was hit by a bomb fully amidships in the engine room but miraculously this did not detonate the ammunition.

At this time it was expected that *Havock* would spend six weeks in Malta undergoing repair but because of dire need of escorts the destroyer was yet again back on convoy duty on 19 February with Operation *MC8* (convoy Malta to Alex) as this signal relates:

> Force 'A' *Barham, Valiant* and *Eagle* left Alexandria today to be about 180 miles north of Benghazi at daylight/21

to meet and cover the passage of *Breconshire* and *Clan MacAulay* which leaves Malta pm/20 escorted by *Havock* and *Hotspur*.

Havock duly left Malta as planned with *Breconshire, Clan MacAulay* and her 'chummy' boat *Hotspur* and arrived in Alexandria.

Late in February 1941, and with great sadness, came news that Commander Rafe E. 'Nutty' Courage DSO, DSC, was being rewarded for his performance by a transfer to the larger Tribal Class Destroyer *Maori* on 9 July 1941, and replaced on *Havock* by Lieutenant Commander Geoffrey Robert Gordon 'Robin' Watkins. All crew that the author interviewed spoke of 'Nutty' with a remarkable reverence. He was a magnificent captain, seaman, leader of men and cavalier of the seas. John Burfield described him in a post war obituary as:

> A big, burly man, with a bright ruddy complexion, who enjoyed life. He was blunt, suffered no fools and was apparently fearless in the face of danger or superior authority. Yet beneath lay a human tenderness and understanding in others.[42]

He inspired great confidence in the men and knew them all. Jim 'Buster' Brown recalled:

> I think all of the crew had a lot of confidence in Commander Courage, particularly when we were being attacked by dive-bombers. He used to look up at them, when they were in a dive, through a piece of smoked glass and as the bombs were released he would calmly give the order 'Hard a port' or whatever manoeuvre was required to evade them. I remember when he left the ship every member of the ships company filed past him, and received a handshake. He was then rowed ashore by fellow officers in a Whaler, as was the custom.[43]

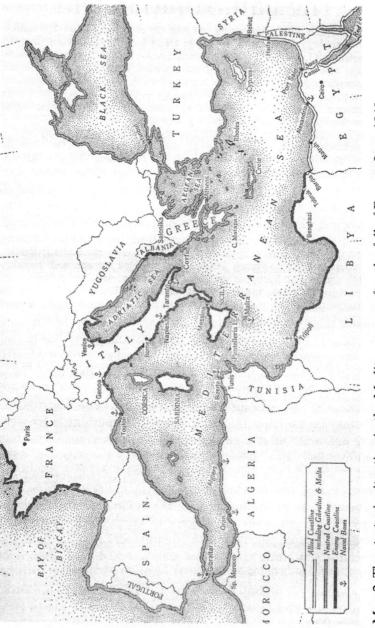

Map 2. The strategic situation in the Mediterranean after the fall of France, June 1940.

Chapter 7

The Battle of Matapan
(27 – 30 March 1941)

The Italian Navy had a marked material superiority over the British Fleet led by Admiral Sir Andrew Cunningham. Thus, Italian ships were generally newer, better armed and, on paper at least, faster than their British counterparts. However, despite these advantages, the Italian Navy also suffered from two serious disadvantages when compared to the Royal Navy. Firstly, it had neither experience in or training for night fighting and, secondly, it possessed no aircraft carriers. Furthermore, the blow inflicted at Taranto coupled with a growing shortage of fuel led to great caution when it came to employing the Italian fleet. For the Italians, the last quarter of 1940 must have seemed particularly depressing with Mussolini's armies being driven back into Albania by the Greek Army and the collapse of the Italian position in North Africa after General Wavell's offensive in early December 1940. The British 13th Corps (later the 8th Army), which was led brilliantly by Major General Richard O'Connor, advanced 500 miles in little over two months capturing 130,000 Italian prisoners, 400 tanks and 850 guns. Amongst the latter were many Breda 20mm AA guns plus tens of thousands of rounds of ammunition and, unsurprisingly, some of the weapons were fitted to ships of the British Mediterranean Fleet in a desperate attempt to improve the close-range AA capability of it ships.

The collapse of the Italian position in Greece led directly to German intervention in the Balkans to safeguard the supply of Rumanian oil and resulted in the deployment of more than 400 German aircraft in airfields in Calabria and Sicily. The effect of this build up was seen on 10-11 January 1941 when, during Operation *Excess*, aircraft from the specialist anti-shipping attack-force Fliegerkorps X sank the cruiser *Southampton* and crippled the aircraft carrier *Illustrious*. Although lacking a Mediterranean Fleet themselves the Germans were insistent that the Italian Navy should be more proactive especially after Churchill decided to send O'Connor's seasoned troops to Greece to counter German expansion in the Balkans. This futile gesture ensured that the North African campaign, which might have been ended in March or April 1941, would drag on until May 1943. Worse still, the already hard-pressed Mediterranean Fleet's cruisers would have to act as fast troop transports while, because there was no dedicated escort force in the Eastern Mediterranean, Cunningham's small and hard-pressed destroyer force would have to escort the convoys carrying troops and equipment to Greece.

In mid-March 1941, pressure from German Admiral Raeder coupled with the promise of air cover over the Italian fleet, led to Italian Naval High Command planning an offensive sweep to disrupt the Operation *Lustre*, the transport of British and Commonwealth troops to Greece which had begun on 4 March 1941. Thus, the German naval staff believed that the appearance of major Italian units south of Crete would disrupt the intense traffic between Egyptian and Greek ports.

Prelude to Matapan – Operation *MC9*

As if to support Raeder's assertion, the British launched Operation *MC9* when the Mediterranean Fleet (Force A) sailed from Alexandria in the forenoon of 20 March to support Malta convoy MW6 while at the same time covering Operation *Lustre* convoys carrying troops and equipment to Greece.[1] Force A consisted of the battleships *Warspite, Valiant* and *Barham*, the aircraft carrier *Formidable* which had arrived on station just ten days previously, DF14 (less *Greyhound* and *Griffin*) and DF2 (less *Hotspur*) from which *Havock* would be detached later to join Force C. Force B, under the command of Vice-Admiral Sir Henry Pridham-Wippell (Vice-Admiral Light Forces, VALF), was built around the 3rd (*Orion* (flag VALF), *Ajax* and *Perth*) and 7th (*York* and *Gloucester*) cruiser squadrons and their respective destroyer escorts which were ordered to join Force A off Gavdo Island at 16.00 hours on 21st March. Force C, which comprised the cruisers *Bonaventure, Coventry, Calcutta* and *Carlisle* and the destroyers *Greyhound, Griffin* and *Hotspur* would be joined by *Havock* on the 22nd, was tasked with getting convoy MW6 (*Perthshire, Clan Ferguson, City of Manchester* and *City of Lincoln*) through to Malta. *Havock* and *Hotspur* had been ordered to leave harbour with mine bow protection gear rigged ready for use. All Force C destroyers were to be prepared to run TSDS when entering Malta and *Havock* and *Hotspur* were to lead the TSDS sweep in front of the incoming convoy. It was stressed that there would be no waiting for pilots, the ships were to go straight in. *Bonaventure, Calcutta, Greyhound,*

Griffin, Hotspur and *Havock* also embarked naval personnel and stores for Malta.

At sunset on the 22nd the cruisers *York* and *Gloucester* plus the destroyers *Nubian* and *Mohawk* were detached from the Mediterranean Fleet to cover the approach of Convoy MW6, escorted by Force C, to Malta which was entered at 07.00 on Sunday 23 March. Soon after their arrival the ships were attacked by Ju 87s and *Bonaventure* suffered minor splinter damage. The returning Force C was met by *York, Gloucester, Ilex* and *Hasty* which had been detached from Force A at sunset on 23 March. At 12.15 on the 24th *Bonaventure, Greyhound, Griffin, Hotspur* and *Havock* were detached for Alexandria while *Orion, Ajax, Perth, York, Gloucester, Ilex* and *Hasty* accompanied *Calcutta* to Suda Bay. Sadly, this was to be the cruiser *York*'s last voyage because on 26 March, while anchored in Suda Bay she was struck by an Italian explosive motor boat and subsequently became a total loss. Force A had arrived back in Alexandria two days previously but had little time to rest before the next westward sortie would take place.

The Protagonists Sail

Italy had tried to strengthen further her naval superiority in the central Mediterranean in the early days of the war by attempting to seize Malta. By early 1941, Italy's failure to capture Malta had become a serious issue because reports from German air reconnaissance suggested that the area south of Gavdo Island and another on the Western Aegean were being used almost daily by important British military convoys.

German political pressure, plus the promise of air support for both Italian and German units, led the Italian Navy's High Command (the Supermarina) to plan a sweep of the waters around Crete in an operation which called for Admiral Angelo Iachino to take the bulk of his remaining surface forces to sea to engage the Allies. Iachino was heartened by false intelligence received from the Germans which indicated that the Mediterranean Fleet had only one operational battleship, *Valiant*, and no aircraft carrier whereas there were in fact three battleships, and the damaged British aircraft carrier *Illustrious* had been replaced by her sister *Formidable*.

On the night of 26 March 1941, Admiral Iachino left the port of Naples on his flagship *Vittorio Veneto* with four destroyers (Force Y) to rendezvous with the 8-inch gun cruisers *Trieste* (Vice-Admiral Sansonetti), *Trento* and *Bolzano* and three destroyers (Force X), three 8-inch gun cruisers *Zara* (Vice-Admiral Cattaneo),

Fiume and *Pola* plus the 6-inch cruisers *Duca degli Abruzzi* (Vice-Admiral Legnani) and *Guiseppe Garibaldi* and six destroyers (Force Z) in the Straits of Messina.[2] Unfortunately, things seemed to go wrong for the Italians from the beginning of the operation because promised air support for the morning of 27 March never materialized, while at 12.20, a Sunderland[3] flying boat from Crete spotted the Italian ships 120 miles south-east of the toe of Italy, steering a south-easterly course. Clearly, the Italians had lost the element of surprise, but rather than terminating the sortie, the Supermarina ordered Iachino to concentrate his forces south of Crete and sweep northward past Cape Matapan at the southern tip of Greece.

When Cunningham received the message from the Sunderland confirming that the Italians were at sea, he ordered Force B, consisting of *Orion* (Vice Admiral H.D. Pridham-Wippell), *Ajax*, *Perth*, *Gloucester* and the destroyers *Ilex* (DF2, Captain H. St L. Nicholson) *Hasty*, *Hereward* and *Vendetta*, to leave Suda Bay and rendezvous with his 1st Battleship Squadron south of Gavdo at 06.30 on 28 March.[4] In the event that Pridham-Wippell encountered the Italians prior to the meeting, he was to lure them south-eastward toward the 15-inch guns of his battleships. Meanwhile the Mediterranean Fleet (Force A) consisting of the battleships *Warspite* (Admiral Sir A. Cunningham), *Barham* (Rear Admiral H.B. Rawlings) and *Valiant*, the aircraft carrier *Formidable* (Rear Admiral D. Boyd) and the destroyers *Jervis* (DF14, Captain Mack) *Janus*, *Nubian*, *Mohawk*, *Stuart* (DF10, Captain Waller), *Greyhound*, *Griffin*, *Hotspur* and *Havock* left Alexandria on the afternoon of 27 March to join Force B.[5] Unfortunately, on leaving Alexandria *Warspite* passed too close to a mudbank as the fleet left harbor and fouled her condensers which limited her speed and that of Force A to twenty knots.[6]

Skirmish off Gavdo Island

At first light on 28 March, the Italians launched two Ro.43 reconnaissance planes, one of which sighted Pridham-Wippell's Force B at 06.50 while en route to join Cunningham. Realizing that he was confronted by a force inferior to his own, Iachino ordered Sansonetti's ships to alter course, increase speed to thirty knots and intercept the British cruisers. He also changed his own course and increased his speed to twenty-eight knots so as to be able to support his cruisers.

Meanwhile, soon after dawn on the 28th, one of *Formidable's* aircraft on reconnaissance reported the three cruisers and four destroyers of Sansonetti's Italian Force X about thirty miles south of Gavdo Island, steering south-south-east. This was in the neighbourhood of Admiral Pridham-Wippell's force of light cruisers and he wondered if his own force was the subject of the sighting report. However, at 07.45 he sighted Force X to northward. They were a long way off but he suspected them to be 8-inch-gun ships, which he knew could outrange his squadron and had superior speed. Consequently, Pridham-Wippell decided to turn to the south-east, feigning flight, and try to entice the enemy towards the British Battle Fleet while at the same time making smoke and zig-zagging.

Sansonetti's force made contact with the British ships at 08.00, with the first Italian salvos being fired at 08.12 hours at a range of 25,000 yards. All the Italians' guns were directed at the last ship in the line, the cruiser *Gloucester*. Pridham-Wippell's ruse succeeded and Force X followed for three-quarters of an hour, firing at intervals, but keeping out of range, with the result that salvoes on both sides fell short.[7]

As the British light cruiser squadron continued its flight to the south, Iachino became concerned that his ships were well within the range of British air cover, and fearing the intervention RAF bombers, he ordered Sansonetti to end his pursuit and head for Taranto. Force X duly broke off the action at 08.55 and turned away to the north-west expecting to leave the inferior British force behind. However, to the Italian's surprise, Pridham-Wippell turned in pursuit. Iachino, who had no knowledge that British battleships were heading his way at about twenty-two knots, ordered *Vittorio Veneto* to alter course towards the British cruisers and destroyers while at the same time ordering Sansonetti's squadron back into the fray. With luck, the Italians would catch the smaller British force in a trap between them. At 10.58 *Orion* sighted a battleship to the northward which, when challenged, responded with an accurate salvo of 15-inch projectiles fired from a range of sixteen miles. Pridham-Wippell had manoeuvred Force B between the jaws of a rapidly closing Italian trap and unsurprisingly, he decided upon a swift retreat. Despite laying smoke and using speed and evasive manoeuvres, the British cruisers still had an unpleasant experience as *Vittorio Veneto* fired ninety-four 15-inch shells mostly at *Gloucester*. *Orion* also attracted the battleship's attention and sustained some splinter damage as a consequence.[8]

Pridham-Wippell was in an uncomfortable position, with a battleship on one quarter and Force X on the other and both were in range of him. To his immense relief, *Vittorio Veneto* suddenly ceased firing, but her reason for doing this was concealed by the smoke. Similarly Force X, which, barely visible from the British cruisers, was also seen to turn away for the same unknown reason.

At this point we must return to the aircraft carrier *Formidable*. Just before 10.00 the Commander-in-Chief ordered a strike-force of six Albacores armed with torpedoes, escorted by a couple of Fulmars, to be flown off to deal with Force X. But on reaching the scene of the action at about 11.00 the pilots dis-covered that what in fact had been delivered into their hands was the Littorio class battleship *Vittorio Veneto*, the Italian flag-ship, escorted by four destroyers. She had just commenced heavy and accurate 15-inch gunfire on the British cruisers and the Albacores were just in time. Under the leadership of Lieutenant Commander W.H.G. Saunt, they dived to attack through an intense barrage. When first spotted by the Italians, they were misidentified as friendly aircraft from Rhodes but after realizing their error, the Italian gunners put up a screen of AA fire while *Vittorio Veneto* manoeuvred to avoid British tor-pedoes. Although they failed to achieve any hits, the Albacores had kept the Italians occupied for about thirty minutes and thereby allowed the British cruisers to escape. Having sur-vived the torpedo attack unscathed but still uneasy about the presence of enemy aircraft and without air cover of his own, Iachino ordered a return to the safety of Taranto.[9]

At 12.30, to the relief of the Commander-in-Chief, his sec-ond-in-command appeared with all his force intact and joined the fleet. Meanwhile a new enemy force was now reported by a patrolling Sunderland as being some thirty-five miles to the westward of Gavdo Island. This consisted of two Abruzzi class cruisers and three Zara class heavy cruisers (Force Z) which was steering to the north-westward and was about a hundred miles in that direction from the British fleet.

The two opposing fleets were still more than sixty miles apart. Cunningham's 1st Battleship Squadron was slow compared with the Italian ships and only air attacks could delay the Italian warships long enough for his ships to intercept. Fortunately, Cunningham had not only *Formidable*'s aircraft under his com-mand but also land-based bombers in Crete and Greece. These machines, along with reconnaissance aircraft from *Formidable*, were tasked with shadowing and continually reporting on the location, speed and composition of the Italian force. Pilots from *Formidable*'s aircraft returning from the morning attack wrongly reported that an Italian battleship had suffered a probable hit thereby giving credence to Cunningham's hopes of slowing the Italian force until his older battleships could arrive on the scene. Land-based Blenheim bombers from Crete repeatedly attacked Iachino's force from a high altitude reporting additional probable hits thereby further building hopes that the Italians were being slowed down. The reality was quite the opposite, no hits had been scored, and the Italians continued to widen the distance between the two forces.

Vittorio Veneto torpedoed

The second carrier-based air attack consisted of three Albacores and two Swordfish torpedo bombers accompanied by two Fulmar fighters. At approximately 15.10, they sighted the Italian battleship fleet as it was being attacked by some of the high-altitude bombers from Crete. Flying low, they were not immediately noticed but, once identified, they were subjected to an intense barrage of AA fire. Ignoring incoming tracers closing on his Albacore, the leader, Lieutenant Commander J. Dalyell-Stead, dropped his torpedo 1,000 yards off *Vittorio Veneto*'s port side shortly before being killed along with his observer Lieutenant R.H. Cooke by enemy fire. The torpedo struck fifteen feet below the waterline just above the port outer propeller. The explosion rocked *Vittorio Veneto* which came to a stop at 15.30 after having shipped 4,000 tons of water. The battleship began to list to port and slowly settled by the stern. Unknown to Iachino, she was stopped sixty-five miles away from a British battlefleet closing at twenty-two knots. Fortunately, the battleship's well-drilled crew managed to recover the situation and *Vittorio Veneto* was soon under way again albeit at ten knots and manoeuvring solely with her starboard screws.[10]

Iachino now organized his fleet columns around his crippled flagship while at the same time ordering his 6-inch gun cruisers home. He placed Cattaneo's 1st Cruiser Division (Force Z) on his starboard side with its destroyer squadron on the outer flank, and Sansonetti's 3rd Cruiser Division (Force X) to his port side, also flanked by its destroyers. Iachino's destroyers were placed both fore and aft of *Vittorio Veneto*. The Italian force now consisted of five columns of ships, with *Vittorio Veneto* in the center of the protective screen. Iachino was determined to return his flagship safely to port.[11]

The Swordfish floatplane carried by the *Warspite* was catapulted off at 17.45. The pilot reported that it appeared that the *Vittorio Veneto* was now doing fifteen knots, to port of her were

8-inch gun cruisers of Force X, while on the starboard wing there were the three 8-inch gun cruisers of Force X with the whole massed force being screened by eleven destroyers.

Pola torpedoed

A final strike for the day, consisting of six Albacores and two Swordfish, was launched from *Formidable* at 17.35. At 18.23 the pilots sighted the Italian formation but remained out of range, circling the enemy fleet, waiting for the cover of darkness to attack. At 19.25 the British aircraft began their attack. The Italians had already created a smoke screen, and the cruisers and destroyers switched on their searchlights to blind the attacking pilots. Suddenly, at 19.46, the heavy cruiser *Pola* was hit by a torpedo amidships on the starboard side between the engine room and boiler room. All electrical power failed, three compartments were flooded and her main engines stopped. *Pola* lay dead in the water, with no electrical power and her boiler rooms flooded. Unaware that *Pola* had been crippled the Italian fleet continued to withdraw until, at 20.15, when Iachino received news that *Pola* had stopped. Cattaneo was ordered to turn back with Force Z to search for *Pola* and decide whether the stricken ship should be towed to safety or scuttled while the rest of the Italian fleet, including the damaged *Vittorio Veneto*, headed for Taranto and safety.[12] Unbeknown to Iachino, the entire British force was now less than forty miles to the south.

It was now nearly dark. Vice-Admiral Pridham-Wippell, pressing on in pursuit of the enemy, saw the sky ahead filled with spouts of coloured tracer ammunition and bursting shells. It was the Italian fleet's reaction to the torpedo air attack. 'They must have been very gallant men who went through it to get their torpedoes home' he commented in his dispatch. The firing died away with the last of the light. The British cruisers held on to their course unaware that, after the attack, the enemy had turned to the south-west. Pridham-Wippell never regained contact with the main body but his radar-equipped cruiser *Ajax* would deliver the Italian Force Z to Cunningham's battlefleet[13].

Cunningham, in deciding to engage in a night action, had to accept certain risks. Apart from the powerful force screening his quarry, there was Force Z, consisting of three 8-inch gun cruisers and five destroyers somewhere in the darkness to the northward. On the other hand, the Italians were 300 miles from home and by daylight would be under cover of their dive-bombers. He could not afford to subject his fleet to air attack on such a scale and consequently decided to accept the hazards involved in a battle-ship night action and at 20.37 he sent most of his destroyers in to the attack the retreating Italians[14].

The necessity for providing the vital Aegean convoys with escorts had reduced the number of destroyers available for fleet work to an absurdly small force and only eight destroyers in two divisions formed the attacking force. The odds were against them and they knew it. Captain Mack (D14) led them in the *Jervis*, with Captain Nicholson (D2) in the *Ilex* while Cunningham retained Waller (D10), the Australian, in *Stuart*, with *Havock*, *Greyhound* and *Griffin*, all of which were old, battle-damaged or efficiency-reduced cripples in one way or another, to act as a screen to the battle fleet. John Burfield observed that:

> As the newer and bigger destroyers came out to the Med, the Tribals and the Ls, we – the Gs, Hs and Is – became known as the Second Division and were often 'relegated' to look after the capital ships. At Matapan our job was to screen *Warspite* and in fact we saw more action at Matapan than all the other destroyers in the Fleet.[15]

Cunningham ordered the striking force to proceed to where he believed the enemy to be but unbeknown to them they were heading for empty water and the action would all be behind them. What at this point nobody knew was that the Italian cruiser *Pola* had stopped after being torpedoed and that two heavy cruisers and four destroyers had turned back to go to her assistance. The rest of the enemy force, after turning to the south-west for some distance, had turned again to the north-west.

The destruction of Cattaneo's squadron

Darkness gave the crews of the Italian heavy cruisers a false sense of security. But the darkness hid little from one of Pridham-Wippell's scavenging cruisers which were sailing westward. A blip appeared on the cruiser *Ajax*'s radar screen at 20.30 and believing it to be the crippled *Vittorio Veneto*, Pridham-Wippell advised Cunningham of the sighting. His battlefleet arrived in the area at 22.00 and the radar-equipped *Valiant* detected a stopped ship approximately 700 feet long off her port bow. Actions stations was sounded and the battlefleet changed course to close on the stationary target which Cunningham must have hoped was the damaged *Vittorio Veneto*.

At 22.20, *Valiant* reported that the target was four and a half miles away and almost immediately detected other incoming ships. Almost simultaneously, at 22.23 the destroyer *Stuart* reported two large enemy ships with a smaller one in front and followed by three smaller ships, bearing 250 degrees at a distance of about two miles. This was Cattaneo's entire cruiser division (Force Z) en route to rescue *Pola*. The British battleships were ready for action and only needed the new bearing for the incoming enemy ships. Using short-range wireless the battlefleet was turned on its original course of 280 degrees which was almost parallel and opposite to the oncoming cruisers who were now steering 130 degrees and totally unprepared for action. *Pola*, mistaking the approaching British battleships for *Fiume* and *Zara*, fired a recognition flare. Force Z had formed a column, led by the destroyer *Alfieri* which was followed by the heavy cruisers *Zara* and *Fiume*, which were then followed by the destroyers *Gioberti*, *Carducci* and *Oriani*. Suddenly, the destroyer *Greyhound* opened her searchlight and a great beam of light fell upon *Fiume*, the third ship of the line while simultaneously revealing the silhouettes of *Zara* and *Alfieri* and greatly assisting the gunnery of Cunningham's battleships.

At 22.27 *Warspite* and *Valiant* opened fire on *Fiume* with 15-inch broadsides at 2,900 and 4000 yards respectively. Five of the six 1920lb 15-inch shells from *Warspite*'s first broadside ('Y turret didn't bear on the target) struck the hapless cruiser along most of her length below the upper deck and blowing 'Y' turret overboard. Thirty seconds later *Warspite* fired a second broadside into *Fiume* before shifting to engage *Zara*, the second ship of the line. After firing her first broadside into *Fiume*, *Valiant* shifted into *Zara* and in three minutes fired five broadsides into the hapless cruiser. By now *Fiume* was ablaze from stem to stern and soon began to list heavily to starboard. The flames were extinguished when the doomed cruiser sank at 23.15.

When the battleships opened fire, the aircraft carrier *Formidable*, which was the third ship in the line of Cunningham's battlefleet, wisely hauled out to starboard at full speed, a night encounter being no place for such a vulnerable and valuable ship. The battleship *Barham*, the fourth ship in line, opened fire on the destroyer *Alfieri*, the leading enemy ship, firing a full broadside into her at 3,000 yards. *Alfieri* was hit along her length and was soon enveloped in smoke and flames. *Barham* now shifted her fire to *Zara* contributing six 15-inch broadsides and seven 6-inch salvoes to the luckless cruiser which had been devastated already by *Warspite* and *Valiant*. By now *Zara* had been reduced to a burning hulk after being hit by at least twenty 15-inch shells and she drifted off, burning fiercely and emitting thick smoke.[16] *Jervis* found her a burning wreck still floating at about 02.40 and sank her with three torpedoes.

'Second Division' sent in to finish off the cripples

Meanwhile, in the terrible illumination of star shell, blazing ships and gun flashes, a number of enemy destroyers appeared astern of the *Fiume* and fired torpedoes at the battleships before making off toward the westward. The leading destroyers were hit by 6-inch shells from the *Warspite*, as the battlefleet swung to starboard to avoid the torpedoes. Instant confusion was caused when *Havock*, being closely engaged with the enemy destroyers, failed to turn on her fighting lights. *Warspite*, believing her to be an enemy ship, fired two salvoes at her. Although straddled the many times lucky *Havock* evaded damage, although it was thought at the time on *Warspite* that she had possibly been hit. The Commander-in-Chief, with the battleships and the aircraft carrier *Formidable*, then withdrew to the north-eastward to avoid the possibility of being torpedoed, in the confusion of a destroyer melee, by his own forces. Before turning, Admiral Cunningham threw his four, as Burfield put it, 'Second Division' defensive screen destroyers in to a classic destroyer melee. The 10th flotilla went off in pairs. *Stuart* led *Havock* towards the burning cruisers whilst *Greyhound* and *Griffin* went off after the fleeing destroyers.

Just before 23.00 *Stuart* saw an enemy cruiser, probably *Zara*, stationary and ablaze with an attendant destroyer, probably the injured *Alfieri* nearby. *Stuart*, judging her moment, fired her full outfit of six torpedoes at the pair of them, observing an explosion in *Zara* which was interpreted as a hit. She also opened fire on the burning cruiser which provoked a brief response, followed by silence. Then she turned her attention to the attendant destroyer, which was found to be lying stopped 1,500 yards away with a heavy list. At this moment, in the glare of the burning cruiser, another destroyer appeared, at about 23.08, probably *Carducci*, which was apparently chasing *Stuart*, which was busy shelling the victim with the heavy list. At 23.15 *Stuart* observed the stopped, burning and listing *Alfieri* suddenly capsize and sink. Two minutes later she saw the burning *Zara* and fired two salvoes at her.

As if this was not crowding the moment with incident enough, a further Italian destroyer, probably *Oriani*, shot past *Stuart* at about 23.20, illuminated by explosions in the enemy ships. *Stuart*, having to go hard to port to avoid ramming, put three salvoes into her as she swept past while *Havock* hurried off in hot pursuit of *Carducci*. Having lost touch with *Havock* and, as Captain Waller puts it, 'feeling somewhat alone' this gallant unit of the Royal Australian Navy, then retired to the north-east and the cover of the battlefleet. On the way, she engaged another the destroyer, *Gioberti*, causing a fire.[17]

We last saw *Havock* disappearing in pursuit of the destroyer *Carducci* that the *Stuart* had engaged earlier. *Havock*'s Lieutenant Commander 'Robin' Watkins fired four torpedoes at her, scoring one hit at about 23.15, which brought her to a standstill. According to Freddie Kemp: 'We were so close the explosion from our torpedo lifted us out of the water'.[18] *Havock* then circled the hapless victim, pouring in a heavy fire until she blew up and sank at 23.30. During this action *Havock* saw the burning *Alfieri* capsize and sink at 23.15.[19]

No. 1 Torpedoman Jack Surridge in command of *Havock*'s after torpedo tubes related: 'We thought we were following one of our own destroyers. When it turned our Yeoman sang out 'It's an Italian, why doesn't someone fire?' My communications number on our tubes heard the word fire and said 'fire'. So I did and the ship was sunk.[20]

It was now about 23.30 and *Havock* reported sighting the burning cruisers *Fiume* and *Zara*. The latter had a single fire abreast the bridge and *Havock* fired her four remaining torpedoes at the crippled cruiser at about this time but scored no hits. At 00.20 *Havock*, passing through a number of rafts and survivors, Watkins, who had fired all his torpedoes, saw, by the light of a star shell, what he took to be a *Littorio* class battleship in the position of the burning cruisers and erroneously reported this to the battlefleet. In fact, this was the stationary *Pola* and he fired a few rounds at her which provoked no reply but caused fires to break out under the bridge and aft. *Pola* appeared undamaged and, in some bewilderment, he ceased fire, hauled off and prepared a boarding party. At 01.10 *Havock* altered her sighting report to that of an 8-inch cruiser.[21]

At this juncture, *Greyhound* and *Griffin* appeared on the scene. *Pola*, her ensign still flying, her guns trained fore and aft, was apparently undamaged but a large number of her crew had unaccountably taken to the water and the remainder, a disorganised rabble on the upper decks, were bawling surrender. Jack Surridge remembered: 'The Italians on *Pola* were drunk, wine bottles in their hands'.[22]

Watkin's problem was whether to sink her, to carry her by boarding, or to go alongside and take the crew grateful prisoner. At 03.14 *Havock* reported being alongside *Pola* and asked whether 'to board or blow her stern off with depth charges', having no torpedoes left.

Watkins was rescued from his quandary by the arrival of Captain Mack and the 14th and 2nd flotillas. They had failed to make contact with the enemy fleet due to its timely change of course to southward and now returned to the scene of the action, sinking the burning hulk of the *Zara* on the way. Ordering his ships to pick up the survivors from the water, Captain Mack took the *Jervis* alongside the *Pola*. Her upper deck was a scene of incredible demoralisation. Many of those who had not jumped overboard were indeed half drunk. The deck was littered with bottles, clothing and packages. The guns were abandoned and had not fired a shot due to a total loss of electrical power.

By 03.40 this strange rescue work was completed. Casting off from the *Pola*, the *Jervis* put a torpedo into her. As she settled very slowly the *Nubian* followed up with another. The *Pola* sank at 04.10 and the two flotillas and the Second Division set off to join the battlefleet.[23]

As ever in these situations the men-at-the-top waited earnestly with great concern to see what carnage had been caused amongst their own friends. The destroyers were sighted from the bridge of the fleet flagship *Warspite* as dawn was breaking, steaming majestically in two divisions of six looking for all the world like a parade at a Spithead Review. The bridge officers counted them through powerful binoculars, reporting, 'There are all twelve there, Sir!' which seemed to the anxious Cunningham almost incredible. Cunningham firmly believed at a minimum that he had sunk *Havock* with his salvoes in the early exchanges[24]. His signal to the Admiralty, reporting the outcome of the battle was succinct and to the point:

> Be pleased to lay before Their Lordships the attached reports of the Battle of Matapan, 27-30 March, 1941. Five ships of the enemy fleet were sunk, burned or destroyed as per margin. Except for the loss of one aircraft in action, our fleet suffered no damage or casualties.

Another view of Matapan is provided by an entry in the Midshipman's Journal Log of Derek Napper on *Havock*. Having arrived on 18 March this young 'Middie' gives a vivid on-the-spot account of the action:

27 March, Thursday. We left harbour at 16.00 with *Hotspur*, *Nubian* and *Mohawk* to screen *Formidable* while she exercised her aircraft. At 19.00 we heard that the Battlefleet was coming out and that we were to RV [rendezvous] with them.

28 March, Friday. At 09.30 Action Stations was piped, as the enemy ships (two 8-inch and one 6-inch cruiser with destroyers) were only fifty miles ahead. *Formidable* flew off a striking force and we increased speed. Our own cruisers were somewhere the other side of the enemy. Further reports came in during the afternoon and from these it became apparent that there were three groups of enemy ships at sea. One seemed to consist of a Littorio Class Battleship with cruisers and destroyers. Another of two Cavour Class Battleships and a third of three cruisers and a few destroyers. We were at Action Stations for the remainder of the day and *Formidable* flew off a force of eight Albacores. On their return, they signalled that there was one Littorio Class battleship damaged fifty miles ahead. Three Swordfish operating from a shore base also claimed to have damaged one enemy cruiser.

With our own cruisers twenty miles ahead we steamed at maximum speed towards the crippled Italian. About 23.00 Valiant got RDF indication of surface ships five miles ahead. A few minutes later *Warspite* fired two or three salvoes at an enemy 8-inch cruiser and sank her

We followed an Italian destroyer for a few minutes and she then turned across our bows. I was on 'A' Gun and ordered the trainer to train right. This he did with great speed and we got off one round local control before she got into our blind position. We fired one torpedo which hit her amidships. The destroyer blew up. At various times we fired about fifty rounds and all our torpedoes.

Soon after this we saw two searchlights ahead and our own searchlight illuminated a large black shape which turned out to be the 8-inch cruiser *Pola* which had been torpedoed. We trained our guns on her but felt rather hopeless as we had no torpedoes left and the range was absolutely point blank. Then they started flashing lights and every floating Italian for miles set up a wail.

'A' Gun's crew were served out with rifles as a boarding party and I collared a revolver and loaded it. The
First Lieutenant came forward and told me I could go on
board with him to get to the bridge and try to find some
Confidential Books. Unfortunately, *Jervis* went alongside
and we were robbed of a pleasant little adventure. When
all the terrified Italians had jumped over the side, *Jervis*
torpedoed her and all the destroyers began to pick up
survivors. They were a very poor lot, and completely lost
all control, biting, scratching and kicking to get to the ladders. It is not hard to see why they cannot compare with
our efficiency, when their manpower is so inferior. Our
ship's company behaved with great coolness throughout
the action, and I think the shooting was brilliant. S.A.P
shells were fired from all guns, except 'B', which fired
star shell. Thirty-five prisoners were taken, mostly from
the *Pola* with a few from the *Zara*, a similar ship. At the
moment, I know two enemy destroyers and two cruisers were sunk, with no loss to ourselves. The Littorio
class battleship reported must have been the *Pola*, which
looks far too large for a cruiser. Altogether this has been
a most satisfactory affair, and I thoroughly enjoyed it,
and to prove beyond doubt (if proof be needed) that our
naval gunnery is still up to standard, and our handling
of destroyers is still executed with great daring. At last
at 05.30, two watch defence stations were assumed and I
turned in to 07.30 having been on my feet for 25 ½ hours.[25]

Jack Surridge who fired the torpedo which sank the destroyer
added:

There are some that say the destroyer that we sank was
the *Carducci*, but they are wrong. It was lit up by our
searchlight and I saw quite clearly the big letters AF on
her bow in red as I fired the torpedo – so it was *Alfieri*
without a doubt.[26]

This appears to be a classic case in which an eye-witness is adamant that they saw a particular sequence of events but is actually
mistaken. Thus, despite his assertion to the contrary, Surridge
could not have seen AF on the bows of the ship he torpedoed,
although I have no doubt whatsoever that he did actually see
Alfieri earlier that night at about 23.00 before she sank at 23.15. This
is exactly the same time that Surridge fired the torpedoes from
Havock and *Carducci* sank fifteen minutes after being hit by one of

them. Furthermore, *Alfieri* was stopped, burning and listing having been blasted by 15-inch shells from the battleship *Barham* and therefore could not have been the destroyer that rushed by both *Stuart* and *Havock*. This means that there can only be two possible candidates for the destroyers that rushed past *Stuart* and *Havock*, namely *Oriani* and *Carducci*. Analysis of the movements made by the respective ships made that night strongly suggest that the latter must be *Havock's* victim – not least because *Oriani* escaped destruction that night and returned to her base albeit in a damaged condition. It is therefore most likely that Surridge, who had seen *Alfieri* earlier that night, also witnessed her capsize and sink as he was firing *Havock's* torpedoes. Then, having witnessed both acts contemporaneously he seems to have conflated them into a single event.

Havock rendezvoused with the fleet at 07.00 on 29 March and formed an anti-submarine screen steering southwest. Course was altered later to the eastwards and the fleet started on its return to its base. At 16.00 the fleet was attacked by dive bombers but without success and one plane fired a few machine-gun shots which all missed. The fleet arrived at its base at Alexandria on the evening of the 30th and started another very brief spell in harbour before sailing once again for an unknown destination.

Further entries in Midshipman Derek Napper's log show how continuous the work was:

> Sunday 30 March the Fleet entered harbour at 17.00. Eight torpedoes were supplied to us immediately on securing. Tuesday 1 April, *Havock* left harbour at 16.00 In company with *Ilex* to escort two large fifteen-knot troopships to Piraeus. Just outside the harbour an A/S trawler signalled that she had a submarine contact and dropped a pattern of charges. D2 ordered us to drop two as well, in order to create as large a volume of explosions as possible, because the Italians are likely to surface even when they are hardly damaged at all. No submarines appeared so I assumed they had got an echo on some other object.
>
> Wednesday 2 April. Just as it got light *Hotspur* and *Breconshire* joined us, and half an hour later *Carlisle* arrived to give AA support. The day passed without incident.[27]

Reflections on Matapan

Historically, the Battle of Matapan is important because it was the first main fleet action in which carrier-borne aircraft played an indispensable role in search, attack and defence. It was also the first time that radar-equipped ships hunted an unsuspecting opponent at night. When set against the background of a powerful Italian fleet and the growing menace of shore-based German dive-bombers which threatened to eliminate British naval supremacy, Matapan was a timely victory. Thus, it had the effect of discouraging Italy from participating with her fleet in the evacuation of Greece and Crete thereby saving many Allied army and navy lives, although the Luftwaffe made sure that the Royal Navy paid a severe price.

Post-war, Admiral Iachino revealed that the Cattaneo's force had been paralysed by surprise when Cunningham's battleships opened fire not least because Italian ships were not fitted with radar and so had to rely on look-outs. Furthermore, the Italians had not prepared for night action and consequently no anti-flash ammunition was provided for the main armaments. The problems of gun laying and fire control at night remained to be addressed. Iachino was full of praise for the accuracy and rapidity of the 15-inch gunfire and was also most impressed by the British use of searchlights and star-shell. Clearly, the time spent learning the lessons from the disastrous night actions at Jutland had paid off and the unfortunate Italians were the victims of British night-fighting skills which had been honed by numerous exercises in the inter-war period.

Needless to say, the British Press reported Cunningham's victory with glee. Thus, on 2 April 1941 the *Daily Mirror* ran the following story:

> **11 ITALIAN CRUISERS IN BATTLE.** Britain's brilliant Mediterranean naval victory was gained although the Italians had eleven cruisers in the battle and we had only four. A naval authority revealed in London yesterday that the British force was three battleships, one aircraft carrier, four cruisers and destroyers. The Italian fleet consisted of three battleships [actually only one] eleven cruisers and fourteen destroyers. When, on 27 March (Thursday) Admiral Cunningham, the- Commander-in-Chief, learned, that enemy ships were off Sicily, he was at Alexandria with the main body of his fleet. Believing that the enemy meant to attack our convoys between Egypt and Greece, he made the following dispositions:- The Vice-Admiral Commanding Light Forces (Vice-Admiral H.D. Pridham-Wippell). with his flag flying in H.M.S. Orion (Flag-Captain G.R.B. Black, R.N.). had with him

the cruisers Ajax (Captain E.D.B. McCarthy). Perth, of the Royal Australian Navy (Captain Sir P.W. Bowyer-Smith R.N.), Gloucester (Flag-Captain H.A. Rowley), and some destroyers. This force proceeded to a position south of Crete. The Commander-in-Chief whose flag was flying in H.M.S Warspite (Flag Captain D.B. Fisher), had with him the battleships Valiant (Captain C.E. Morgan) and Barham (Flag Captain G.C. Cooke), the aircraft carrier Formidable (Flag Captain A.W. la T. Bissett), in which was flying the flag of Rear-Admiral D.W. Boyd and some destroyers.

On the afternoon of 27 March the Commander-in-Chief took his main fleet to sea. The British ships had to travel miles before joining action with the enemy. At 07.49 on 29 March enemy force of one Littorio class battleship, six cruisers and seven destroyers was about thirty-five miles south of Gavdo Island. It was joined by two cruisers. Our cruiser force made contact and the Vice-Admiral turned towards the enemy Battle fleet. Later our aircraft reported a second enemy force eighty miles west of Gavdo Island. The Vice-Admiral got in touch with the enemy just after dusk. H.M.S. *Greyhound* (Commander R. Marshall-A'Deane) illuminated the leading heavy cruiser. Our Battle Fleet at once opened fire. The first salvos hit at a range of about 4,000 yards and practically wrecked two cruisers of the Zara class. What followed is still obscure. None of our ships suffered either damage or casualties.

Chapter 8

Convoys and the Tripoli Bombardment (April – May 1941)

After Matapan, *Havock*'s Midshipman Derek Napper's log continues to give us a contemporaneous view of the Tripoli bombardment and repeated convoy work starting with a journey to the Greek port of Piraeus:

> Thursday 3 April. During the night, we passed through the Kithera Straits into the Aegean, reaching Piraeus about 12.30. First, we came to single anchor and then, when the oiler was ready for us at 16.00, we went alongside her. As soon as *Breconshire* was ready, she went to sea, and *Hotspur* and ourselves followed later, making a rendezvous outside. We were bound for the island of Moudros where *Breconshire* was to be unloaded by her men and fifteen hands from each destroyer. We were instructed to wear Greek colours approaching the island, in case, I suppose, some ignorant battery commander should open fire, not being able to differentiate between ships of different nationalities.[1]

Jim 'Buster' Brown also recalled:

> At one time, whilst operating in the Greek islands, we sailed under the Greek ensign. We thought there was a chance we might not be bombed if spotted by German aircraft. We were approached by a Greek fishing vessel which gave us fresh fish and no doubt wondered why we never spoke Greek.[2]

Napper's log clearly demonstrates the relentless pressure suffered by the Mediterranean Fleet's cruisers and destroyers:

> A message from *Calcutta* on an A.N. convoy (fast) informed us that a merchant ship was damaged and on

fire from enemy air action. With *Bonaventure* sunk by a submarine[3] on the surface and *York* badly damaged in Suda Bay by human-controlled torpedoes.[4] we have suffered one or two reverses, but they fade into nothingness besides the achievements of our Fleet on the 28th and 29th March, the advance of our army in Africa and the success of our air force at home and abroad. Only today comes the news of three more Italian warships sunk in the Red Sea. Three destroyers, two set on fire by aircraft attack and one disposed of by the surface craft.[5]

The more the German air force takes a hand in the Mediterranean the more chance we will have of shooting down their aircraft and nobody but a fool thinks that the air has any real mastery over the sea – only a certain influence in maritime affairs.

Friday 4 April. Our speed during the night was twenty-five knots, but it was considerably reduced when a thick fog settled down about 05.00. We lost touch with *Breconshire* and *Hotspur*, but found *Hotspur* again a little later when the fog cleared and we entered Moudros Bay in company only to find *Breconshire* already anchored. The harbour at Moudros is completely landlocked and makes a very good anchorage, but the low-lying hills would be very favourable to aircraft making a dusk torpedo attack. We lay at single anchor so as to cover the three entrance channels and swept with our asdics. As regards aircraft, *Breconshire* made a signal 'It is most important that the Germans should not know that we are landing troops here. To this end fire may be opened on sight at Italian aircraft but NOT, repetition NOT, on German, unless they have actually dropped a bomb or used a machine gun'. I'd forgotten that in our guise as Greeks, we were not at war with Germany!

Saturday 5 April. At 18.30 we went to sea to do an A/S patrol outside the harbour for the night, returning at dawn to take up *Hotspur*'s old berth. We were put at two hours' notice for steam.

Monday 7 April. As *Breconshire* was unloaded (she had been carrying troops and supplies to form a base at Moudros Bay) we left the island of Lemnos for Piraeus, at 16.00, to join a southbound convoy.

Tuesday 8 April. The harbour of Piraeus we found unsafe because of mines, so we oiled alongside *Breconshire* in Phaleron Bay, until we were told it was alright to go in.

There was a strong wind blowing, turning the land into an unpleasant lee shore and I kept anchor watch on the bridge the whole afternoon. There seemed to be some doubt as to our correct sailing time and the captain received written orders to proceed to sea at 17.00, only to find the remainder of the convoy and escort underway at 16.00. *Hotspur* waved us out of harbour as she passed and being at immediate notice for steam in any case, we lost little time in catching up. The convoy was A.S.F.24., part of the general troop movement 'Lustre' and consisted of five large ships, with a speed of eleven knots. A gale warning was in force and dust storms were in progress along the north coast of Egypt.

Wednesday 9 April. During the afternoon, an enemy aircraft (it may have been a Dornier) came out of the clouds and dropped half a dozen bombs amongst us. None caused any damage and the bomb aiming was poor I am told (for I did not actually see it, having been sent down to the T.S. [Transmitting Station] to liven them up there). I hope to go back to 'A' gun now as the Transmitting drill seems nearly faultless and I much prefer being on the upper deck for any kind of action, be it AA or low angle. The weather improved considerably as night fell and a full moon made conditions ideal for enemy torpedo carrying aircraft and M.T.Bs. This was unfortunate, for we went to action stations at 24.00 and did not revert to night defence till 03.30. Having the morning watch it was useless turning in then.

Thursday 10 April. Having passed through the Kaso Straits we found the Mediterranean rougher than the Aegean and the merchant ships seemed to find it even harder to keep station. The Germans have captured Salonika, which gives them a base in the northern Aegean, so I expect we may have some more lively experiences. I hope so.

Convoy ASF 24, *Breconshire* (fast merchantman), *Havock* and *Hotspur*, was due to arrive at Alexandria and Port Said on the 10th and 11th and was duly delivered unmolested.

Friday 11 April. By 1000 on the morning of the 11th we had secured alongside the oiler, after nearly ten and a half days at sea. Although our 'Boiler Hours' were slightly under the Boiler cleaning figure of 680, we were put at twelve hours' notice for steam and went alongside *Woolwich* [destroyer depot ship] to do it.

Tuesday 15 April. We went out at 1330 to calibrate our R.D.F. [radar]. The AA cruiser *Carlisle* was assisting by giving us R.D.F. and rangefinder ranges to compare with our own … The Fleet was to have sailed at 1900 to carry out Operation *M.D.1.*, but this was cancelled.

Thursday 17 April. News has just come through of the sinking of an entire Italian convoy of 8 ships by our destroyers, with the loss on our side of H.M.S. *Mohawk*.[6] Apparently, two of the enemy ships were 5,000-ton ammunition ships and one a 4,000-ton ship laden with M.T. [Motor Transport]. Two others were thought to be transports and the remaining three Italian destroyers.

In the forenoon, I went over to *Woolwich* to watch a bombardment exercise on the table. I have also carried out some runs on the A/S attack teacher in the same ship. During the bombardment exercise, the Captain arrived at *Woolwich* on his way to *Havock* to tell us we were going to sea. M.D.1. had finally been cancelled, so we only went out to do a Degaussing Range. It was exactly the same as the one I saw in *Gloucester*, except that it lasted a shorter time and by 14.30 we were secured again. There was a thick dust storm and a strong wind which made it very hard for the whaler to reach the buoy with the 'jumpers'. Two bridles were used and the slip rope as we were emergency destroyer.

Friday 18 April. The battleship *Warspite* and *Formidable*, *Phoebe*, *Calcutta* and destroyers left harbour at 06.00. We were on the right wing of the screen. I do not know what the operation is to consist of, but I hope we have another chance of a surface action, though I suppose that is rather a lot to expect.

Saturday 19 April. The now familiar passage of the Kaso was made at 04.00 the next morning and a course shaped for Suda Bay. On arrival, we oiled quickly and left again at 15.00. This is one of the few times that all the capital ships have been into the Bay together. *Phoebe* and *Calcutta* left to join a convoy which *Gloucester* and *Ajax* were covering.

The Bombardment of Tripoli 21 April 1941

After Churchill's unfortunate decision in March 1941 to send military aid to Greece, an unfavourable situation developed in Cyrenaica, which had been overrun the previous winter by a brilliant offensive launched by the C-in-C Middle East, General Sir Archibald Wavell. His Army, which had been already weakened in December 1940 by the despatch to Abyssinia of an Indian Division, was now called upon to provide for this new commitment an expeditionary force of two infantry divisions as well as mechanized and other troops. Meanwhile, Germany had been sending strong reinforcements of infantry and armoured divisions to Tripoli to stiffen the battered remnants of the Italian army.

The Italo-German offensive, led by General Erwin Rommel, began on 2 April and the depleted forces holding positions at El Agheila were driven back quickly. The enemy soon reached Benghazi, which was abandoned hastily, and Mechili, where the 2nd Armoured Division was surrounded and lost over 2,000 men and all its equipment. After falling back on Derna, the British forces continued their retreat to the Egyptian frontier, leaving a garrison to defend Tobruk, which was invested on 11 April. In just fourteen days all the gains of Wavell's winter campaign, except Tobruk, were lost and the defence of Egypt had become a cause for concern.[7]

Tripoli, which was the only port capable of serving as the main supply base the Italo-German army, had a harbour roughly a square mile in area enclosed by two breakwaters. Its entrance, which was about 350 yards wide, was closed by a boom. A seaplane base with a hangar was situated at the southern end of the Karamanli Mole where destroyers could be moored. Halfway along the first arm of the northern breakwater there was Naval Mole, extending about 600 feet to the southward and enclosing the Naval Basin where, destroyers and escort vessels could moor stern on to the breakwater. Officers' quarters, barracks, sheds, officers and workshops were situated on the Naval Mole. Up to twenty-four merchant vessels, ranging from 2,000 to 8,000 tons, could be accommodated, either at the quays or moored stern on to the breakwater. Other vessels anchored in the north-east of the outer harbour. Several oil and petrol depots were situated inside the defended perimeter of Tripoli with most of the storage tanks being underground. The seaward defences consisted of batteries, mounting 5-inch, 6-inch, 7.5-inch and 10-inch guns. There were also many A.A. batteries, searchlights and smoke-making devices as well as a minefield outside the harbour. There were two airfields were in the vicinity, one at Mellaga, six or seven miles east of Tripoli, and another at Castel Benito, fifteen miles to the south of the town[8].

The calamitous situation in North Africa led Churchill to pressurise the Admiralty to attempt either to block the port by sinking the battleship *Barham* and an A.A. cruiser in the main entrance or destroy the port facilities by a heavy bombardment by the Mediterranean Fleet. Unsurprisingly, Cunningham preferred the latter alternative and because of the expected scale of air attack he decided on a night-bombardment, the operation being masked by the passage of *Breconshire* to Malta and convoy ME7 (Operation *MD2*) of empty merchant ships (*City of London, Clan Ferguson, City of Manchester* and *Perthshire*) from Malta to Alexandria. Having opted for the night-bombardment, Cunningham relied on flares for illumination. Zero time was accordingly fixed for 05.00 [Zone minus three] 21 April, when moonrise was at 04/36, dawn at 06.50 and sunrise at 07.30.

Orders for the forthcoming operations were issued on 18 April, the Fleet being organised in two forces Forces, B and C. The organisation adopted for Force A included practically the full strength of the Mediterranean Fleet including three battle-ships, one aircraft carrier, five cruisers, one A.A. ship and fifteen destroyers. Force B, the bombarding force, was to be composed of the battleships *Warspite* (C-in-C Mediterranean Fleet, Admiral Sir Andrew Cunningham), *Barham* (Flag Rear Admiral H.B. Rawlings) and *Valiant*, the cruiser *Gloucester*, and the destroyers *Hotspur, Havock, Hero* (SO Sweeping Force), *Hasty, Hereward, Jervis* (Captain DF 14), *Janus, Juno,* and *Jaguar.*[9] In order to help the Fleet to make an accurate landfall, the submarine *Truant*, which at that time on patrol in the Gulf of Sirte, was to act as a 'lighthouse' and asdic beacon in a position four miles north (true) of Ras Tajura.[10]

Havock left Alexandria with the Mediterranean Fleet at 08.00 on 18 April 1941.[11] Having detached the Carrier Force at 21.00 on the 20th, the Commander-in-Chief formed Force B in line ahead in the order *Warspite, Valiant, Barham, Gloucester,* with the four T.S.D.S destroyers *Hotspur, Havock, Hero* and *Hasty* sweeping ahead. The *Hotspur* and *Havock*, with bow protection [paravanes] out, led the van while *Hereward* stood by to replace any one of the T.S.D.S. destroyers if necessary. Fortuitously, the weather condi-tions were ideal with a calm sea, no wind and excellent visibility. The light exhibited by the *Truant* was sighted at 04.10 seven miles ahead and proved to be a most effective beacon. Four minutes later *Havock* made asdic contact with *Truant* which was rounded by the bombarding ship ships at 04.38.[12]

The tense approach period passed without any indication that the enemy was aware of the Fleet's presence. At 05.00 the har-bour of Tripoli was fully illuminated by some ten to twelve flares and spotting aircraft had reported 'Ready to observe'. *Warspite* opened fire just after 05.02 and within a minute all the other ships, except the destroyers, were in action with their main and second-ary armaments engaging their allotted targets. The sweeping destroyers joined in at 05.04, firing in divisional concentration, while the *Janus* and *Hereward* fired independently. A vast cloud of dust and smoke rising from the bombs dropped shortly by the Torpedo Strike & Reconnaissance (TSR) aircraft from Malta and the shell bursts, hung over the harbour and town, making direct observation practically impossible. All that could be seen from the ships was an occasional explosion or the top of a splash of a 15-inch salvo when it landed in the harbour. In spite of the brilliant flare illumination, the spotting aircraft experienced difficulty in observing until they could see the flash of shells bursting inshore. There is no doubt that complete surprise had been achieved, for, while the defences kept up a fine display of coloured AA tracer directed against the flares and aircraft, the coastal batteries made no reply until the Fleet had commenced to turn eastward, fully twenty minutes after the start of the bombardment.[13]

The four T.S.D.S. destroyers, which had got out their sweeps at 20.02 hours, formed to port in the order *Hotspur*, *Havock*, *Hero* (S.O.) and *Hasty* with *Hotspur* acting as the guide of the Fleet. The *Havock*'s sweep became knotted and it was cut away but she got out her bow protection gear in position.[14]

Napper relates the story in his Log:

> Sunday 20 April. At dawn *Gloucester*, *Ajax*, *Orion*, *Perth* and *Breconshire* joined the fleet, with a few destroyers. *Breconshire* was bound for Malta. The rest of us are to do a bombardment of Tripoli. The scheme is roughly as follows: At 03.30 the RAF start bombing the harbour and finish an hour later. At 05.00 the battleships swept in by *Havock* and *Hotspur* streaming bow protection and T.S.D.S. gear, open fire. *Gloucester* and the 'J' destroyers are to stand by as a counter attacking force to deal with any enemy surface craft which venture against us. We are to steam for twenty minutes in towards the harbour from a range of 12,500 yards to 10,000 yards and then out again. Our particular target in *Havock* is to be the ships just inside the breakwater. The whole thing should provide a nice little surprise for the enemy and I can be thankful that I am to participate in the destruction from really close quarters.
>
> The aircraft carrier and her escort (the 7th cruiser squadron]) parted company about 21.30 and steered a course to keep her well to the north of the final scene

of operations and out of harm's way. By midnight we were about eighty miles off the coast, so we assumed 2nd degree readiness and continued at fifteen knots towards our objective. When streaming paravanes at dusk out port bow P.Vs. ran all right but in the T.S.D.S. the depressor started turning round and round pulling the towing wires together. Eventually we cut the depressor towing wire, but found it impossible to recover the T.S.D.S. as the depressor itself was still snatched up on and completely tied up. So the Captain decided to increase to twenty knots (having veered the full amount again) and let the towing wires part if they had to. This they both did and consequently when we took up battle formation at 03.00 to sweep the big ships in, we were without T.S.D.S. altogether.[15]

Jim Brown remembered:

As we closed Tripoli to carry out the bombardment star shells were fired over the harbour to illuminate it. Warships and AA batteries in the harbour were firing at the flares as they believed, at first, it was an air raid. But later they began to return our fire and ships could be seen moving in the harbour. After a time, the order to retire was given as there was a report of 'E' boats or similar vessels in the vicinity. As we were operating our mine-sweeping gear these had to be cut away as there was no time to get them in. This was done by putting a wooden block under the cables and cutting them with 'Tankies Cleaver' [the ship's meat axe]. We managed to get away alright.[16]

The screen destroyers opened fire in a flotilla concentration using a corrected bearing which was signalled for each salvo, *Hero* being the master ship. Salvoes were laddered across the target area in 300-yard steps working and down 900 yards. At 05.11, when a large merchant vessel was illuminated by a flare, fire was shifted on to her. Throughout the bombardment, no splashes were seen short of the breakwater. To enable a look-out to be kept for surface craft, the *Hotspur* did not fire her forward guns. *Hotspur* led round to course 090 degrees at 05.13, fire being checked for the turn.

At 05.17 a few shells fell near the screen, apparently from a large-calibre gun situated one and a quarter miles east of the harbour. During the turn the *Hotspur* became involved with the *Juno* and *Jaguar*. Apparently, these ships had not intercepted the signal ordering the screen to alter course, and one of them fired at *Hotspur* with Breda and pompom guns. Happily, no damage was done, and firing ceased when *Hotspur* switched on her fighting lights.[17]

Midshipman Napper:

> Monday 21 April. The R.A.F. had already started operations by this time and the flash of A.A. fire, the glimmer of tracer bullets and the glare of bursting bombs were plainly visible. The attack was a very heavy one, the aircraft coming over in waves and the enemy were further disconcerted by the dropping of parachute flares. These last played a very important part in the operation because when the Fleet Air Arm dropped more flares at 05.00 to illuminate the target for the ships, the enemy thought it was a continuation of the air attack. They must have got the surprise of their life when *Warspite* opened fire.
>
> On the run in from 12,500 yards to 10,000 we fired about twenty-five rounds per gun. The shoot was a concentration one, with *Hero* as master ship. Eventually the shore batteries woke up and started firing, but they did not worry anybody and they were engaged by our cruisers to seaward. Some small diversion was provided when *Jaguar* of the counter attacking force, tried to finish off *Hotspur* with Breda fire. A large fire was burning ashore and I think considerable damage was done. The Battleship shooting, as far as I could see, was again very good and all my gun's crew behaved very well and remained cool, with the possible exception of one 'hostilities only' ordinary seaman who kept on mentioning to me that he'd seen shell splashes close on our starboard bow. Eventually I told him that he was being very stupid and we weren't going to be hit and even if we were, talking about it didn't do any good.[18]

At 05.24 the Fleet checked fire and turned together at 090 degrees; the destroyers having turned ten minutes earlier. Fire was re-opened at about 05.29 hours and many more spotting reports of hits began to come in. Three ships of the T.S.D.S. destroyer group fired again during the second run. However, Commander Biggs on *Hero* decided not to fire again, as the blinding effect of his own and the adjacent ship's gun-flashes interfered with the look-out for enemy surface craft. As far as could be estimated the great majority of the rounds fired by the destroyers fell in the target area.[19]

During the bombardment, *Warspite* fired 135 15-inch and 106 6-inch shells, *Barham* delivered fifty-five salvoes of 15-inch shells, *Valiant* fired 208 15-inch and 602 4.5-inch shells, *Gloucester* fired 456 6-inch shells and the destroyers *Hero*, *Hasty*, *Havock* and *Hotspur* fired, ninety-nine, 100, ninety and forty-five 4.7-inch shells respectively.[20]

The bombardment of Tripoli was the first full-scale bombardment carried out at night, no previous bombardment of importance having been planned or executed entirely as a night operation. It also exemplified the use at night of air attacks preceding the bombardment; of flares for illuminating the target area; of aircraft for spotting; of a submarine as a navigational beacon. The operation was carried through without a hitch but the results, although impressive, were regarded as disappointing. The contributory causes of difficulty may be summed up as:

(a)   The target areas as defined were too close together.
(b)   Smoke prevented distinction of salvoes.
(c)   The flare illumination was too shallow in depth.
(d)   Initial ranges were in some cases inaccurate.[21]

It is not surprising that, in an operation of this nature, the town and its inhabitants suffered far more damage than the shipping or the port facilities. To what degree the material destruction is comparable with that of a strong concentrated air attack remains open to question. In either case the results obtained could not be expected to be more than temporary, as the enemy's supply route remained open. In fact, shipping movements from Naples to Tripoli were suspended for only twenty-four hours as the result of this bombardment. Far greater damage was done to fortnight later, when a 5,000-ton ammunition ship blew up in the port.[22]

An Italian report dated 29 April 1941 claimed that:

> Numerous salvoes struck the city and the harbour. Altogether about 100 dwelling houses were hit. The principal buildings named as having been hit: Banca d'Italia, Banca di Napoli, Banca di Sicilia, Post Office, Municipal Baths, Church of the Madonna della Guardia. Palazzo of the R. Prefettura, Provident Society and the Grande Albergo. The casualties were stated as having been 100 civilian dead and 300 wounded.[23]

Lieutenant R.O.B. Long R.N.V.R, who arrived in Tripoli on the day of its occupation on 23 January 1943 and examined captured documents, reported that:

> It is clear that a very great impression was made by the Naval bombardments of the town and that confusion reigned throughout them. They do not appear to have done much damage but the moral effect was tremendous and lasting.[24]

The Italians recorded that one torpedo boat, *Partenope*, was damaged, one merchant ship, laden with fuel and bombs, and a 'few others' damaged. Buildings on wharves and in the city suffered considerably.[25] Derek Napper:

> At 07.00 *Formidable* and escort joined C-in-C and we proceeded in company. The day passed without incident and the Germans made no attempt to avenge themselves for our bombardment of Tripoli. A signal was made from R.A.A. [Rear Admiral Aircraft Carriers] saying that Fleet fighters encountered five troop-carrying J.U. 52s on the 21st and shot down four without loss themselves.
>
> The original intention was to attack Benghazi with aircraft during the night, but this was cancelled, and we continued east through the dark hours and the whole of the 22nd.[26]

The expected counter-attack from the air did not materialise. There was almost a feeling of anti-climax. As dawn rose astern, a pall of smoke and dust, tinged with the glow of fires, could be seen. The fleet returned to Alexandria with the loss of one of the *Formidable's* Fulmars – they had accounted for ten enemy aircraft, mainly shadowers, on passage. The operation took the fleet 900 miles from its base, within range of enemy airfields capable of releasing clouds of bombers and torpedo carrying aircraft against the bombarding squadron. It was an exploit of shrewdly calculated audacity.

Napper's log continues:

> Wednesday 23 April. Alexandria was reached at 11.00 the next morning and after oiling we went alongside *Resource* to facilitate work on the T.S.D.S. gear and P.V. derrick forward. The results after bombardment appear to be highly satisfactory. Six merchant ships were destroyed, the destroyer berth hit and one severely damaged, four

other merchant ships out of action probably, the Spanish Wharf (a most important target) hit by two 15-inch salvoes, and the station, stores, warehouses and military headquarters practically demolished. In addition, naval aircraft torpedoed one 10,000-ton enemy tanker, one 6,000-ton supply ship and a 7,000-ton full ammunition ship, which blew up.

I consider that their position in Libya will rapidly become most insecure and we will finally destroy or capture the lot. The situation in Greece is more serious. The Greek army in the Epirus sector has capitulated, but the main Allied Greek line is intact. The government has left the country for Crete and the Greek cruiser *Averoff* and three destroyers are now in Alexandria.[27]

Chapter 9

Evacuation of Greece and Crete (April – June 1941)

The ship had been involved in almost continuous action for many weeks. Thus, *Havock* had escorted multiple convoys, been involved in a major action at Cape Matapan followed almost immediately by the Tripoli bombardment and was next off to assist in the evacuation of Allied troops in Greece. Although her crew could not know it, this would be followed by participation in the evacuation of Crete which would turn out to be one of the most bloody and sacrificial periods for the Royal Navy in the whole war.

No sooner had she arrived back in Alexandria from her latest convoy than news was received that the Allied situation in Greece had become untenable. Plans were being pushed ahead with great haste to evacuate troops from Greece to Crete and Egypt. *Havock* was about to enter a period which severely tested the Royal Navy's ships and men causing significant casualties to both.

The Afrika Korps had opened its offensive in Libya in April 1941 and at the same time the Germans also invaded Greece. Churchill's decision to strip Wavell's small, battle-hardened and successful army of the equivalent of fifty battalions and transfer them from the desert to the mountains of Greece might have been noble but was a strategic blunder of the first order. Thus, it denied Wavell the necessary reserves to complete the conquest of Italian Libya, or to withstand Erwin Rommel's Afrika Korp's March offensive, thereby prolonging the North African Campaign, which might have been concluded during 1941. The magnitude of the impending disasters was increased because, thanks to the pacifism of the interwar period, successive British governments had failed to maintain the nation's defences at an appropriate level. Consequently, in 1941 there simply weren't enough armaments in the United Kingdom to support the military needs of the Middle East Command. The end result was that the expeditionary force sent to Greece was not only outnumbered but also lacked armour and vital air-support. The inter-war pacifist chickens were coming home to roost with a vengeance and it would be the Royal Navy which would have to 'pick up the tab'.

Evacuation of Greece

Unsurprisingly the Greek campaign was short lived ending in the middle of April just as the Eighth Army was retreating towards the Egyptian frontier. Rear Admiral Baillie-Grohman, whose son, Lieutenant Michael Baillie-Grohman was one of *Havock*'s officers, was sent to Athens to assess the situation. It was not an occasion to dabble in half measures. The decision was taken to evacuate 50,000 Allied soldiers from the Greek mainland without delay and as soon as beaches for embarkation and shipping could be organised.

Six beaches in southern Greece, Rafina, Raftis, Megara, Navplion, Monemvasia and Kalamata, were chosen and the army's long march south commenced. The lack of air cover meant that any movement on land or sea was only safe at night. By day the army had to take cover amongst the olive groves and the navy had to be out of the range of Ju 87 Stukas and other marauding German aircraft.

In early April *Havock* had found herself escorting troopships into Greece and by the end of April she was taking troops off the beaches and escorting troopships out. The shallow draft vessels, the destroyers, commandeered caiques, LCTs (Landing Craft Tank) and other landing craft came into the beaches and ferried the waiting soldiers out to the cruisers and troopships before finally cramming their own decks with as many men as possible to be clear of the shore and well out to sea by daylight and the inevitable bombers.

On Thursday, 24 April 1941, *Havock* left Alexandria with seven other destroyers and the transport *Triumph* to assist the evacuation. The last RAF fighters in Greece had been destroyed by overwhelming German air superiority, so no protection could be expected from that direction.

The dawn of 25 April heralded the start of Operation *Demon*, the evacuation of Imperial Forces from Greece. In all, 50,672 troops were brought to Crete and Egypt using ships under the command of Vice Admiral Light Forces, Sir Henry Pridham-Wippell. These included the cruisers *Orion, Ajax, Phoebe, Calcutta, Carlisle* and *Coventry*, the destroyers *Stuart, Voyager, Vendetta, Waterhen, Vampire, Wryneck, Diamond, Decoy, Defender, Griffin, Hasty, Havock, Hero, Hotspur, Hereward, Isis, Nubian, Kandahar, Kingston* and

Kimberley, the sloops *Grimsby, Flamingo* and *Auckland* the corvettes *Hyacinth* and *Salvia,* the infantry landing ships armed merchant-men *Glenearn* and *Glengyle.* The latter, which were sister ships to the armed transport *Breconshire,* would provide many of the landing craft used in the evacuation of both Greece and Crete. A further nineteen transports of varying size, including the ill-fated *Costa Rica, Pennland, Slamat* and *Ulster Prince* were employed in the operation.[1]

Part of the dispositions for 25 April had Pridham-Wippell arriving at Suda Bay, Crete at 18.00 hours. His force was the cruiser *Orion* (flagship) and the destroyers *Havock, Hasty, Decoy* and *Defender.* Pridham-Wippell retained *Defender* in Suda but detached *Havock, Hasty* and *Decoy* to Nauplia to discover the fate of the transport *Ulster Prince* and to investigate the situation there. They discovered that on 24 April *Ulster Prince* had grounded in the fairway while attempting to go alongside the wharf, thereby denying access to destroyers on successive nights. The next day an air attack turned the grounded ship into a total loss.[2] Consequently ships now had to anchor in the bay and tenders would be needed to bring troops and equipment out to them from the shore. That being the case, the landing ship infantry (LSI) *Glenearn* was sent to deliver several Landing Craft Assault (LCA) to Nauplia to facilitate the evacuation. At 17.45 hours on 24 April, whilst on passage to Nauplia, *Glenearn* was attacked by two Heinkel bombers and was hit on the forecastle. The anchor and cable gear were destroyed and a fire started forward. The fire was extinguished and the ship proceeded at 18.45.[3] On the afternoon *Glenearn* was bombed and hit in the engine-room by a Ju 87 and was towed to Suda Bay by *Griffin.* However, *Glenearn* was ordered to send her landing craft to Monemvasia, since they could not reach Nauplia in time for that night's evacuation.[4]

Convoy AN 29, consisting of *Coventry, Wryneck, Diamond* and *Griffin* plus the transports *Pennland and Thurland Castle* was scheduled to arrive in Megara to evacuate 5,000 men during the night of 25/26 April.[5] Unfortunately, during the afternoon of the 25th *Pennland* was bombed and damaged. *Griffin* was ordered to stand by until dark. Later, *Pennland* which was to take off troops at Megara, was again bombed. Pridham-Wippell heard of her loss, and he diverted *Havock, Hasty* and *Decoy* the three destroyers from Nauplia to Megara to take on board all those troops which might have embarked on *Pennland* that night.[6]

The plans for the night of 26/27 April envisaged that *Glenearn, Diamond, Griffin* and *Havock* would embark troops from Tolon but *Glenearn* had been put out action by a bomb in the engine room and *Havock* was detailed to embark the GOC, his staff, F.O.A.M (Flag Officer Attached Mediterranean, Sir H.T. Baillie-Grohman) and staff at Myli opposite Nauplia. Soon afterwards, Baillie-Grohman and his staff were landed at Monemvasia.[7]

Derek Napper's log provides a graphic account of these desperate days:

> Thursday 24 April. At 15.00, *Orion* made a signal 'Destroyers raise steam for 24 knots' and all the ship's companies were recalled from leave. We left harbour in company with *Orion* and 3 other destroyers at 19.30, to assist in the evacuation of our troops from Greece. It is a foul task and I only hope that I get a chance to assist in the destruction of some of the enemy en-route. I know, and everybody British should know, that a local reverse means little in the general scheme of the war and will make no difference to our ultimate victory, but our apparent defeat will have a bad effect on the tender nervous systems of easily frightened neutrals.
>
> At 24.00 (night of 24th/25th), we anchored in the Bay of Nauplia and I went inshore in the motorboat to bring off troops. Of course, we got a piece of waste around the screw and eventually the Jollyboat came out and towed us back to the ship. I transferred to the whaler and finally reached the stone jetty astern of the Jollyboat. We took off mostly Australian troops, with two stretcher cases amongst them. They seemed quite confident of beating the Germans on land at any time, but dive bombers had caused some nervousness. One trip consisted of taking a boatload of nurses (from the base hospital) out to a merchant ship, the *Thurland Castle*.
>
> Saturday 26 April. When the Captain brought a Brigadier on board at 03.00, we weighed and proceeded to sea, reaching Crete at 12.30. After oiling we sailed for Nauplia again. On the way we were bombed by 3 Junkers 88s. I was a little surprised as the first thing we saw were the aircraft overhead. It wasn't a determined attack at all and I think they must have seen us on their way to bomb Suda Bay or somewhere. Exactly the same drill was carried out as on the previous night, except that we took off F.O.A.M. and staff with only a few soldiers and also a caique came alongside which saved our boats many trips. We landed F.O.A.M. again off a cape 60' from Nauplia to arrange for a further evacuation.[8]

By Sunday, 27 April 27 5,000 men still remained at Rafina and
Raftis. This force included the rearguard formed by the 4th
New Zealand Brigade. Fortunately, the enemy had not discov-
ered their presence and on the night of the 27/28th *Ajax, Havock,
Kingston* and *Kimberley* lifted the entire party without incident.
Midshipman Napper's log recorded:

> Sunday, 27 April. Suda Bay was again reached during the
> forenoon and oiling began. The night operations were
> to consist of evacuating the remaining 3,000 men from
> north of the Corinth Canal. The signal from *Ajax* said that
> the enemy might already be in possession, so we might
> get a chance to do a bombardment. About 23.00 we were
> diverted to take off 800 men who had been surrounded.
> Having commandeered a caique we went inshore to do
> so. They were all collected in two damaged steamers
> some 200 yards from the shore and one officer told me
> they had just about given up hope of being rescued and
> were making plans to take to the hills. We managed to
> get them all on board and sailed at 0400 for Suda Bay.[9]

This was the final evacuation north of the Corinth Canal during
which *Ajax, Kingston, Kimberley*, and *Havock* embarked 2,500, 640,
700 and 800 troops respectively from Rafina Cove.[10] Midshipman
Napper's log continued:

> Monday 28 April. We arrived off Monemvasia, on the Elos
> Peninsula, at 22.30, and our boats went in to assist in load-
> ing *Ajax*. The operations were very speedily carried out
> as there were a few 'assault landing craft' helping, which
> carried a large number of men at a time. F.O.A.M. and
> General Freyberg, the New Zealand V.C. went to *Ajax*.[11]

Torpedoman Jack Surridge remembered that:

> On one trip, we picked up [Rear] Admiral Baillie-
> Grohman and he had the pleasant surprise of finding his
> son as an officer on board *Havock*. We evacuated a lot of
> Australians and RAF personnel to Crete. The last troops
> we took were New Zealanders (26 Battalion). They were
> gentleman and appreciative. I liked them. They had
> good manners.[12]

Many years after the war Stoker Albert Goodey met a New
Zealander who had been picked up in the evacuation. He shook

Albert's hand firmly and thanked him. He said they had always believed the British Navy would not leave them and sure enough at the last possible moment in the darkness *Havock*'s bow nosed in toward the beach and they were lifted. He movingly said that a ripple went round the troops that it was *Havock*, as she was well known.[13]

The final embarkation occurred on the night of 28/29 April at Monemvasia when *Ajax, Havock, Hotspur, Griffin* and *Isis* embarked 1,050, 850, 800, 720 and 900 troops respectively.[14] Midshipman Napper, who was ill at the time, remembered:

> Tuesday 29 April. During the forenoon, I found that I had a temperature of 102 degrees and feeling generally unfit I turned in, sleeping heavily until Thursday morning. Our movements on Tuesday and Wednesday nights were as follows. On Tuesday, we left Crete to do a further evacuation and were recalled remaining in Suda Bay till Wednesday night, when we went to the island of Milos, due north of Suda, on the same parallel of latitude approximately as the Elos Peninsula.[15]

Around this time an extraordinary event occurred which involved the Walrus/Seagull (A2-17) amphibian from the Australian Cruiser *Perth*. Out on reconnaissance near Monemvasia, over the Anti-Kithera channel, they were jumped by two much more powerful and well-armed German Dorniers. After a real battle, with damage to both sides, the lumbering Walrus was shot down in flames. The Australian crew, Beaumont, Brian and Bowden, took to the dinghy and suffered a long period swirling around in the currents of the channel. Eventually at 14.00 hours, they fired Verey flares as a Sunderland flew overhead at about 5,000 feet. But sadly, the big flying boat flew on. They were shivering with cold when darkness blotted out the sea and sky. For hours, they huddled together in the rocking craft, then suddenly Brian sat bolt upright and shouted, 'Look there's a destroyer over there'. Beaumont fired the last two flares. The flares were fortunately spotted by *Havock* and *Hotspur*. *Havock*, believing a submarine was in the vicinity, set off ready to depth charge the position. What they found was a rubber dinghy with a trio of freezing cold and soaking wet Australian airmen inside it. Beaumont, Brian and Bowden heard the destroyer's engines and there she was, dark and towering and lovely. Minutes later they were sipping hot cocoa in *Havock*'s Wardroom. The rescue took place in the early hours of 29 April 1941.[16]

That day the Naval Officer in Command reported that 2,000 troops, believed to be mostly Greek, were still in Milo.[17] *Havock* and *Hotspur* were detailed to visit the island during the night 29/30 April. That night *Havock* and *Hotspur* discovered 700 British and Palestinian troops on the island of Milos and took them all off. This final action concluded the dangerous withdrawal of forces from Greece. Her luck was holding, but not for much longer. Derek Napper explained

> Wednesday 30 April. There was some fear that the Germans had already taken the place, so the boat's crews went in armed with Thompson submachine guns and Brens. I'm glad nothing happened, as I would hate to have missed it.[18]

In this adventure, Lieutenant Commander Ian Robertson led the *Havock* motor boat contingent along with Colonel Waller and a trio from *Hotspur* in their motor boat. Most of *Havock*'s Thompson submachine-guns had been 'liberated' from troops evacuated earlier. They chugged into the harbour under the cover of darkness. Soon they were challenged in Greek and answered '*Inglesi*' which prompted a mobbing by a crowd of very pathetic looking Greeks. The boats pushed off to avoid being boarded and swamped. After a much-garbled question and answer session in a variety of languages the *Havock* boat moved off to the east to a harbour wall. Robertson soon found the required evacuees, and a full-bore evacuation took place using all available boats, with some difficulty as the Palestinians could not speak a word of English (and vice-versa). By 03.30 hours both destroyers were fully laden with 6-700 assorted British, Palestinian and Cypriot troops and two nurses, plus some locals who begged to be evacuated. On leaving the harbour and out to sea heading for Suda Bay, *Hotspur*'s lookout thought he saw a submarine and *Havock* was ordered to 'chuck a couple of depth charges at it' to keep its head down while they withdrew. Subsequently, Napper recorded:

> Thursday, 1 May. While in Suda we received the very welcome news that after taking some refugees from Candia at about 22.00, we should proceed to Alexandria. To this end we finally left the harbour at 19.00. The BBC has now announced that 80% of the Imperial troops in Greece have been re-embarked.
>   Having embarked the Legation Staff from Candia (including three women and two small children escorted by Peter Fleming (the travel author) we sailed

to Alexandria, only to find the port closed to shipping because of mines laid by enemy aircraft.

Friday 2 May. After steaming up and down outside for about an hour, we were told to go to Port Said. Arriving in the late afternoon, we stayed there throughout Saturday and left for Alexandria at 01.00 on Sunday morning securing to the buoy at 15.00.

Sunday 4 May. *Dido*, the minelaying cruiser *Abdiel*, two 'N' class destroyers and some more submarines had joined the Mediterranean Fleet.[19]

Operation *Tiger* and the bombardment of Benghazi

With the Greek evacuation complete there was an urgent need to get back to the business of resupplying Malta while at the same time reinforcing the 8th Army in Egypt. Operation *Tiger* was an ambitious attempt to pass five fast merchant ships loaded with 295 tanks and fifty-three crated Hurricane fighters from Gibraltar to Alexandria, thereby avoiding the much longer haul around the Cape of Good Hope. Admiral Cunningham, whose Mediterranean Fleet would be covering the passage of the *Tiger* convoy from the Sicilian Narrows to Alexandria, decided to take the opportunity to resupply Malta with two of the convoys from Alexandria namely MW7A and MW7B which would be covered by his ships. The Fleet sailed from Alexandria on 6 May, on Operation *MD4*, covering Malta convoy MW7A consisting of merchantmen *Thermopylae, Talabot, Settler* and *Amerika*. *Havock* left Alexandria as part of the huge supporting contingent of escorts. Napper recorded:

Tuesday 6 May. The battlefleet, *Ajax, Orion, Perth*, and destroyers left Alexandria at 12.30. We were temporarily forming part of the 7th D.F. comprising the two 'N' class and *Abdiel*. Before leaving harbour, our bow protection wires were shackled onto the stem towing position, so I suppose another attack on an enemy port has been planned. The day passed without incident, though the thick dust laden atmosphere made station keeping rather difficult. A few days of weather like this, with the Germans short of water, should make a great deal of difference to the Western Desert situation. The news from the other parts of the world is good, or fairly so.

Our night fighters having brought down 16, 5, 7 and 9, German bombers in successive raids on England. The two German Battle Cruisers sheltering in Brest have been hit by R.A.F. bombers. All resistance in East Africa seems to have ceased.[20]

The following morning, 7 May, at 11.30 hours, the cruiser *Ajax* with *Havock*, *Hotspur* and *Imperial* detached from the operation to bombard Benghazi. Benghazi was duly bombarded at about 01.00 on the morning of the 8th. Hits were obtained on several ships docked alongside. Also, on retiring, two laden ships, *Tenace* (1,142 tons) and *Capitano Cecchi* (2,321 tons) were spotted approaching inshore from the south. These were promptly eliminated by the destroyers; *Havock* delivering the *coup de grace* on the first. *Capitano Cecchi* was evidently an ammunition ship and was blown to pieces with the loss of all twenty-six of her crew. *Imperial* reported observing a lorry or tank passing over her as the target blew up. *Havock* also claimed hits on a ship at the Giuliana Mole and sank one motor vessel. The force, having completed its task, re-joined the Fleet at 17.00 on 8 May, reporting the destruction of the two freighters.[21] Derek Napper's log provides a graphic account:

Wednesday 7 May. At 11.00 *Ajax*, *Hotspur* and *Imperial* and ourselves parted company with the rest of the Fleet, to attack shipping anchored in Benghazi and just outside. As we approached the harbour at midnight, we were treated to a little firework display by the Benghazi AA gunners, who were trying vainly to stem an R.A.F. attack. Fires were started and I should say, from their size, that an oil tank must have been hit. By 01.00 (on Thursday 9 May) we were in position, at 5,000 yards range, and *Ajax*, to seaward of us, illuminated the target with star shell. *Hotspur* did not immediately open fire and I had some time to try to discern what shipping there was about. Outside the breakwater there was nothing but a few half-submerged wrecks, so when we finally opened fire, it was at vessels actually inside the harbour. We did a run lasting about 15 minutes, then turned round and gave it to them the other side. At the critical moment, the manila rope, which had been badly lashed, was blown off 'B' gun deck and draped itself over my gun barrel and shield, so that it was impossible for the trainer to move the mounting at all.

I had the gun put to the 'half-cock' position and reported to the T.S. that we couldn't fire. Meanwhile 'B' gun's crew affected a temporary clearance, but this was not enough, as will be seen later.

After we had finished with Benghazi harbour itself, we carried out a sweep for convoys, etc. Only a short time had elapsed when we sighted an oil tanker and set it on fire in a very short time by gunfire. I have a great respect for our shooting and am very glad I am not in the enemy's shoes. The tanker burnt fiercely and it soon became apparent that no assistance would be required from us to send it to the bottom.

Meanwhile *Ajax* and the other two destroyers had found a large ammunition ship. In a few minutes a direct hit was registered and the vessel blew up with an enormous explosion.

By this time, the manila had fouled 'A' gun even more effectively and if we had been engaged it would have been just too bad. While I was getting it clear (standing forward of the gunshield) the thing fired! I very soon made certain that the gun was not loaded and the interceptor left open and we lashed the offending manila to the blast screen where it remained out of the way for the rest of the night.

The gun's crew behaved in the efficient manner I have come to expect of them, with the exception of the same O.D. who betrayed signs of nervousness at the bombardment of Tripoli. He was jumping about like a cat on hot bricks.

When it became obvious that there was no further sport to be had, we withdrew. In the course of the night's operations we lost both our bow P.Vs.

A rendezvous was made with the Battle Fleet at 16.00 and we steered a course to reach Malta about 08.00 on Friday morning. Later in the evening *Hotspur*, *Imperial* and ourselves were detached with *Breconshire* and entered Marsaxlokk the next morning to oil.[22]

After the Benghazi bombardment, *Havock* and her accompanying ships re-joined the Operation *Tiger* convoy and its formidable escort, on 9 May 1941. Derek Napper follows on and further describes the event in his Midshipman's log:

Friday 9 May. This was completed in the forenoon and we sailed to join the important convoy *Tiger* bound for

Alexandria loaded with tanks and motor transport. In addition, *Queen Elizabeth*, *Fiji* and *Naiad* were coming through to join the Mediterranean Fleet. *Tiger* was sighted about noon and consisted of 5 merchant ships escorted by *Queen Elizabeth*, *Phoebe*, *Dido*, *Naiad*, *Fiji*, *Gloucester*, the 3 A.A. cruisers and a screen of Force F (Home Fleet) destroyers. In addition to this formidable collection of ships, further protection from the air was afforded by a constant patrol of the new twin engine Beaufighters.

It was altogether a most heartening sight and should give even the most fainthearted faith in an ultimate victory. I think the situation in Libya will very soon show a turn for the better as the Germans must be feeling the pinch of our stranglehold on their Tripoli supply route. Another very good piece of news was that we sent about 400 bombers over Hamburg and Bremen in the biggest raid ever attempted by either side this war. It shows that our air striking force is increasing at a considerable rate.

Queen Elizabeth left the convoy during the dog watches to join up with the Battle Fleet. Saturday and Sunday passed without any unusual incident.[23]

The *Tiger* convoy passed through the Sicilian Narrows on the night of 8/9 May with the loss of only one ship, the ill-fated *Empire Song* which was mined and sunk. The convoy and the Mediterranean Fleet arrived in Alexandria during the forenoon of 12 May without further loss. Operation *Tiger* was a considerable success because only fifty-seven of the 295 tanks and ten of the crated Hurricanes were lost in *Empire Song*. Sadly, it would be another two years and fourteen days before another British convoy would be able to sail from Gibraltar to Alexandria.[24]

The Battle for Crete

By mid-May 1941 the Allied Command had clear evidence from Ultra decrypts that the Germans were planning to invade the island of Crete. Despite having been present on the island since the previous November, the British Army had made no serious attempt to prepare defences against invasion, protect vital airfields or even improve the roads to the south of the island thereby facilitating the arrival of seaborne supplies. The German invasion of Crete could not have come at a worse time for the British forces in the Eastern Mediterranean because the Army was still reeling from defeats in North Africa and Greece, while about half of the troops in Crete had been evacuated from Greece and had almost no equipment. Frequent changes of command on the island had hindered meaningful preparation to defend the island. The situation was exacerbated by the almost complete absence of any effective air cover for the troops on Crete or the ships operating off its coast. Thus, wear and tear had greatly reduced the serviceability of what aircraft remained after the recent campaigns in Cyrenaica and Greece and replacement machines were still en route to the theatre. The stage had been set for yet another British defeat in that long litany of reverses suffered during 1940 – 1942.

The object of the Commander-in-Chief, Mediterranean, was to prevent the enemy landing in Crete from the sea. The most likely places for an enemy seaborne landing were thought to be Canea, Retimo and Heraklion whilst Kissamo Bay and Sitia were possibilities. On 15 May, the British forces were at sea, to the south of Crete, ready to move to any threatened point. The Commander-in-Chief, Mediterranean signalled his intentions as follows: Force C (the cruisers *Dido* and *Coventry* with the destroyers *Kandahar*, *Nubian*, *Kingston*, and *Juno*) was to be available to deal with landings at Heraklion and Sitia, Force D (the cruisers *Naiad*, *Phoebe* and two destroyers) would deal with any landing west of Retimo and Force B (the cruisers *Gloucester* and *Fiji*) would deal with enemy forces north west of Crete, or support Force D. Meanwhile, Force A (the battleships *Queen Elizabeth* and *Barham* plus five destroyers) was to take up a position to the westward of Crete to act as cover for the other forces. The battleships *Warspite* and *Valiant*, the aircraft carrier *Formidable* which had only four serviceable aircraft, the cruisers *Orion* and *Ajax* plus all remaining destroyers were held in reserve at Alexandria. Cunningham's intention was that night sweeps would be carried out and that all forces were to retire to be close to the north of Crete by dawn and then retire to the south of Crete. Force B was to sweep the west coast of Greece from Matapan, Force D was to sweep from Anti-Kithera to Piraeus and C was to sweep from Kaso towards Leros. The Commander-in-Chief, Mediterranean, would control the operation from Alexandria but the Senior Officers of the various forces were informed that they were expected to take independent action to intercept any enemy forces reported. *Formidable* would be unable to provide fighter protection to his naval forces until 25 May and the fleet could expect no assistance from the few shore-based fighters in Crete.[25] Sweeps referred to above were carried out on the night 16/17 May, without result and the forces taking part withdrew to the south of Crete. On 18 May, arrangements were made to relieve and rotate forces at sea.

Early on 16 May 1941, Force A, *Queen Elizabeth* (Vice-Admiral Pridham-Wippell), *Barham, Naiad* (Rear Admiral King), *Phoebe, Jervis, Jaguar, Greyhound, Hasty, Nizam, Defender* and *Imperial* sailed from Alexandria for Cretan waters. They were joined by the destroyer *Ilex* and later by Force B, consisting of *Gloucester* (Captain H.A. Rowley S.O.) and *Fiji* and the destroyers *Hotspur* and *Havock* which had landed reinforcements at Suda Bay the previous night.[26] Derek Napper recalled:

> 15 May 1941. When at 08.00 we were told to go to 2 hours' notice for steam it was obvious something was brewing. *Gloucester* and *Fiji* went out early in the forenoon and then we got the order to slip at 14.00. While leaving harbour our stern swung on to the bows of the Greek merchant ship *Point Clear* removing an escape hatch in the First Lieutenant's cabin and bending the frame. It was most unfortunate that during a most difficult piece of manoeuvring a tug and a lighter should be right astern, not to mention an oiler some distance further away. In my opinion the only way the accident could have been avoided would have been by going astern and making a detour right round the harbour and not attempting to cross the merchant ship's bows at all. This would have meant that we would have been very late passing the breakwater and would have held everything up. As (bad) luck would have it there was a fairly heavy sea and a considerable amount of water came in through the ship's side. Nevertheless, we easily maintained a speed of 25 knots and made a rendezvous with *Gloucester* and *Fiji* during the forenoon of Friday 16th May. Later in the day we joined *Queen Elizabeth, Barham, Naiad, Perth* and destroyers.
>
> At 17.30 we went alongside *Queen Elizabeth* to oil. Just as they had started pumping we yawed away to starboard and parted the hose, covering the foc'sle in oil before the supply could be shut off. Eventually they rigged another hose and we started pumping only to be interrupted by a yellow Air Raid Warning. We were cast off in a remarkable short space of time and when the Air Raid Warning was cancelled it was too late to go back alongside.
>
> During the night, we carried out a sweep up the West Coast of Greece in company with *Gloucester, Fiji* and *Hotspur*. I heard people say that they hoped we wouldn't

meet anything during the night. I cannot understand this sentiment, as my whole interest at the moment is in meeting the enemy and destroying him.

Saturday 17 May. On rejoining V.A.1. at 08.00 we went alongside *Queen Elizabeth* again to oil. This time the operation was completed without a hitch and we finished about 1030. For the remainder of the day we steamed S.E. and then at 20.00 parted company with V.A.1. and carried out a similar sweep to the night before meeting the Battleships at dawn and oiling again alongside *Queen Elizabeth*. [27]

The invasion of Crete

The attack on Crete began on the morning of 20 May, when German paratroopers and glider troops began an airborne assault on the island, striking at the vital Maleme airfield. That day the Germans suffered heavy losses and the Allied troops were confident that they would defeat the invasion. Unfortunately, the next day a combination of communication failures, Allied tactical hesitation and German offensive operations, meant that Maleme airfield in western Crete was captured. This enabled the Germans to land reinforcements and overwhelm the defensive positions, such as they were, on the north of the island. Axis attempts to land troops from the sea were frustrated by the Royal Navy until towards the end of the battle. Although not immediately obvious at the time, the loss of Maleme airfield on 21 May coupled with the paucity of Allied air power meant that the battle of Crete was over. At 08.40 on 27 May, General Wavell informed Churchill that Crete was lost. All that remained was to evacuate as many British and Dominion troops as possible before the island came under German control on 1 June 1941.

When the Germans launched their attack upon Crete, *Havock* was one of twenty-nine destroyers available at Alexandria. Midshipman Derek Napper's log picks up this next serious and bloody adventure as follows:

Tuesday 20 May. At 07.00 the next morning we entered Alexandria and went alongside *Woolwich* to make good our defects. We were supposed to be at 12 hours' notice for 2 days, but the news announced a German attack on Crete by parachute troops and it soon became apparent that we should be required in the Aegean.

Wednesday 21 May. On Wednesday afternoon, a signal was made telling us to raise steam for 24 knots and at
01.00 on the 22nd we left harbour in company with D.14
(*Jervis*), D.2 [*Ilex*] and *Nizam*.[28]

The four destroyers together with the cruisers *Orion* and *Ajax*
constituted Force E, and under the command of Captain P.J. Mack
in *Jervis* entered the Aegean via the Kaso Strait and maintained a
patrol off Heraklion during the night of 22/23 May without incident, returning to Alexandria in the morning. On the return journey, they were dive-bombed for five hours, the *Ilex* and *Havock*
being damaged by near misses.[29]

The most serious damage to *Havock* was caused by a near miss
which was fifteen feet from the starboard side and the ship's plating abreast the bridge. It caused severe splinter and blast damage
in the vicinity of the bridge. The ship's side plating was holed
by splinters from three feet below the waterline to the upper
deck level. The foremost oil fuel tanks were holed and opened to
the sea. No. 1 boiler was put out of action because of punctured
main steam and feed pipes, cut tubes and partial flooding of the
boiler room. Important electrical cables were severely damaged
and a fire was started in the decontamination store but was extinguished rapidly. *Havock*'s fighting efficiency was impaired and
speed reduced because of the damage to No. 1 boiler room, while
her radius of action had been reduced by flooding of the forward
oil fuel tanks.[30] The damage would keep *Havock* out of action for
three weeks and consequently she had the good fortune to miss
the carnage associated with the evacuation of Crete. At least six
were killed in the attack, including Able Seaman Donald 'Ginger'
Glenister, Leading Seaman Edward 'Lofty' Forsyth, Ordinary
Seaman Gordon Green, Ordnance Artificer Albert Abnett, Able
Seaman Ronald Allen and Electrical Artificer George Sinclair and
up to ten wounded including 'A' Gun Layer Rodney Bridge and
Gunner (T) Daniels. *Havock* was out of action and in Alexandria
for repair until 16 June.

Although not immediately affecting *Havock*, the tragedy that
struck the Mediterranean Fleet on 22 May was described by Derek
Napper whose previous ship to *Havock* was the cruiser *Gloucester*:

Thursday 22 May. The whole of Thursday passed without incident and we didn't see a single German aircraft.
It gave, in fact, no indication of the wrath to come.
During the dog watches, I heard the most depressing
news that *Gloucester* had been sunk by dive-bombers

while standing by to support *Kandahar* and *Kingston* who were picking up *Greyhound's* survivors. The story I put together on the strength of later information was that *Greyhound* had left the Battlefleet screen to sink a trawler full of German soldiers. Having done this, she was attacked by about 12 Ju 87s and eventually hit aft, sinking in 5 minutes. The two 'K' class destroyers came to her rescue, in spite of continued heavy aircraft attack and let go all their boats and Carley rafts. *Greyhounds's* crew were machine gunned in their whaler and in the water by ME 109s and nearly all the officers and a large number of men were killed. In the meantime, *Gloucester* and *Fiji* were standing by and were heavily attacked in their turn by waves of aircraft. Both ships exhausted all their H.A. ammunition and were firing star shells and smoke shell from their 4-inch guns and C.P.B.C. from their 6-inch.

Gloucester received several direct hits from heavy bombs and sank on an even keel. No survivors were picked up by our own ships as it was impossible owing to bombing, but they were only a few miles from land and *Fiji* dropped all her rafts and most of her boats. A few hours later she shared the same fate, but remained floating bottom up for some time. Other ships damaged were *Carlisle, Warspite* and *Valiant*, while the destroyers *Kelly, Kashmir* and *Juno* were sunk.

During the night, *Orion* and *Dido* ran into a convoy of merchant ships and many caiques and sank the lot. Other forces also encountered convoys and I have heard various estimates as to the number of German soldiers destroyed, the largest being 40,000.

We carried out an uneventful patrol in the Kaso Straits until dawn when the A.S.V. gear picked up an aircraft 4,000 yards astern.

Friday 23 May. This was the beginning of the attack. To start with, we were bombed by Ju 88s and Heinkels, with no result. It was annoying, but hardly dangerous. Then they disappeared and 6 Stukas arrived on the scene. Each destroyer was dived at in turn, sometimes by 3 aircraft together, sometimes by less. We had to be very careful of our 4.7-inch ammunition as we had exhausted a large percentage of it, but our supplies of .303 were limitless. I myself had a Bren gun, with which I tried to hit the aircraft when they got too low for our 4.7-inch to elevate to the required angle. Some of the tracer bullets seemed to be going straight into the propellers. One air-craft crashed into the sea soon after and the pilot bailed out. Two others went away very low over the water with smoke pouring from them.

At last after about 5 hours of spasmodic bombing, we had a very near miss, which flooded the boiler room and killed several people including a man on my gun who was standing just next to me and had a piece of shrapnel through the head. I had my cap blown off and sat down hard on the deck but was otherwise unhurt.

For a few moments we were stopped completely while the boiler was changed over and from then until we finally reached Alexandria, we left a trail of fuel oil behind.

In addition to the rating killed on my gun, one was badly wounded and another slightly, so that I had to take over gun layer for the latter part of the firing. My job was fairly easy, as by this time the aircraft were diving and it was only a question of keeping the telescope on the target and not below.

The last visit we had was about 11.30 when an 88 dropped a stick close ahead. Making good 25 knots we reached Alexandria at 2000 and went alongside 46 shed to disembark wounded. After this we shifted to along-side *Resource*, where we were given hot baths, food and beds.

Throughout the bombing the men behaved very well, especially one man on my gun [Able Seaman Rodney Bridge, subsequently awarded the Conspicuous Gallantry Medal], who went on doing his job (gun layer) after having half his back shot away, and refused to be looked at.[31]

Torpedoman Jack Surridge adds a sad note regarding the effects of the dive-bombing of *Havock* on 23 May:

There were three men sitting together on a hatch. The two outer ones were killed outright by shrapnel. The middle one survived without a scratch. We buried our dead at sea.[32]

Jim 'Buster' Brown stated:

My mate 'Ginger' Glenister was hit and lying on his back moaning. We turned him over and found a big wound in his back. Nothing could be done. There was a lot of damage. The funnel was peppered as well.[33]

Albert Goodey, being a stoker, spent most of his time in the boiler and engine rooms where he said the effect of the bombings and strafing was always terrifying, not knowing whether the next one would be the one. Having been on the ship since the beginning he often wondered how long his luck would last. The ship shuddered with every bomb, loose fittings and tools were flung around, footing was lost, massive movements of the helm made balance difficult while trying to operate the systems, machine-gun bullets rattled the plates in a staccato drum beat, the heat was stifling and smoke and cordite infiltrated all areas. He was fortunate to not be in the boiler room when the bomb exploded extremely close alongside killing some of his crewmates. When back at HMS *Resource*, a depot repair ship, he and two torpedo-men thought it highly amusing that they had been 'discharged dead' having slept on *Resource* and reported as missing presumed killed.[34]

Midshipman Napper's log records:

> Monday 26 May. Went on leave and stayed with some charming people for a week, returning to the ship at 09.00 on Tuesday 3 June. We had the funeral of one of the ratings, who died on board, at the Military Cemetery in Alexandria.[35]

While *Havock* was in for weeks of repair, *Bismarck* was sunk in the Atlantic on 27 May and two days later *Havock*'s sister-ship *Hereward*, was bombed and sunk by German aircraft off Crete. However, some clouds have a silver lining and the opportunity, whilst under repair, was taken to update *Havock*'s anti-aircraft armament and not before time in view of the absolute carnage of the Crete evacuation. The after quadruple torpedo tube mounting was removed and replaced with a very popular and efficient 3-inch-High Angle AA gun, believed to be of First World War vintage. Two Oerlikon cannons were fitted, which augmented the batteries of twin Lewis guns and a variety of 'free-lance' Bren guns which, in naval parlance, had been 'liberated' from passing soldiers from time to time.

On 11 June a signal was sent from the C-in-C Mediterranean: 'If *Kipling, Havock* and *Nizam* cannot be repaired in Red Sea ports they should be repaired in India. FOC RIN being asked to state port'. This signal was followed a few days later, on the 14th, with: 'Intend to sail *Naiad, Kingston, Nizam, Havock*, from Alex pm 16 to arrive Haifa am 17. Request you transfer your flag to *Naiad* and send *Phoebe* and three destroyers to Alex'.[36]

Havock had been originally fitted with two sets of ineffective four-barrelled 0.5-inch machine-guns, one each side between the funnels and four 0.303 machine-guns. This proved to be woefully inadequate when the Luftwaffe showed only too clearly that power had shifted significantly towards the air. It is interesting to count the number of AA weapons she was fitted with by the middle of June 1941 after the Crete debacle. Derek Napper records:

> Wednesday 18 June. During the night, we stayed at our buoy, going alongside 46 shed at 0600 to fire the 3-inch H.A. gun. This work occupied us on Thursday as well and so it wasn't until noon on Friday that we went to sea in company with *Decoy* and *Hotspur*.
>
> Friday 20 June. As soon as we'd passed the breakwater we began extensive tests of the H.A. armament. The new 3-inch gun was tested by firing single rounds at a small elevation and then the maximum, followed by 4 rounds rapid. Every machine gun in the ship was tested. Our close-range armament now consists of a Bren gun either side below the bridge, a Breda either side of the Flag deck, 0.5s, 2 Oerlikons, a close range battery abaft the 3-inch consisting of 3 twin Lewis guns and a Bren, beside several 'wandering' machine-guns to be used when convenient.
>
> After we were satisfied everyone knew their action and defence stations, cruising watches were piped and conditions reverted to more or less normal. With 4 per cent new ship's company we shall need a considerable amount of working up before our general level of efficiency is as high as it was prior to the bombing.

Evacuation of Crete

Crete was, in every respect, a dead-end. There were only two ports of any size, Suda Bay and Heraklion, both in the north, where there were no facilities. In a carbon-copy of the Greek campaign, a withdrawal to the southern beaches was the only realistic answer and the evacuation of Crete was ordered within a week of the initial assault and, thanks to damage sustained on 23 May. *Havock* missed this melancholy duty. Again, much of the army was plucked from the beaches, but the cost to the navy was horrendous. The roll of ships bombed, damaged, set on fire and sunk by enemy aircraft operating from airfields on the Greek mainland, the Dodecanese and Crete itself seems endless. The situation in the eastern Mediterranean grew rapidly worse until eventually the light cruisers *Naiad,* and *Euryalus* were the only ships larger than a destroyer which were operational. The sinking of the *Bismarck* distracted British opinion to the loss of Crete and in particular to the failure of the Allied land forces to protect vital airfields. The debacle in Crete and that in Malaya later in the year led to the formation of the RAF Regiment which was tasked with the specific objective of protecting airfields.

After the fall of Crete Allied Commanders were concerned that the Germans might use Crete as a springboard to invade Cyprus and Egypt. However, Hitler's invasion of Russia on 22 June made it obvious that the occupation of Crete was a defensive measure designed to secure the Axis southern front.

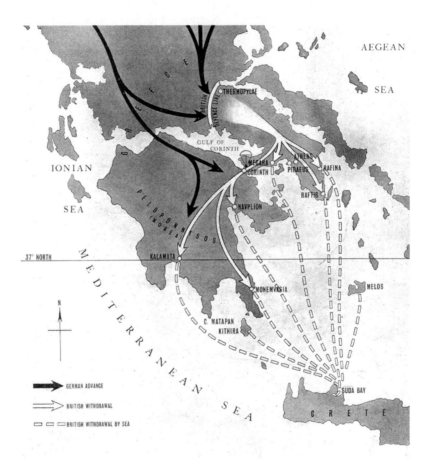

Map 3. The evacuation from Greece.

Chapter 10

No Rest for the Wicked: Syria, Tobruk, Groundings and more convoys (June 1941 – March 1942)

A fter a month of repairs *Havock* was finally reasonably fit for service again, somewhat covered in patches to cover her wounds, and was therefore respectfully invited to join the war again with the following signal from Admiral Cunningham, sent at 1055 on 19 May, to Flag Officer Destroyers (Mediterranean):

> Request you will sail *Hotspur, Havock, Decoy*, pm/20 to arrive Haifa 0700/21 as relief for three destroyers of Force B. Request you will ensure bow protection gear in *Havock* and *Hotspur* is fully efficient.

The Syrian Campaign June – July 1941

At the far eastern end of the Mediterranean lay the Levant Coast, divided almost equally into two with French mandated Syria to the north and British administered Palestine to the south. By mid-1941 both were causing concern. In Palestine was the port of Haifa, important not only because it was a British base, but also because it was the terminal for the oil pipeline from Persia. The uneasiness arose from the fact that it was only 600 miles, or three hours flying time, from the German airborne troops in Crete. The second concern was that a few miles, not a few hundred, away to the north was a potential, if not actual, Axis ally – Vichy France.

Clearly, in view of the delicate situation in the Eastern Mediterranean, some sort of pre-emptive action was called for and units of the British Army in Palestine, reinforced by some Free French contingents, moved north. There was a Vichy French naval presence on the Syrian coast, harbour-bound for most of its life, but operational nonetheless. Of necessity, therefore, the Mediterranean Fleet became involved in the operation, partly as mobile artillery and partly to ensure that the French navy kept its distance.

Havock entered the affair on 21 June 1941[1] when together with *Decoy* and *Hotspur* she left Alexandria to relieve *Hero, Kimberley* and *Jackal* at Haifa where they joined a force of three cruisers and some six destroyers. She remained based there for over three weeks until the land operations came to an end with the Vichy French asking for terms during the second week of July. The days between were spent creating swept channels with the much-disliked TSDS gear or bombarding targets ashore at the request of the army.

Midshipman Napper recorded:

> Saturday 21 June. An uneventful passage was completed at 07.00 on Saturday when we entered Haifa. *Ilex* and *Isis* (both damaged, the latter very seriously) were already alongside. About 10.00 C.S.15 in *Naiad, Leander, Jervis, Nizam, Hasty* and *Jaguar* came in. In addition, *Coventry* was berthed at the entrance of the harbour. At 18.00 *Decoy, Hotspur* and ourselves went out to intercept and search a suspected French Hospital ship [*Canada*]. She was sighted a blaze of lights during the middle watch and *Decoy* was detached to bring her into Haifa while we acted with *Hotspur*.
>
> Sunday 22 June. The whole of Sunday was spent in harbour and it wasn't till the evening that we proceeded to sea in company with *Jervis, Decoy* and *Hotspur* to form the 'searching force' in an operation designed to seek out and destroy some Vichy warships. The 'striking force' consisted of *Naiad, Leander, Jackal, Jaguar* and *Nizam*. This latter force located 2 French destroyers about 8 miles from Beirut and engaged them, probably sinking one. We suffered no damage.[2]

So, in the blink of an eye, *Havock* had moved into yet another theatre and period of war, known as 'Syrian Operations'. The *Guepard*, a Vichy French warship, tried to break the British blockade of Beirut on 23 June. There followed a night engagement involving the cruisers *Leander* and *Naiad* supported by *Jaguar, Kingston* and *Nizam* which swept close inshore. Meanwhile, the destroyers *Jervis, Havock, Hotspur* and *Decoy* carried out an anti-submarine sweep to seaward to protect the strike force led by *Naiad*.[3]

The ship had a pet monkey, imaginatively named 'Monkey'. Able Seaman Hugh 'Bob' Langton, along with AB Wally McDoughall from Tasmania, also on *Havock* but subsequently lost with *Sydney*, came across a spider monkey in Alex that was being mistreated so they 'rescued' it and smuggled it on board. The crew adopted him and he was often seen swinging through the rigging above the bridge. His favourite trick was to swing down to the galley and steal the cook's eggs. The Captain tolerated him because of the morale lift it gave the crew during a pretty tough time. The First Lieutenant, John Burfield, was less impressed having been bitten by it. Sadly, Monkey the monkey was killed in the rigging by shrapnel during an air raid.[4]

Picking up Derek Napper's log again:

> Monday 23 June. On entering harbour again at 06.00 on Monday morning, we were greeted with the news that Germany had declared war on Russia. Also, that in offensive sweeps with aircraft over Germany and enemy occupied territory, during daylight, we destroyed 65 German planes in the space of 3 days, with a total loss on our side of 9 fighters. Monday night was spent in harbour as it was our turn for a rest.
>
> Tuesday 24 June. On Tuesday, again we had a stand-off, except an enemy aircraft dived over the harbour at 04.30 and dropped a single H.E. bomb close to *Leander*. A large fire was seen burning in Acre as a result of a raid, but no damage was done to Haifa.
>
> Wednesday 25 June/Thursday 26 June. *Leander*, *Decoy*, *Nizam* and *Havock* left harbour at 19.30 [25th] to carry out a bombardment. We arrived in position at dawn on Thursday morning and took station ahead of *Leander* to carry out A/S sweep while *Decoy* and *Nizam* proceeded to bombard. There were five separate targets – a wood, a machine gun post on a ridge, a house used as an HQ, some other buildings and various strong points. The wood was well covered by *Leander*'s 6-inch guns and *Decoy*, steaming close inshore, put 3 direct hits on her appointed target. Long range shore batteries fired a few rounds from Beirut direction and one salvo straddled *Decoy*, the shot over being out for line astern, which was fortunate, as otherwise she might have suffered casualties from splinters. She withdrew a little after this and

although we were unable to locate the shore guns, they suddenly ceased firing. We fired six rounds per gun at the wood for practice and then the whole force steered for Haifa. *Leander* parted company just outside to go back to Alexandria and the destroyers went in together.

Friday 27 June. The operation on Friday night consisted of a searching sweep with *Kandahar* (streaming T.S.D.S. and bow protection) with *Perth* and *Griffin* in close support, to locate a suspected minefield. No mines were swept up during the period and we returned to Haifa at 05.30 on 28th.

On Monday night [30th] we were engaged on a routine sweep which produced no results and a similar type of thing was carried out on Tuesday [1 July], with the same dismal lack of incident.

Wednesday, 2 July. At 10.00 on Wednesday we left harbour with *Naiad, Perth, Kandahar, Kingston* and *Griffin* to bombard the Syrian coast near Beirut. The two main targets were an artillery position on the slope of a hill and an important road junction, while a wood much favoured by the enemy was a secondary target for the destroyers to fire at. When we got into position at 13.00, the two 'K' class proceeded close inshore and opened fire, whilst *Perth* tried to find her targets. This she did slowly, assisted by a forward military observation post in W/T communication. Eventually she scored direct hits on the road junction, for I observed the fall of shot through the layer's telescope on 'Y' gun. The battery was hidden from view by the shoulder of a hill, so it was impossible to observe anything but the smoke columns. No shore batteries fired at us and we continued our bombardment unmolested by aircraft. On our way back however, a Maryland or Glen Martin dropped a stick of 5 bombs close to *Perth*. There seems to be some doubt as to whether the pilot was a Vichy Frenchman or R.A.F. as the latter reported bombing an enemy convoy of a somewhat mythical character in almost exactly the same place during the afternoon.[5]

First Lieutenant John Burfield added:

To use a destroyer to bombard was really bloody silly, although we did sight a tank from the Director and set its course and speed on the Clock and found that it was going due north at four knots, so we fired a shell or two at it. When the French surrendered, they were allowed either to go to Vichy France, or join De Gaulle. We later found that our gaolers at Laghouat had been shelled by us in Syria.[6]

Napper continued:

On reaching the searched channel, C.S.15 signalled that Force 'B' would remain at sea during the night to try to intercept the afore-mentioned enemy convoy, now reported by the North Somerset Yeomanry ashore as 3 four funnelled French destroyers escorting motor landing craft, which were in dangerous proximity to Tyre, 60 miles south of Beirut and behind our advanced positions.

Nothing happened, as usual, through the dark hours and there seems to be some doubt now as to whether any convoy existed at all. I consider it quite possible that our force was continually reported by the aircraft as hostile.

Thursday 3 July. *Jackal* and *Hasty* entered harbour soon after we did at 0800 on Thursday and *Hasty* came alongside us at 'V' berth. They were intended as relief for *Kandahar* and *Decoy* who sailed for Alexandria soon after. Thursday night was spent in Haifa and then we sailed on Friday to bombard our usual position of the coast, round about the village of Damour. A similar thing was done on Saturday, and Saturday night spent on patrol with *Ajax*, *Perth* and *Kingston*.[7]

The days 5-7 July, were spent shelling near Damour the last fortified position before Beirut in the Lebanon. Allied troops were fighting their way up the coast from Palestine, now Israel, towards Beirut.[8]

Napper:

Sunday 6 July. At 05.00 on Sunday morning we were in position again off Damour. The original intention was to carry out a clean bombardment and return to Haifa at 07.00, but when *Carlisle* and 4 more destroyers joined us I began to suspect that we should be seeing the same piece of coastline the whole day. I was certainly right. We remained at the disposal of the Army, firing at the shore targets as required and steaming backwards and forwards off Beirut. One thing only distinguished the day from many other similar. We ourselves carried out a shoot in concentration with the other destroyers, *Jackal* being the master ship. 20 rounds D.I.P. were fired from each gun and about 25 S.A.P. No untoward incidents occurred, except that the tray worker on 'X' gun nearly put the cordite charge in the gun without removing the clip. I was lucky enough to see it in time and snatch it off before a breech jam resulted.

The shore batteries amused themselves by putting a few rounds over *Nizam* and the remainder about 2000 yards short of our ships.

Under cover of our bombardment, our army crossed the river Damour in several places and made a substantial advance toward Beirut.

The berthing arrangements at Haifa are so fantastically bad as to be hardly creditable. We were kept waiting outside the harbour for a full 50 minutes, had our berth changed about 6 times and finally were told to move directly we secured alongside *Ajax*. Twelve o'clock found us with our bows to the jetty astern of *Jackal* and our stern secured to *Ajax's* forecastle, as there was not room for us to get properly alongside.

Monday 7 July. At 09.20 we got sailing orders for 09.30 and were consequently 10 minutes adrift in leaving harbour. However, we easily caught up with *Carlisle* and *Hasty* who were already outside and made for our usual beat at 21 knots. *Ajax, Perth* and 4 destroyers followed later at 28 knots. We might just as well have stayed in harbour, for the army did not require any assistance and not a ship had fired a single round.

In the evening, D.7., detailed ourselves, *Nizam, Hotspur* and *Jackal* to rendezvous off the searched channel with *Naiad* and *Phoebe* while *Perth, Ajax, Hasty* and *Kingston* went in. A very half-hearted night sweep followed and then, to go from bad to worse, we found the harbour entrance mined and the port closed on our return to Haifa in the morning.

Tuesday 8 July. There was nothing for it but to steam up and down outside, which we did ad nauseam. I did think that we ought to have gone up and bombarded, instead of providing the inhabitants of Haifa with Naval manoeuvres on a small scale. During the dog watches we indulged in a little rather futile 'general' knowledge – most of the questions requiring knowledge of a very specialised character, or a vast capacity for assimilating unimportant facts, coupled with extreme deftness in extracting information from such publications as the *Daily Mail Year Book* and *Pears* [encyclopaedia].

Wednesday 9 July. On Wednesday morning at 06.00 it really looked as though we were going to enter harbour, but our hopes were not to be realised till 12.00, for *Naiad* and *Phoebe* anchored outside the harbour, while *Jackal* and ourselves carried out an A/S patrol. There was at least an improvement in the berthing arrangements, for when we eventually did get inside, we went alongside the oiling jetty at 'V' and remained there in peace.

It now appears that the Vichy authorities are sueing for peace in Syria. In fact, they have at last been convinced, in spite of our half-hearted policy to start with, that we mean what we say and cannot permit a German occupation.[9]

Napper's thoughts on the campaign were expressed succinctly in his log:

Sunday 13 July. An agreement has now been reached between ourselves and the Vichy government and all hostilities have ceased. One or two salient points emerge from the campaign. It appears that the intrusion of Free French Troops into Syria was most fiercely resented by the Vichy French in Syria. Indeed, some people go so far as to say that if Free French Troops had not been employed there would have been no fighting at all.

It is also evident that people of Syria would much rather be controlled by Great Britain than any Free French administration. I put this down to the fact that they know England treats her Mandated Territories with all consideration, but they are not so sure of their own countrymen.

Ajax, Phoebe, Jackal, Kingston and ourselves went to sea on Sunday night for a patrol, in order to keep the number of ships in harbour down to a reasonable figure in view of possible air attacks. On berthing at 07.00 (14th), we received orders to raise steam for 24 knots by 18.00.[10]

At 20.00 on 14 July the Vichy Forces in Syria signed the Armistice document and consequently, there was no longer a requirement for a heavy naval presence in Haifa. The following disposition signal sent at 18.00 on 13 July reflected the new situation: '*Kimberley, Griffin, Havock* and *Hotspur* return to Alexandria'. At 10.00 on 14

July *Naiad*, *Phoebe*, *Perth*, *Kimberley*, *Griffin*, *Havock* and *Hotspur* left Haifa en route for Alexandria.[11]

This was Derek Napper's last voyage in *Havock*:

> Tuesday 15 July. *Naiad*, *Perth*, *Phoebe*, *Griffin*, *Kimberley*, *Hotspur* and ourselves arrived back in Alexandria at noon Tuesday. I left *Havock* and joined *Valiant* on Wednesday thus coming to the end of one of the best periods of my life. The 4 months spent in *Havock* were instructive ones indeed.[12]

Operation *Guillotine*

The capture of Crete led to concerns that the Germans would use the island as a base to seize Cyprus or other strategic assets in the Eastern Mediterranean. An obvious counter was to reinforce the garrison of Cyprus. Consequently, on 16 July Admiral Cunningham issued the orders for Operation *Guillotine* which involved the movement from Port Said and Haifa to Cyprus of the Army's 50th Division as well as 259 Wing, Royal Air Force, and their attached artillery, motor transport, and stores. The ships used for this task were the cruisers *Leander*, *Neptune*, *Hobart*, units of the 14th Destroyer Flotilla, the sloops *Parramatta*, and *Flamingo* plus a number of merchant ships.

On 22 July, *Havock* left Alexandria with the battleship *Queen Elizabeth* and fourteen other warships arriving back on the 24th with the same group after an uneventful voyage south of Crete during which the fleet covered the first phase of the long-running *Guillotine*. Once again, the Mediterranean Fleet's hard-pressed, overworked cruisers and destroyers and their crews were transporting British and Dominion troops between disparate parts of the Middle East Command. *Havock*'s turn to participate in this operation came on 15 August when she left Port Said in company with the cruiser *Hobart*, the fast minelayer *Abdiel* and the destroyer *Decoy* en route for Famagusta with troops. After disembarking the military passengers at Famagusta on the night of 15/16 August, *Abdiel* sailed for Alexandria while *Hobart*, *Decoy* and *Havock* proceeded to Haifa where she remained until the 20th of the month.

The Tobruk 'Run' August – October 1941

The peace and tranquillity of these relatively quieter times was soon shattered as *Havock* was about to experience the horrors of the 'beef and spud run' or 'suicide run' to Tobruk which was to be regular nightmare of an operation for some time. Tobruk was utterly isolated and could only be supplied from the sea at night as the Germans had air cover all along the coast to the Egyptian border at this time. It was a fearfully dangerous exercise which was executed at maximum speed because of the very real possibility of air attack during the day and night.

The problem had arisen because Operation *Battleaxe* failed to relieve Tobruk in June 1941. Consequently, the British began the long process of building up strong-enough forces to launch a major offensive to drive back the Africa Korps and thereby relieve Tobruk. In the meantime, the surrounded garrison at Tobruk had to be supplied with all the necessities to enable to it to withstand the siege. This included military equipment, ammunition, fuel, food and replacement troops as well as evacuating the sick and wounded. This new commitment fell upon Cunningham's sorely pressed Mediterranean Fleet which had taken a severe battering during the battle for Crete. The troops defending Tobruk were supplied from Alexandria by all sorts of craft ranging from destroyers to sloops and lighters and even small sailing ships which together made up the 'inshore squadron'. This included the Australian DF10, the so-called 'Scrap Iron Flotilla', which was led by Captain Waller and consisted of the Scott class flotilla leader *Stuart* (D10) and the V/W class destroyers *Voyager*, *Vampire*, *Vendetta* and *Waterhen*. The latter was crippled by bombs at 19.45 on 29th June 1941 off Sollum while making yet another 'run' on the so-called 'Tobruk ferry service' in company with the destroyer *Defender*. Attempts to get *Waterhen* back to Alexandria were in vain because the old ship rolled over and sank at 01.50 the following day. To their great credit and glory, the ships and men operating this run had to endure all kinds of hazards, including air attacks and later U-boat torpedoes. They suffered heavy losses but they kept the men of Tobruk supplied and so helped to frustrate the operations of Rommel's Afrika Korps.

While running supplies to Tobruk on Saturday, 2 August, *Havock* and *Vendetta* were attacked at 20.00 by twenty to thirty German aircraft (Ju 87 Stukas and Bf 109s). No damage was caused to the ships. Twelve Hurricanes on patrol intercepted and shot down three of the Ju 87s, one Bf 109 and possibly two more 109s. Three Hurricanes were reported missing.[13]

Derek Napper later related:

The First Lieutenant (Lieutenant John Burfield) of my last ship (*Havock*) told me what an exciting time they were having on the Tobruk run. The first time they went out with *Vendetta* they were carrying 47 tons of dynamite stowed on the upper deck. While on passage they were attacked by 40 Ju 87s. The fighter patrol of 12 South African Hurricanes broke up the enemy formation, but 20 Junkers got through to the ships. By a miracle and good shooting by *Havock*'s Oerlikons neither ship was touched. On the second trip *Havock* was attacked by a few Heinkel 111s during the night. The ships were shelled by the enemy land batteries while anchored in Tobruk harbour and *Havock* beat all records by unloading her cargo in 22 minutes.[14]

Havock and *Decoy* were due in Alexandria on Wednesday, 6 August following a supply drop to Tobruk overnight. 'Buster' Brown observed that:

When running supplies to Tobruk we used to carry several tons of ammunition on the upper deck together with some food stuffs. This was loaded onto one of the wrecks in the harbour at night. We then got away as quickly as possible before daylight and the usual Stukas.[15]

Torpedoman Jack Surridge recalled that:

The Captain would look at the Stukas through a piece of smoked glass. Once they had got into their vertical dive he would steer under them. Once tied up alongside everyone would be involved in the unloading. After one bombing I was left under bags of potatoes. We took the wounded, mail and even German prisoners, who were very surly and resented being taken prisoner.[16]

Able Seaman Harry Jenkins remembered that:

Going to Tobruk we had to get along before the moon rose or we would be spotted. We were doing 30-35 knots and leaving a huge white wake behind. These were known as 'Suicide runs'. We carried ammunition, fuel, food, stores, troops, even Gurkhas who were terribly seasick. The Army provided most of the labour for unloading. We had to unload and get out before German aircraft could be called. They bombed us in the dark, but we couldn't see them. We hid behind cases of land mines when the bombs were dropping!

Sometimes we had to turn back as it was too dangerous
in the harbour or on land.[17]

A typical signal sent on 10 August, gives a vivid insight into a
frenetic passage along the North African coast '*Havock* and *Decoy*
expected time of departure from Tobruk 0130/11 passing through
R 0335/11, B 0555/11 thence to Alex.' Able Seaman Gunner Harry
Jenkins also recalled bombardments of Bardia:

> They had a big shore battery gun that ran out on rails
> from a protected position. It easily outranged us. We
> called it 'Bardia Bill'.[18]

In all, *Havock* made eight supply trips to Tobruk in August and
September and was subjected to many air attacks. Also, when
Havock spent four days in harbour at Alexandria, her Commanding
Officer, Lieutenant Commander Robin Watkins was married to
his fiancée who had travelled from South Africa with her mother
with the blessing of Admiral Cunningham and General Smuts.
Interspersed with her duties on the Tobruk run *Havock* was still
involved in Operation *Guillotine* transporting troops and stores to
Cyprus – these seemingly endless and potentially very dangerous operations must have been very hard on both the ship and
her crew.

The garrison defending the 'fortress' Tobruk was consisted of
Australian, British and Indian units and under the command of
Major-General Leslie Morshead who was also the commander of
the Australian 9th Division. Unfortunately, Australian domestic
politics added to the burden because in the summer of 1941 the
Australian Government began to insist on the withdrawal of all
Australian troops from Tobruk to fulfil an agreement between the
British and Australian governments that all Australian troops in
the Middle East should operate as a single force.

Not surprisingly, because of the limited and seriously over-
stretched forces at their disposal, the naval, military and air
forces commanders in the Middle East felt that this an unrealis-
tic request. Furthermore, if carried out, it would cause unnecessary casualties while at the same time diverting scarce resources
away from their main task of defeating the Axis forces in North
Africa. However, the Australian Government was adamant that
the Australians in Tobruk must be relieved regardless of casualties. Such was the genesis of Operation *Treacle* which involved the
replacement of the Australian 18th Infantry Brigade and the 18th
King Edward VII's Own Cavalry of the Indian Army with the

Polish Carpathian Brigade. The Australian 9th Division was to be replaced later by the British 70th Division.

Operation *Treacle*

On 19 August, the first night Operation *Treacle*, destroyers *Jervis*, *Kimberley* and *Hasty* left Alexandria to make the high-speed dash to Tobruk under cover of darkness returning late on the 20th. Earlier that day, *Havock*, which had been relieved at Haifa by *Hotspur*, returned to Alexandria in preparation. On 26 August the Leander class cruisers *Ajax* and *Neptune* departed Alexandria escorting fast minelayer *Latona* and the destroyers *Jervis*, with Rear Admiral Destroyers, Mediterranean Fleet, embarked, *Griffin* and *Havock*, in the seventh of the *Treacle* operations returning to Alexandria the following day. Two days later *Griffin* and *Havock* sailed from Alexandria to undertake the tenth and final run of Operation *Treacle* returning on 30 August.

A total of 6,116 men of the Polish Carpathian Brigade and 1,297 tons of stores were disembarked in Tobruk from the fast minelayers and the destroyers during Operation *Treacle* and 4,432 able-bodied men and 610 invalids were brought out of Tobruk. It was then necessary to consider whether the further relief of the garrison was desirable or feasible not least because it could only take place during the moonless period of each month. Just as Operation *Treacle* was coming to an end, the Australian Prime Minister Robert Menzies resigned and on 29 August was replaced by his deputy Fadden. Australian domestic politics of the time meant that Fadden was insistent that the 9th Australian Division must be brought back from Tobruk regardless of cost in lives and scarce equipment. Consequently, in early September plans were made to replace the 9th Australian Division with the British 70th Division during the next two moonless periods, during Operation *Supercharge* in September and Operation *Cultivate* in October.[19]

Operation *Supercharge*

The object of Operation *Supercharge* was the reinforcement of the garrison of Tobruk by part of the 6th Division from Syria. The arrival of these troops would enable the withdrawal of an Australian infantry brigade and some auxiliary troops. These shipping movements, which were undertaken during the moonless period of 17-27 September 1941, would at the same time bring in stores, petrol and a few tanks. The ships employed included the fast minelayers *Abdiel* and *Latona* as well as the destroyers

A port quarter view of *Havock* showing "Y" gun at its maximum elevation of 40° which was adequate against torpedo and high level bombers but totally inadequate against dive bombers. (Richard Osborne Collection)

The destroyer *Havock* in the Mediterranean – note the Nyon patrol marking on the shield of "B" gun. *Havock* was completed as a TSDS-equipped destroyer and the paired davits can be seen right aft along with a pair of Oropesa floats on the quarterdeck together with the starboard minesweeping winch on the upper deck abreast the aft mast. (Richard Osborne Collection)

Stoker Albert William Goodey, aged 20, photographed in Malta in 1938-39, served in *Havock* from 28 September 1938 until 14 November 1941. (David Goodey)

The Second Destroyer Flotilla photographed in Marseilles in 1939. From right to left: *Hotspur* (H01), *Havock* (H43), *Hostile* (H55), *Hunter* (H35), *Hero* (H99), *Hyperion* (H97), *Hasty* (H24) and the flotilla leader *Hardy*. The latter can be identified by the black top to her fore-funnel, the fifth 4.7-inch gun between the funnels and the absence of a pennant number. (David Goodey)

A pre-war photograph of *Havock*'s complement showing Lieutenant Commander Rafe Courage in the front row immediately beneath the barrel of "A" gun. (David Goodey)

During the First Battle of Narvik on 10 April 1940, *Havock* was hit by debris from the exploding German ammunition ship *Rauenfels*. Here the destroyer's "X"-gun crew (left to right: John Dodds, J.A. Brown, Jim 'Buster' Brown, Gun Captain 'Shits' Gilbert and Seaman Grimes) stand alongside a hole made in the gun shield. (Lieutenant J. Burfield via David Goodey)

A piece of the debris that rained down on *Havock* after the destruction of *Rauenfels* on 10 April – note the pair of 4.7-inch shells in the ready use rack. (Lieutenant J. Burfield via David Goodey)

This historically important but damaged photograph of *Havock* in Alexandria in July 1940 shows that the destroyer was still in her pre-war condition immediately before the action off Cape Spada on 17 July 1940. Note the interned French 8-inch gun cruiser in the background – either *Duquesne* or her sister *Tourville*. (David Goodey Collection)

The Australian 6-inch gun cruiser *Sydney* seen in British waters on 18 October 1935. (World Ship Society)

Havock's sister *Hyperion* fired the torpedo that finally sank *Bartolomeo Colleoni* at 0959 on 19 July 1940. Note the battlecruiser *Hood* in the background of this pre-war picture. (Richard Osborne Collection)

The crippled and stationary Italian cruiser *Bartolomeo Colleoni* on 19 July 1940. (Historic Military Press)

Recently promoted Commander Rafe Courage on *Havock*'s bridge supervises the rescue of the survivors from *Bartolomeo Colleoni* who can be seen in the water close to the destroyer's starboard bow. (Lieutenant J. Burfield via David Goodey)

Survivors from *Bartolomeo Colleoni* on board *Havock* on 19 July 1940. (Lieutenant J. Burfield via David Goodey)

Bomb damage to *Havock*, suffered while returning to Alexandria after the action off Cape Spada, being repaired in Port Tewfik during August. When she returned to service in early September *Havock* had been camouflaged. (David Goodey)

The destroyer *Hasty* standing by the sinking Italian submarine *Berillo* on 2 October 1940. (Lieutenant J. Burfield via David Goodey)

The aircraft carrier *Illustrious* in 1940. On the night of 11 – 12 November 1940 *Havock* was part of the force escorting the carrier when she carried out the attack on the Italian Fleet in Taranto. (US Navy)

The 31,000-ton battleship *Valiant* seen in early 1940 soon after the completion of a major reconstruction. On 3 December of that year, while returning to Alexandria, she was involved in a collision with *Havock* which subsequently spent several weeks under repair. (Richard Osborne Collection)

During early 1941 Cunningham's cruisers and destroyers were used extensively to transport men, equipment and munitions to Greece and Crete. Here a Bren-gun carrier is being unloaded from the cruiser *Ajax* in Suda Bay. Note the AA cruiser *Coventry* in the right of the picture. (Richard Osborne Collection)

The AA cruiser *Carlisle* firing at enemy aircraft while in Suda Bay in early 1941. Note the Type 279 air-warning radar at the head of the cruiser's mainmast. (Richard Osborne Collection)

This poor quality, but historically important, picture, taken from the bridge of the cruiser *Perth* on 24 March 1941, depicts the cruisers *York* (right) and *Gloucester* during an air attack while returning from the Malta convoy operation MW6. This is probably the last picture of *York* taken as an operational warship at sea because two days later she was crippled by an Italian explosive motor boat in Suda Bay and subsequently became a constructive total loss. (Richard Osborne Collection)

The battleship *Warspite*, Admiral Cunningham's flagship at the Battle of Matapan on 28/29 March 1941, seen leaving Portsmouth in July 1937. (Wright and Logan)

Havock leaving Alexandria in early 1941 showing the camouflage scheme that she sported at the Battle of Matapan. Note that the destroyer's second funnel is still at its original height and that both banks of torpedo tubes and the mainmast are still fitted. (David Goodey Collection)

The Italian destroyer *Carducci* which was torpedoed and sunk by *Havock* during the night action off Cape Matapan on 28/29 March 1941.

The destroyer *Nizam*, pictured in Alexandria in mid-1941, was one of 29 destroyers, including *Havock*, available at Alexandria at the start of the battle for Crete. (Richard Osborne Collection)

Havock (H43) and *Hotspur* (H01) at Alexandria in the autumn of 1941. Note that the after funnels of both ships have been reduced in height and their after masts removed to improve the AA arcs of the 3-inch HA gun installed in lieu of the after set of torpedo tubes. (David Goodey Collection)

Isis down at the head in Haifa having been badly damaged by near misses off the Syrian coast on 15 June 1941. The destroyer, which suffered shock and whip damage, was out of action until November 1943. Note the destroyer *Kimberley* alongside the crippled *Isis*. (Richard Osborne Collection)

Havock in Alexandria in the autumn of 1941. Note that she still retains the ineffective quadruple 0.5-inch AA guns between her funnels and has Type 286 radar at her foremasthead. (David Goodey Collection)

The Australian destroyer *Vendetta*. On 2 August 1941, she and *Havock* survived an attack by twenty to thirty German aircraft while ferrying supplies to Tobruk. (Richard Osborne Collection)

The cruiser *Ajax* returning to Alexandria in August 1941 after providing cover for a Tobruk "run". Like *Havock*, the cruiser had been present at Matapan as well as participating in the evacuation of Greece, the battle for and evacuation of Crete, the Syrian campaign and numerous Malta convoys. (Richard Osborne Collection)

An on board view of *Havock* carrying troops during Operation *Cultivate* in October 1941. Note the single 20mm gun abreast the searchlight platform. (Robert Wilford Collection)

The Leander-class cruiser *Neptune* which was lost after striking four mines off Tripoli on 19 December 1941 during a sortie by Force K. There was only one survivor from *Neptune*'s crew. *Havock* escorted the mine-damaged cruiser *Aurora* back to Malta. (World Ship Society)

The destroyer *Kandahar* which went to *Neptune*'s assistance but was also mined and sunk. Some 830 Allied seamen were killed during this failed operation. (Richard Osborne Collection)

Havock pictured in late 1941/early 1942 in her final configuration with a single 3-inch gun in lieu of the aft torpedo tubes and single 20mm guns between the funnels and abreast the signal platform. Note that her camouflage scheme has also been changed. (David Goodey Collection)

The Hunt-class destroyer *Southwold* (L10) at Alexandria in late 1941. She was Commander Jellicoe's ship during the Malta convoy operation that led to the Second Battle of Sirte and was sunk by a mine on 24 March while escorting *Breconshire* to the besieged island. (Richard Osborne Collection)

The burnt-out wreck of *Havock* about 300 yards from the shore and approximately 2.5 miles from Kelibia Lighthouse. (World Ship Society)

Another view of the wreck of *Havock*. (World Ship Society)

Hotspur after her conversion to an anti-submarine destroyer in 1943. Note "Y" gun has been removed to facilitate increased depth charge stowage on the quarterdeck, single 20mm guns in the bridge wings, between the funnels and abreast the searchlight platform, HF/DF aerial on a new mainmast, Type 291 air warning radar on the foremast, surface warning radar on the bridge and a split Hedgehog ahead throwing weapon to port and starboard abreast "A" gun mounting. Had *Havock* survived it is highly likely that she would have been converted to a similar configuration. (Richard Osborne Collection)

Jervis, Jaguar, Jackal, Kandahar, Kingston, Kimberley, Griffin, Hasty, Havock, Hotspur, Nizam and *Napier* sailing out of Alexandria and 'A' lighters operating out of Mersa Matruh.

Havock participated in the second run which started on 17 September when she arrived at Mersa Matruh to embark fifteen tons of equipment for 100 men of the Royal Tank Regiment as well as twenty-five tons of stores. The destroyer sailed the following day to rendezvous with the fast minelayer *Latona* which was accompanied by the destroyers *Napier* and *Nizam*. The force arrived at Tobruk at 23.12 on the 18th and disembarked 678 personnel and 189 tons of stores and evacuated eighty-seven personal and sixty-six wounded. *Latona* and her consorts arrived back in Alexandria on 19 September.[20]

Everything changed on 20 September 1941, when a minor disaster struck, as this signal reveals: '*Havock* grounded, starboard propeller blades damaged. Port propeller ¼-inch of each blade missing'.[21]

Jim Brown recalled:

20 September 1941. *Havock* grounded whilst closing the shore in darkness to bombard Bardia. As the ship was fitted with bow sweeps, which were attached to the stem of the ship, together with the usual TSDS (Two Speed Destroyer Sweeps), this meant that we were first in line and could sweep a channel for the rest of the task force. After running aground, we limped back to Alexandria at a few knots with damaged screws and at least one 'A' bracket (shaft support) bent. This set up a terrific vibration even at only a few knots. We went through the Suez Canal to Port Tewfik for repairs. The dockyard workers at Tewfik amazed us by carrying out the repairs with little more than hand tools. The 'A' bracket was straightened by bolting sheets of perforated steel round it and a fire lit inside the cage to make it malleable. The shaft was changed on our next trip to Malta, this entailed taking up the deck amidships. I believe the new shaft was taken to Malta by a mine-laying submarine.

Whilst in Tewfik late leave was granted only to ratings if they intended going to the local open air cinema. The film showing at the time was 'The Wizard of Oz' and late leave became known as 'Oz leave' to circumvent the rules on shore leave.

Also, whilst in Tewfik quite a few of the ship's company were affected by 'Gypo Tummy' and all green vegetables, fruit, etc., had to be washed in a 'fluid' before eating. There was also an air raid on a local oil refinery. We thought we were in for problems, but the raid was not repeated during our stay.

Operation *Cultivate*

This operation was intended to complete the transport of part of the 6th Division from Syria to Tobruk while simultaneously withdrawing the remainder of the Australian troops in the besieged 'fortress'. Stores, petrol, guns and tanks were also landed at the same time. Once again, all movements were made during the dark moon period of 12-25 October. Troops were transported to and from Alexandria aboard *Abdiel, Latona, Hotspur, Napier, Nizam, Kandahar, Kipling, Kingston, Jaguar, Jackal, Griffin, Hasty, Hero, Decoy* and *Havock*. Tanks and guns were run into Tobruk aboard 'A' lighters from Mersa Matruh.

A programme of ten voyages, designated serials or flights, was drawn up of which eight were to be composed of a mix of fast minelayers and destroyers while two consisted of 'A' lighters from Mersa Matruh. The second serial of *Latona, Jackal, Nizam* and *Havock* sailed from Alexandria at 08.00 on 17 October and arrived at Tobruk without incident. All four ships completed very good turn-round times an hour ahead of schedule before departing at 23.40 that day. They arrived at Alexandria having transported seventy-seven officers, 1,195 other ranks, nine guns and 153 tons of stores into Tobruk and evacuated sixty officers, 929 other ranks, 140 invalids and ten prisoners of war.[22] The tenth and final serial did not reach Tobruk because of the loss of *Latona* and damage to *Hero* – needless casualties which were yet more victims of Australian domestic politics.

To damage the screws once is misfortune but to do so twice is careless. But, on 19 October, one month after the earlier grounding, Lieutenant Commander Watkins did it again and, this time, both propellers were badly damaged. This propensity to run the ship aground, largely due to having to work close inshore, was eventually to lead to her demise in April 1942. As a result of this grounding *Havock* remained in Alexandria until 4 December, having shaft damage repaired. Few of the crew complained about this forced rest from the rigours of war.

However, 28 October 1941, was a particularly dark day, for an incident for once not caused by the enemy. An accident occurred which cast a shadow for a while over the lucky and happy ship. The event is best described in the words of Jim 'Buster' Brown:

There was a most unfortunate accident whilst lying on our buoy in Alexandria harbour. As usual a forecastle sentry was posted, whose duty was to challenge any boats approaching the ship. He was armed with a rifle and carried several rounds of ammunition in the magazine. It was the habit of some ratings to sleep on their hammocks slung on the after end of the foredeck, particularly on hot nights. The sentry was cracking jokes with one of these ratings [Able Seaman William Bagnall aged twenty-three] and in jest pointed the rifle at him and pulled the trigger and sad to say the rifle went off and the rating was shot dead. There should not have been a round in the breech.[23]

First Battle of Sirte

Following repairs to her propellers and shafts, *Havock* was back on duty on 15 December with another convoy, this time with Rear-Admiral Vian in *Naiad* with *Euryalus, Carlisle, Jervis, Kimberley, Kingston, Kipling, Nizam, Havock, Hasty* and *Decoy*. The group set out to cover the passage of the fast merchantman *Breconshire* to Malta. Force K, consisting of the cruisers *Aurora* and *Penelope* accompanied by the destroyers *Lance* and *Lively*, left Malta at 18.00 on 16 December to meet Vian's force and take over the job of escorting *Breconshire* into Valletta. Numerous air attacks were made during the afternoon of 17 December and alarming reports were received that the Italian Fleet was at sea and consequently, Force B – the cruisers *Neptune* and the destroyers *Kandahar* and *Jaguar* – sailed from Malta to reinforce *Breconshire*'s escort. Naturally the British assumed that the Italian fleet had put to sea to undertake a set-piece attack on their much weaker force. However, in fact, the recent successes against Italian convoys by the cruisers and destroyers of the Malta-based Force K had forced the Italian battlefleet to sea to cover the passage of Axis convoys to Tripoli and Benghazi.

Just before dusk at 17.42 hours, the Italian ships were sighted 300 degrees, seventeen miles distant from *Naiad*. The Italian fleet consisted of the battleships *Andrea Doria* and *Giulio Cesare*, an 8-inch gun cruiser squadron and destroyers. When the range was down to fourteen miles, the two Italian battleships opened very accurate fire with their 12.6-inch guns on Vian's small force, which turned away. *Havock* and *Decoy* were given the task of screening the *Breconshire* away as the cruisers engaged the Italian battle fleet in what became known as the First Battle of Sirte. Axis aircraft also attacked the British force during the brief engagement. The destroyers *Jervis, Kimberley, Kingston, Kipling, Nizam* and *Hasty* turned to attack the Italian battlefleet but were forestalled by a recall signal, sent at 17.57, from Rear Admiral Vian. By 18.00 the Italians had turned away and Force K, Force B, *Breconshire* and *Havock* headed for Malta arriving at 15.00 on 18 December.

The Second Battle of Sirte some three months later was to have the direst of consequences for the battle weary and battered *Havock*. In the meantime, the British had realised that an Italian convoy was at sea and, arguing that it was unlikely that the Italian battlefleet would escort it all the way to Tripoli, decided to send the Malta striking force out to destroy it on the night of 18/19 December. The stage had been set for a tragedy of epic proportions.

The destruction of Force K

At 18.00 on 18 December Captain Rory O'Conor led the Malta striking force, consisting of Force B, the cruiser *Neptune* and the destroyers *Kandahar* and *Havock* and Force K, the cruisers *Aurora* and *Penelope* and the destroyers *Lance* and *Lively*, from the Grand Harbour in an attempt to destroy and Italian convoy known to be en route to Tripoli. All went well until the early hours of 19 December when the force was about twenty miles from Tripoli harbour in 100 fathoms of water. Unexpectedly, it entered a hitherto unidentified minefield of special German contact mines which had been laid by Italian cruisers to counter just such a raid by Force K. The minefield took the British by surprise as the depth of water was 600 feet which was thought to be too deep for mines. At 01.06 *Neptune* struck the first of four mines and sank at about 04.00 with only one survivor[24]. The cruiser *Aurora* detonated a mine abreast 'B' turret at about 01.07 suffering serious damage forward of her bridge. Her sister *Penelope* was luckier suffering only minor structural damage when an explosion occurred abreast her bridge on the port side. The destroyer *Kandahar* informed *Lance* that she was going to go alongside the stricken *Neptune* and ordered *Lance* to take command of the destroyers. *Lance* and *Havock* escorted the damaged *Aurora* back to Malta arriving without further incident at 12.30 on 19 December. Subsequently, after temporary repairs, *Aurora* sailed for Gibraltar and was out of action for thirteen weeks. *Penelope* and *Lively* arrived back in the Grand Harbour at 11.00 that day.

Meanwhile *Kandahar* also struck a mine under her stern at about 03.04 causing severe damage and was scuttled by a torpedo fired by *Jaguar* at 05.40 on 19 December. *Jaguar* rescued eight officers and 160 ratings of *Kandahar's* crew. A further sixty were killed by the explosion of the mine and seven were lost during rescue operations. Some 830 Allied seamen, many of them New Zealanders from *Neptune*, lost their lives in this disaster. The Malta Strike Force which had been such an active threat to Axis shipping to Libya during the last quarter of 1941 had been reduced to impotence. It was later forced to withdraw to Gibraltar.[25]

By 21 December, *Havock* was back in Malta for yet more running repairs. On 3 January 1942, whilst still in Malta repairing, *Havock* and *Zulu* were both damaged by bomb splinters and sustained casualties. *Havock* had one officer and two ratings killed and two ratings wounded during these persistent air attacks.[26] Those killed on board *Havock* were Lieutenant Thomas Ellison Godman DSC, RNVR, Able Seaman William Ernest Bidmade and Stoker First Class Walter Morehen – their deaths are reported as 4 January 1942.

On 5 January 1942, Operation *MF2* left Alexandria for Malta with the fast merchantman *Glengyle* protected by Force B (Rear Admiral Vian) with *Dido, Euryalus, Naiad* (cruisers), *Gurkha, Sikh, Kipling, Kingston* and *Foxhound*. The next day, 6 January, *Breconshire* left Malta for Alexandria with Force C, *Lance, Lively, Jaguar* and *Havock*. Both convoys met on 7 January. The transports, plus *Sikh* and *Havock* were exchanged and *Havock* arrived back in Alex on 9 January.[27] Jack Surridge remembered that: 'On convoys to Malta we were under attack all daylight hours by aircraft, submarines and surface craft.'[28]

Jim Brown recalls the experiences of Malta at this time:

> When we came back from Port Tewfik they put us in dock in Malta to check us over. While we were there the ill-fated convoy came in with the *Essex*. A bomb had gone down through the bridge and exploded in the engine room. She was loaded with ammunition. We sent working parties over to unload her and worked down in her holds loading the slings and operating the derricks. To help keep morale up, a Royal Marine Band played on a lighter alongside the ship.[29]

Operation *MF3* to Malta was initiated on 16 January and involved convoy MW8A leaving Alexandria (transports *Ajax* and *Thermopylae*, twelve knots) at 08.30 in company with the AA cruiser *Carlisle* and the destroyers *Arrow, Griffin, Hasty* and *Hero*. Convoy MW8B (transports *City of Calcutta* and *Clan Ferguson*,

fourteen knots) left Alexandria at 1530 that day escorted by the
destroyers *Isaac Sweers, Legion, Maori* and *Gurkha* followed by
Force B (Vian) with the cruisers *Naiad, Dido, Euryalus* and *destroyers Kelvin, Kipling, Havock, Foxhound* and *Hotspur*. Special fighter
protection had been arranged for these forces from aerodromes
in Cyrenaica and a strong air reconnaissance of the Ionian Sea
was cleared for 17 and 18 January.[30] The carnage of war continued when the next day, 17 January, *U133* torpedoed *Gurkha. Isaac
Sweers* had to tow her out of burning oil and rescue the crew
before she sank.[31]

Force B and convoys MW8A and MW8b joined up at 11.00
on 18 January and Force K, from Malta, made contact at 13.15
that day. There were a number of attacks by lone Ju 88s during
the day. At 11.30, for example, SS *Thermopylae* was detached
with *Carlisle, Arrow* and *Havock* to make for Benghazi because of
engine defects. She was later able to make thirteen knots and was
ordered to steer for Alexandria.[32]

However, at about 09.30 on the 19th, aircraft attacked and hit
her, setting her on fire. Because of the large amount of ammunition on board she was sunk by *Arrow* in position 33°02′N, 24°16′E
after she had taken off fifty-four survivors and *Havock*, in difficult
sea conditions, lifted 207, out of a total of 385 crew and passengers[33]. Jim Brown related:

> When *Thermopylae* was detached from the convoy she
> was directed to Benghazi. But we didn't make Benghazi
> as I understand the town had been taken by the
> enemy. So once again we changed course, this time for
> Alexandria. It was then that the air attacks started and
> the *Thermopylae* set on fire. We went alongside to take
> off South African soldiers. Unfortunately, as we closed
> alongside some of the soldiers tried to jump from one
> ship to the other and were crushed between the two. To
> prevent this, we dropped fenders, made from bundles
> of sticks, between the two vessels to keep them apart.
> Nevertheless, all survivors were taken off before she was
> sent to the bottom.[34]

Havock returned to Alexandria on 20 January but was clearly not
serviceable because she did not participate in Operation *MP4*
which sailed on 24th of the month when CS 15 sailed to cover the
passage of *Breconshire*.[35]

At 17.00 on 4 February 1942, the destroyers *Jervis* (D14), *Jaguar,
Kelvin, Lance, Griffin, Hero, Arrow* and *Havock* left Alexandria to

carry out an anti-submarine sweep to the westward in conjunc-
tion with ASV-equipped Swordfish and Wellington aircraft which
maintained a patrol five miles ahead of the destroyers. The sweep
was continued throughout the next day in co-operation with the
aircraft. The force turned eastward when in the vicinity of Derna
and arrived back in Alexandria in the afternoon of 6 February.[36]

Having survived into February 1942 *Havock* was now allotted
to the 22nd DF whereupon she entered into the calculations as
Operation *MF5* was being planned. This operation was to pass
the loaded convoy MW9 of three ships into Malta and retrieve
four empty ships in convoy ME10. The possibility of success was
much lower than on previous operations as the enemy had largely
neutralised the Malta fighters and ejected the army from western
Cyrenaica, control of the air now rested with the Luftwaffe and
the Italian air force.

Operation *MF5* began on 12 February when convoys MW9A
to Malta, consisting of *Clan Campbell* and *Clan Chattan* escorted
by *Carlisle, Lance, Heythrop, Avon Vale, Eridge* and MW9B *Rowallan
Castle* was escorted by *Beaufort, Dulverton, Hurworth* and
Southwold and left Alexandria covered by Force B (Rear Admiral
Vian), *Naiad, Dido, Euryalus* plus *Jervis, Kipling, Kelvin, Jaguar,
Griffin, Havock, Hasty* and *Arrow*. These convoys were desperate
measures to supply Malta and huge risks were taken. Despite the
considerable escort strength such was the superiority of enemy
air power that all of the merchantmen on these convoys were lost
or damaged. A very costly affair as the operation was abandoned
and Force B returned to Alexandria on 16 February.[37]

On 2 March the Hunt class destroyers *Dulverton* and *Hurworth*
and the Flower class corvette *Gloxinia* sailed from Alexandria
with convoy AT32 en route for Tobruk. The destroyers *Havock*
and *Hasty* were detailed to act as a striking force covering the
passage of this convoy.[38]

At 04.00 on 10 March CS15 (Rear Admiral Vian) with *Naiad,
Dido, Euryalus, Sikh, Zulu, Lively, Havock, Hero, Hasty, Kelvin,
Kipling* and *Jervis* left Alexandria to cover the passage of convoys
to and from Malta. At 08.00 on the 11th, the cruiser *Cleopatra* and
the destroyer *Kingston* met CS15 and the whole force returned to
Alexandria at high speed. Unfortunately, at 20.05 hours that day
the cruiser *Naiad* was torpedoed and sunk by *U565* in position
32°01′N, 26°20′E. *Dido* (now flying flag CS15) arrived at Alexandria
at 08.00 on 12 March in company with *Cleopatra, Euryalus, Sikh,
Havock, Hasty, Hero, Kelvin,* and *Kingston.* [39]

Less than forty-eight hours later Operation *MF8* began when
the cruisers *Dido, Euryalus* and the destroyers *Zulu, Lively, Hero,*

Havock and *Hasty*, under the command of *Dido*, left Alexandria at 01.00 on 14 February to bombard Rhodes.[40] The bombardment was carried out successfully from 01.30-01,45 hours on the 15th with the cruisers each firing 160 rounds of 5.25-inch shells. *Hero*, *Havock* and *Hasty* used their TSDS equipment to provide minesweeping protection. Hits were observed on the Alliotti flour mills and adjacent hangars and workshops before the force withdrew to the westwards at 01.45 and returned to Alexandria. RAF Beaufighters drove off one attacker during the force's return to Alexandria and the ships arrived unscathed at 09.30 on 16 March.[40]

David Masterman Ellis, who had an unfortunately short stay on *Havock* when he joined her on loan from the crippled *Queen Elizabeth*, as a Midshipman, in the first week of March 1942, recalled:

> Our first trip after I joined was escorting two of the cruisers from Alexandria to meet and escort back a third cruiser arriving from the west. This may have been *Cleopatra*. After dark on our way back to Alexandria *Naiad* was torpedoed and sank (11 March 1942).
>
> On Friday, 13 March, we sailed with a cruiser force and carried out a night bombardment of Rhodes. Presumably there was some important military target, but I believe the real object was to create a diversion in the hope of drawing off some of the Luftwaffe from their task of bombing Malta. Cruisers and destroyers joined the bombardment and the trip passed off without incident.[41]

Chapter 11

The Slow Death of HMS *Havock*: The Second Battle of Sirte and Beyond (March – April 1942)

During the autumn of 1941 ships, submarines and aircraft based in Malta had inflicted catastrophic losses on Italian warships and shipping, thereby causing major supply problems for the Axis army in North Africa. On 18 November, General Auchinleck launched his Operation *Crusader* offensive which drove Rommel's army out of Cyrenaica and back to the borders of Tripolitania by 12 January 1942. The Eighth Army's success owed not a little to British sea power but the balance began to swing back in favour of the Axis with the return of Fliegerkorps II from Russia.

At this critical moment, a series of disasters had occurred which greatly reduced British naval strength in the Mediterranean with the aircraft carrier *Ark Royal*, the battleship *Barham* and cruiser *Galatea* being torpedoed and sunk on 14 November, 25 November and 14 December respectively. Five days later, Force K, based in Malta, was crippled when the cruiser *Neptune* and the destroyer *Kandahar* were sunk by mines and the cruiser *Aurora* badly damaged.

The strategic situation had substantially changed on 19 December when three Italian Charioteers crippled the battle-ships *Queen Elizabeth* and *Valiant* by attaching delayed action mines. Fortunately, the two capital ships settled vertically onto shallow mud in Alexandria harbour and it was some weeks before the enemy realised what had been achieved. This action dramatically changed the balance of power in the Eastern Mediterranean and led to speculation in the Admiralty that it might be necessary to withdraw what was left of the Mediterranean Fleet. Fortunately, wiser counsels prevailed, although the absence of capital ships made increasing demands on the dwindling numbers of cruisers and destroyers which were available to Admiral Cunningham. The situation was exacerbated by the outbreak of war in the Far East and the loss of *Prince of Wales* and *Repulse* off Kuantan on 10 December. The cumulative effect of these losses was to rob the Royal Navy of any strategic reserve which could be moved to bolster the position in the Eastern Mediterranean. Any such ships as could become available had to be sent to the Indian Ocean to counter the Japanese threat.

Thus, by early 1942 the British Mediterranean Fleet had been reduced to a shadow of its former self and consisted of four light cruisers, fifteen destroyers and twenty-five submarines. In comparison, their rival Italian fleet could muster four operational battleships, four heavy cruisers, five light cruisers, more than fifty destroyers and torpedo boats as well as fifty submarines. The principal difference between the two forces was that the Italians seemed to have adopted a 'fleet in being' strategy and therefore spent far more time in port than their British counterpart which often spent more time at sea than in harbour.

The retention of Cyrenaica was essential to provide air cover for the fleet and convoys to Malta. However, Rommel launched a lightning counter-attack on 21 January 1942, and in two weeks drove the Eighth Army out of most of Cyrenaica and laid siege to Tobruk once again. The availability of Fliegerkorps II was a major factor and ensured Axis aerial domination over the land and sea battles. The threat posed by Malta's striking forces was such that the Germans decided that the island must either be invaded or rendered unusable – a decision which made the defence of the island a priority at a time when the Allied naval resources in the eastern Mediterranean were already seriously weakened. Axis domination in the air was partly caused by numerical superiority and partly because the obsolete Hurricanes had become totally outclassed by Messerschmitt Bf 109s. Clearly the introduction of the much more capable Spitfire to the Mediterranean theatre was long overdue. The first fifteen arrived in Malta on 7 March, followed by a few more two weeks later. Unfortunately, at this stage of the war there were never enough to counter the attacks mounted by Fliegerkorps II which wrought destruction on the island's airfields and harbours almost without hindrance.

Operation *MG1*

During late 1941/early 1942 Malta had been kept resupplied with occasional trips made from Alexandria by the fast transport *Breconshire* and her sister *Glengyle*. However, the threat to Malta was considered so severe that General Dobbie, the Governor of the island, felt that it would take a convoy of ships to bring in the necessary ammunition, fuel, food and other essential stores. Unfortunately, Dobbie must have known that he could not guarantee air cover as the ships approached Malta or even once they were in harbour.

Nevertheless, the need was so great that a four-ship fast convoy (MW10) from Alexandria to Malta – *Clan Campbell* (7,255 grt), *Pampas* (5,415 grt), the Norwegian *Talabot* (6,798 grt) the ubiquitous commissioned transport *Breconshire* (9,776 grt) – had to be risked and was escorted by the totally inadequate force of light cruisers and destroyers available at Alexandria. *Havock* was to be one of their number.

The Plan[1]

At that time of year and assuming the convoy could make twelve knots or above, the approximately 900-mile journey from Alexandria could be split into three periods of twenty-four hours with almost equal hours of daylight and darkness. During the hours of daylight on D + 1 the convoy would pass through the so-called 'bomb alley' south of Crete but could expect some fighter cover from aircraft based in Egypt. The real dangers would arise on D + 2 when the convoy would be passing the Gulf of Sirte without fighter protection but in range for Axis aircraft and the Italian fleet which could sortie from Taranto. All being well, the convoy would arrive in Malta at dawn on D + 3, Monday, 23 March.

During D + 1 the convoy was protected by relays of fighter aircraft but by about 09.00 on D + 2 even the long-range Beaufighters had reached the limits of their radius of action and would have to return to airfields in Egypt. Axis air attacks began about thirty minutes after the last fighter cover was withdrawn at 09.30 hours.

Vian planned to counter an intervention by the Italian Fleet, organizing his force so that a certain disposition could be achieved rapidly and then use the speed and initiative of his small ships to harass and threaten his superior enemy by repeated assaults and withdrawals under cover of smoke screens. The latter would also cause the Italians to worry about sudden torpedo attacks from one of more destroyers emerging from smoke to deliver a deadly blow against an attacking battleship.

Thus, once the Italian Fleet was sighted, close AA escort for the convoy would be provided by *Southwold* (Commander Jellicoe),

Beaufort, Dulverton, Hurworth, Eridge and *Heythrop* while *Carlisle* and *Avon Vale* would be responsible for laying smoke across the wake of the convoy. In order to attack and harass the Italians Vian organized his ships to five strike force divisions:

1st *Jervis* (Captain Poland, D14), *Kipling*, *Kelvin* and *Kingston*.

2nd *Dido* (Captain McCall), *Penelope* and *Legion*.

3rd *Zulu* (Captain Graham) and *Hasty*.

4th *Cleopatra* (Rear Admiral Vian) and *Euryalus*.

5th *Sikh* (Captain Micklethwait, D22), *Sikh*, *Lively*, *Hero* and *Havock*.

Captain H.W.U. McCall of *Dido* recalled that: 'In the waters off Alexandria his captains had rehearsed the tactics to be used should we encounter the Italian Fleet e.g. divisions acting independently to a large extent with the minimum of signals and using smoke as a cover.'[2]

Captain (later Admiral) Guy Grantham the commanding officer of Vian's flagship *Cleopatra* wrote:

> Vian had all the commanding officers of HM ships and the merchant ships to a conference on board before we sailed. He explained to them what he thought would happen and what he intended all ships should do. In the event his forecast was correct, and the only signals he had to make to start the action were 'Enemy in sight' and 'Engage the enemy bearing …'[3]

Captain Bush of *Euryalus* was also very complimentary about Vian's preparation for the operation: 'He had the 15th Cruiser Squadron so well trained that it was hardly ever necessary for him to make a signal: the Nelson touch. We all knew what we had to do.'[4]

The convoy sails

Convoy MW10 sailed from Alexandria at 07.00 on 20 March escorted the AA cruiser *Carlisle* and DF22 which consisted of *Sikh, Zulu, Lively, Havock, Hero* and *Hasty*. The convoy consisted of *Breconshire, Clan Campbell, Pampas* and *Talabot* and naval liaison officers and signalmen were embarked in each of the ships of the convoy. CS15 consisting of the cruisers *Cleopatra* (Flag Rear Admiral Vian), *Dido* and *Euryalus* with the destroyers of DF 14, *Jervis, Kipling, Kelvin* and *Kingston*, sailed after dark that day to cover the passage of the convoy to Malta. CS15, DF14 and DF 22 together constituted Force B.

The Hunt class destroyers of DF 5 led by Commander Jellicoe in *Southwold* with *Dulverton, Hurworth, Eridge, Heythrop* and *Avon Vale* joined the escort of MW10 at daylight on the 21st and CS15 joined soon thereafter. *Beaufort,* another Hunt class destroyer, left Tobruk at 09.45 that day to join the convoy. Together with the AA cruiser *Carlisle* these six would form the close escort of the convoy which was apparently not sighted by aircraft on the 20th or 21st. This successful action by the Army in shelling the Martuba landing ground and threatening Tmimi probably contributed to this immunity.[5]

At 01.30 on 22 March the submarine *P36* reported heavy ships leaving Taranto. Continued large scale bombing of Malta aerodromes prevented the intended reconnaissance being flown from Malta. The cruiser *Penelope* and the destroyer *Legion,* all that remained of Force C, sailed from Malta after dark on 21st and joined CS15 in the morning of 22nd. Light enemy air attacks commenced during the forenoon and developed into heavy air attacks in the afternoon. A total of about 150 torpedo-, dive- and high-level bombers were employed and concentrated on the convoy which was escorted by *Carlisle* and the six Hunt class destroyers of DF5. No ships were hit. Five aircraft were shot down and at least four more damaged. Two more aircraft were shot down by *Euryalus* during the later surface action. Beaufighters covered the convoy until 09.00 on the 22nd.[6]

The convoy made a tempting target. As expected, the Luftwaffe rose to the occasion, but unusually this time, so did the Italian Battle Fleet which sailed from Taranto in an attempt to intercept and annihilate it.

The Second Battle of Sirte 22 March 1942[7]

At 14.10 hours *Euryalus* sighted and reported smoke bearing 350 degrees and seven minutes later reported three ships bearing 360 degrees. At 14.27 *Euryalus* sighted four ships bearing 015 degrees, distant twelve miles and Italian masts came into view and were taken to be those of battleships. Subsequently, at 14.30 Vian was able to report that 'in position 33°55′N, 17°47′E CS15 sighted four cruisers to the north east which were successfully driven off'.

CS15 moved to meet the threat while *Carlisle* and the six Hunt class destroyers became the sole defenders of the convoy which was bombed heavily. Vian was well aware that his force could not refuel at Malta nor could the convoy continue too far to the southwest as every hour's delay decreased their chance of reaching Malta before daybreak. Consequently, he knew that the Italian had to be driven off before dark. As his striking force moved off to the north and away from the convoy, his ships formed divisions in line ahead as instructed at Alexandria. *Penelope* and *Legion*, which had sailed from Malta had not been party to such instructions and initially followed astern of *Dido*. A number of shell splashes fell near *Penelope* but the Italians soon turned away.

At 14.33 Vian's divisions turned east to lay smoke which, thanks to the freshening south-easterly wind blotted out the convoy in less than a minute. By 14.42 Vian could see that he was opposed by heavy cruisers and not battleships. *Cleopatra* and *Euryalus* closed the range to about ten miles and began to fire on the leading Italian heavy cruiser at 14.56. The Italians turned away to the north-west and by 15.15 Admiral Parona's ships were steaming northward. Throughout this engagement, the convoy, and also Vian's cruisers and destroyers, were heavily bombed but the barrage put up by the six Hunt class destroyers was such that not a single ship was hit while several attacking aircraft were brought down. However, the expenditure of AA ammunition had been prodigious with *Carlisle* reporting that she had expended one third of her total while the Hunts had expended 60 per cent.

Between 14.45 and 15.00 *Carlisle* and *Avon Vale* had succeeded in putting up a smoke screen which hid the convoy from the Italians. Both ships had been the subject of several air attacks and, while manoeuvring to avoid bombs in thick smoke, *Carlisle* collided with *Avon Vale* fortunately causing only minor damage.

Admiral Iachino in *Littorio* had been steaming southward all day at twenty-eight knots intending to make rendezvous with Admiral Parona's cruisers at a propitious moment. At 16.18 *Littorio* joined Parona's cruisers but by this time the sea had become very rough, the wind had risen to thirty miles an hour and visibility was very poor. Rear Admiral Vian had barely re-joined the convoy when, at 16.40, Italian ships were sighted to the north-east and just ten miles away.

The second phase of the battle began at 1640 when the battleship *Littorio* with the three cruisers seen earlier and escorting destroyers appeared on the north horizon, At about this time, Admiral Vian, worried by the dangerously high rate at which the 'Hunts' were expending their ammunition, ordered the first division under Captain Poland to fall back in support of the convoy which had now turned south behind smoke and was getting further and further by the hour from its destination, Malta.

It soon became clear that there were two enemy groups which were identified as two 8-inch gun cruisers (actually *Trento* and *Gorizia*) and the 6-inch cruiser *Giovanni delle Bande Nere* plus four destroyers. The second group consisted of the battleship *Littorio* and three destroyers. Both groups, which were steaming at high speed, were well placed to intercept the convoy. There seemed little to stop the Italians from getting through to the convoy and annihilating it. Iachino's 15-inch and 8-inch guns could easily outrange those of CS15 but the British continued to lay down smoke screens. Consequently, the Italians could only see glimpses of some of the British ships while the convoy was more or less invisible to them thanks to the strong south-easterly wind blowing the smoke towards the Italians. Meanwhile, the British ships, which were enveloped in the smoke manoeuvred almost aimlessly with little knowledge of the relative position of the forces engaged.

Vian was concerned that the Italians might slip round the smokescreen and attack the convoy from the east and consequently led *Cleopatra, Euryalus, Dido, Penelope, Legion, Zulu* and *Hasty* to the east to counter such a move. As DF14 was supporting the convoy, this left Micklethwait's 5th Division consisting of *Sikh, Lively, Hero* and *Havock* covering the western flank. At 16.49 Micklethwait sighted an Italian battleship and two cruisers bearing north-east about six miles distant. Consequently, he altered course and engaged the Italian ships with his four destroyers for approximately six minutes, making use of smoke until the battleship came into view. The hour between 17.00 and 18.00 was the most critical of the day, when Captain Micklethwait's four destroyers, *Sikh, Havock, Hero* and *Lively*, were all that stood between the Italian fleet and the convoy. At 17.05 he turned his ships away to avoid highly accurate Italian gunfire but his division's luck ran out at 17.20 when *Havock* was very seriously damaged by shell splinters from a 15-inch shell fired by *Littorio*.

At 17.20 in a hail of fire and whilst making smoke to position for a mock or real torpedo attack *Havock* was struck what turned out to be a mortal blow, when a 15-inch shell burst with enormous explosive power alongside, heavily damaging the boiler room and killing seven of the crew and wounding many more. Those killed in the attack were Signalmen Claude Brown and Arthur Crane, Supply Assistant Alexander Gimblett, Sub-Lieutenant Walter Orpen the Gunnery Control Officer/Navigating Officer (G.C.O./N.O.), Able Seaman Frederick 'Blood' Reid, Gunner (T) James Thompson and Able Seaman James Hulme. Able Seaman George Gordon Frederick Carter died of his wounds in Malta two weeks later. Maurice Douglas was one of the many wounded.

Able Seaman John Dodds remembers the action as the worst ever:

> I was on the 3-inch high angle anti-aircraft gun and my
> opposite number was standing beside me and we were
> talking. He was instantly killed by a shrapnel splinter to
> the head. I didn't feel anything at the time other than 'oh
> dear, he's gone'. However, it affected me later and after
> the war. There was a rough sea and gunfire and people
> being killed. We didn't get much protection from the
> smoke because of the strong wind. We could see sheets
> of flame from the battleship as she fired at us.[8]

Havock shuddered to a near standstill for a period before fast and
efficient damage control and repair recovered her sufficiently to
turn and limp back to reinforce the convoy escort as far as her
half-sinking capability would allow. The remaining three destroyers of the fifth division pressed on meanwhile in an endeavour to
reach a favourable position on the bow from which to launch a
torpedo attack, but the Italians were too fast for them and they
could not gain a bearing as the range continued to decrease.

Eighteen-year old Midshipman David Masterman Ellis, less
than three weeks on board *Havock*, recalled:

> Leaving the Hunt Class destroyers, the Fleet destroyers
> headed northward at full speed and proceeded to lay a
> smokescreen between the convoy and the enemy. By this time
> the wind, which had been steadily increasing, was blowing
> hard from a southerly point towards the Italian Fleet and
> to some extent the destroyers, crossing the enemy's line of
> advance from east to west, were hidden by their own smoke.
>
> The enemy had been ranging on the point at which
> the destroyers, steaming in line ahead, turned away to
> the southward in succession, and by the time that *Havock*
> reached this point, *Littorio's* main 15-inch armament
> straddled her with a salvo. The nearest shell was close
> alongside her, amidships on the port side, and made a
> large hole in her forward boiler room. The director was
> put out of action and the Navigator (Sub-Lieutenant
> Walter Orpen) was killed. The ship lost way, but was
> already hidden by the smoke and was not hit again.
>
> While the engineers were trying to get steam back
> into the engine, the Gunner (James Thompson) was sent
> onto the forecastle with a party to rig a bottom line, with
> the intention of getting a collision mat over the hole in
> the boiler room. Before they could complete the task, the

engine room reported the engines ready and the forecastle party was ordered aft. At the same time the engines were ordered full ahead and as the Gunner, following the rest of the party, was making his way off the forecastle, the ship dipped her bows into the head sea and the Gunner went overboard. To have tried to recover him would have meant the probable loss of the ship, and the Captain was obliged to abandon him.

From then on *Havock*'s speed was limited to 15 knots and she was ordered back to join the convoy's anti-aircraft screen. Meanwhile the cruisers, making full use of the smoke screen which was blowing down towards the enemy, were engaging him at decreasing range as they emerged from the smoke and taking cover in it before being hit themselves. The L class destroyers were sent in to attack with torpedoes. To avoid these, the enemy turned away and being unwilling to risk another torpedo attack, taking them by surprise if they came through the smoke, broke off the action and went home.[9]

As soon as Watkins informed *Sikh* that *Havock* had been crippled, Micklethwait signalled Vian requesting instructions and was told to send the crippled destroyer to join the close escort of the convoy.

On 13 April, Lieutenant Commander G.R.G. Watkins, *Havock*'s Commanding Officer sent a cablegram to his wife from the internment camp in Laghouat, Algeria in which he briefly outlined the events of 22 March:

I would not have believed so many misfortunes could have overtaken me since we left home [Alexandria] three weeks ago. I got clouted by the largest type of enemy and very nearly sank, came to a standstill and had 10 minutes on my own with a lot of firing going on in local control. The Director Officer [Sub Lieutenant Orpen] was killed. We just got the old boiler going and got away and had a nightmare of the night following. Very rough and quarter sea. We very nearly capsized. Staggered into harbour [23 March] and had to be held up by dockyard wires.[10]

Meanwhile, as *Havock* limped away to join the convoy, Micklethwait's three remaining destroyers continued to challenge the oncoming Italian force by suddenly emerging from their smokescreen to fire at *Littorio* while at the same time attempting to gain a position from which torpedoes could be fired with the possibility of achieving some measure of success. By 18.05 hours, the Italians were clearly gaining on the convoy which would be annihilated if spotted through a gap in the smokescreen. At 18.02 *Cleopatra* and *Euryalus* arrived to support Micklethwait's over-matched destroyers and opened fire with their 5.25-inch guns on the battleship at a range of only six and a half miles. Four minutes later *Cleopatra* fired her starboard torpedoes and almost simulta-neously *Littorio* disappeared behind smoke. At about this time, Poland's destroyers were arriving to support Micklethwait's ships.

At 18.34, while steaming north, Poland sighted *Littorio* about six miles away bearing west-north-west and ordered his destroyers to make an immediate torpedo attack. At the time *Jervis*, *Kipling*, *Kelvin*, *Kingston* and *Legion* were in line ahead and they now turned together so as to put them in line abreast and opened fire on the battleship as they tried to get within range. Eventually the range came down to two to three miles and at 18.41 the destroyers turned to fire their torpedoes. Unfortunately, not one of the twenty-five torpedoes fired hit *Littorio*, but the battle-ship was observed to turn away as the weapons were launched. During the attack the destroyer *Kingston* was hit by a 15-inch shell in the engine room and boiler room but still managed to fire her torpedoes before being brought to a halt. However, her crew got her underway again and she was despatched to join the convoy.

The Italian withdrawal gave Micklethwait the opportunity to carry out a torpedo attack on the Italian force at 18.55. *Sikh* and *Hero* were unable to fire torpedoes because their target was obscured by smoke but *Lively* managed to fire all eight even though she was damaged by a splinter from a near miss by a 15-inch shell. By now it was getting dark and the Italians, who had neither radar nor much night fighting capability, realised that it was time to withdraw or risk a night action. The last shots were fired at 18.56 and, as the Italians ships sailed for Taranto, Vian set about getting the convoy back on course for Malta.[11]

Unfortunately, the intervention of the Italian fleet had forced the convoy to the south-west of its intended course which meant that its ships would not arrive until well after daybreak on 23 March and consequently would be vulnerable to Axis air attacks. Consequently at 19.00, on his own initiative, the convoy com-modore, Captain Hutchison of *Breconshire*, ordered the convoy to disperse during the night in the hope that some of the ships might make it to the swept channel to Malta. At this point, the convoy and its escorts would be concentrated so that *Carlisle* and the six Hunt class destroyers would cover their entrance into the

Grand Harbour. *Penelope, Legion, Kingston* and *Havock* were also detached to Malta while CS15 returned to Alexandria.

Losses after the action

At this stage of Operation *MG1*, despite the best efforts of the Italian Navy and Axis air power, the convoy and its close escort remained intact although the latter had expended a worryingly large percentage of its AA ammunition. Force B had also expended much of its AA ammunition as well as most of its torpedoes, but had suffered only limited damage with the flagship *Cleopatra* being hit on the bridge. Although the destroyers *Kingston* and *Havock* had been reduced to fifteen or sixteen knots by damage to their engine and boiler rooms respectively and *Lively* had suffered some flooding caused by splinter damage, Vian's force was otherwise intact.

The returning Italian fleet had likewise suffered only minimal damage but became victims of the severe gale that developed overnight after the battle. The storm was of such severity that the destroyers *Scirocco* and *Lanciere* foundered on 23 March while the cruiser *Giovanni delle Bande Nere* was badly damaged as her slender hull was battered by the raging sea. Subsequently, the cruiser, which had struggled into Messina on 24 March, was torpedoed and sunk by the submarine *Urge* on 1 April while on passage to La Spezia for repairs to her storm damage. The battleship *Littorio*, which had great difficulty making headway, also suffered damage as she shipped tons of water in the heavy seas.[12]

The War Diary of the C-in-C Mediterranean recorded that:

> Ships of convoy *MW10* were again subjected to a very heavy scale of bombing from daylight on 23rd as they approached Malta. *Clan Campbell* was hit and sunk in position 35°33′N, 14°35′E. *Eridge* rescued 112 officers and men. *Breconshire* was hit in the engine room at 10.30 when about 8 miles from the Grand Harbour. She was disabled and an attempt by *Penelope* to tow her in was unsuccessful. She drifted towards the shore and came to an anchor off Zanker Point.
>
> Owing to the very heavy gale and swell attempts to tow her had to be abandoned. *Pampas* and *Talabot* arrived safely in Grand Harbour. *Legion* was hit but reached Marsaxlokk harbour and anchored in shallow water. Fighters did an excellent job despite the weather and enemy action. *Carlisle* and the Hunts remained at

Malta to give *Breconshire* AA protection. *Avonvale* [*Avon Vale*] was damaged in collision with *Breconshire* and by a near miss and was rendered unseaworthy. *Kingston* and *Havock* arrived safely in harbour. Meanwhile, CS15 arrived Alexandria on 23 March 1942.[13]

The 'safe haven' of Malta

Sadly, Malta proved to be anything but a safe haven because, despite their best efforts, the defending fighters were simply overwhelmed by the Luftwaffe whose planes seemed to surround the island and strike at any target almost at will. Generalfeldmarschall Kesselring's air assault on Malta had begun on 20 March and concentrated on the islands airfields and gun batteries flying an average of 300 sorties each day. By now the convoy's escorts were so short of ammunition that they could only fire when threatened with immediate danger. The heavy weather made it impossible to bring in *Breconshire* and, after lying at anchor off the Island, she was towed into Marsaxlokk, south-east of Malta and berthed at 10.45 on the 25th.[14] *Southwold*, (Commander Jellicoe, DF5) one of the Hunt Class destroyers screening her while she was at anchor on the 24th, struck a mine and sank some hours later.

The arrival of the convoy on 23 March meant that the Luftwaffe began to concentrate on the dockyard and that day *Havock* suffered minor damage during an air raid as, together with the cruiser *Penelope*, she became a primary target of enemy aircraft whilst in dock.

The following day, on 24 March, Vice Admiral Malta sent a message to the C-in-C Mediterranean Fleet repeated to the Admiralty in which he described the damage to *Havock*, *Kingston* and other cripples from the Operation.

> *Havock*: Holes under water in boiler room. Docking 23rd March at least two days in dock depending on result of examination. Vital structural strength members cut at corner of upper Port side of number one boiler room. Necessary for seaworthiness to restore strength. Two weeks required. Possible extensive damage to number three boiler.
> *Kingston*: Serious damage to upper deck which has impaired structural strength. In addition, extensive damage to structures of Pom-pom supports and platforms.

Oerlikon guns and searchlight platforms. Time-required to effect repairs was two months. Minor damage in engine and boiler room.

Legion: had near miss starboard engine badly damaged. Engine room and after boiler room leaking water and kept under by trailer pumps. No detailed information at present.

Avonvale:[15] Serious damage to structural strength starboard side amidships at corner of upper deck and ship's side. Necessary to repair to restore some of original strength. Ship has been in collision. Permanent repairs to bow damage all above water requires four weeks.[16]

The War Diary of C-in-C Mediterranean noted that *Havock* was expected to be seaworthy at Malta by early April but had suffered considerable further damage while *Kingston* should be seaworthy on 25 April but would require a further two month's repairs.[17]

Although *Talabot* and *Pampas* had arrived on 23 March neither was unloaded that night because the Maltese stevedores stopped worked at 18.30 and no service personnel were detailed to do the work either. Furthermore, unsurprisingly, the stevedores would not work during air raid warnings and consequently no work was done to unload either ship during the next two days. The work of unloading finally started on the morning of 26 March and less than 1,000 tons had been discharged by the time Axis air raids began that afternoon. During three very heavy dive-bombing attacks that day *Talabot* was hit twice and set on fire and scuttled to avoid explosion of ammunition. *Pampas* also hit and grounded on even keel with its deck awash. About 4,000 tons was salvaged from the two ships over several weeks. That day *Breconshire* was bombed again and set on fire. At 11.30 the following day *Breconshire* sank at No. 1 buoy Marsaxlokk, at 11.30, with part of her remaining above water. It had not been possible to get the fire entirely under control. C-in-C Mediterranean made the reasonable assumption that her cargo of oil fuel was now reasonably safe from enemy action and hoped that most of it could be saved. Much of her cargo was indeed unloaded gradually from her wreck off Kalafrana over several weeks.[18]

The very heavy air raids on 26 March which sank *Pampas* and *Talabot* also badly damaged *Penelope*, which was holed, while the submarine *P.39* was damaged by near misses and the destroyer *Legion* sunk. The Fleet Oiler *Plumleaf* was hit and beached and destroyer *Avon Vale* was slightly damaged. Four days later, the latter sailed from Malta en route for Gibraltar in company with the mine-damaged cruiser *Aurora* which had been undergoing repairs in the Dockyard.[19]

The trials and tribulations experienced by convoy MW10 and its escorts led Cunningham to make strong representations to the Admiralty in a signal sent at 12.48 on 28 March about the serious situation concerning future convoys to Malta. He pointed out that before any further attempts could be made it would be necessary for (a) destroyers to be reinforced, (b) strength and quality of Malta fighters to be increased and (c) to plan some form of diversion to disperse Axis air strength – fortunately this would prove to be a wasting asset during the next twelve months.[20]

Life in Malta

In a report written on 1 December 1942, *Havock*'s Commanding Officer, Lieutenant Commander G.R.G. Watkins, described graphically the conditions in Malta:

> H.M.S. *Havock* had taken part in Rear Admiral Vian's action on 22 March 1942 in which she had been severely damaged and just managed to make Valetta [now Valletta] harbour. Sub Lieutenant Orpen my trained gunnery control officer (G.C.O.) and navigator had been killed; Mr Thompson my Gunner (T) was lost over the side and the remaining officers, including for the first time myself, were severely shaken. Conditions in Malta at the time were not conducive to a speedy recovery of nerves. On the contrary, the reverse was the case. The island was being subjected to the most severe pounding yet from the Luftwaffe. Life in the Dockyard narrowly approximated to the Biblical conception of Hell. And what little rest there was obtainable was to be found in the underground dressing stations. It was futile to even man the guns in the berth the ship occupied in, or close by No. 1 dock, Dockyard Creek as the view on all sides was obscured by buildings. Fire watchers only remained on board, and after each lull in the bombing I rushed out of my shelter to see if the ship had survived the attack and to deal with the damage in and near her.
>
> The ordeal was nerve-wracking. In the shelter, every big explosion seemed to be striking my ship. But she survived, although everything round her was devastated and she herself was constantly covered in masonry and dust from the surrounding ruins. No direct hits were

received and it was only when she was fit for sea and in stream some four days before she sailed on her last voyage that important damage was done. The after magazine and shell room were holed and roughly repaired with cement which had hardly set on our departure.

The morale of my officers and men remained high. Although my doctor Surg. Lieut. Royds R.N.V.R., who has since died in internment, was of the opinion that it was on the point of cracking. As a result of this sequence of events, the situation was extracting more from our constitutions than we could stand. I myself, although I did not realise it at the time, was deeply affected. I did not report my nervous condition to Vice-Admiral Malta, as there was no one to relieve me, and my brother officers were no fitter than myself. But it was my intention on the advice of my medical officer to demand fourteen days leave immediately the ship reached any other port. I considered that I was able to do my duty efficiently until such time was the case.[21]

The Mediterranean Fleet's War Diary reports that by 31 March *Havock* was ready for sea, although further repairs would be necessary. The Commander-in-Chief decided that she should remain at Malta as a possible escort for *Penelope* until a further report was received concerning the latter.[22]

During air raids on Floriana on 2 April some of *Havock*'s plating and framing aft was damaged by near misses and the decision was taken that the destroyer must leave Malta as soon as possible or become a total loss. The blast from the near misses blew a hole in the ship's side abreast after magazine.[23] The hole was filled with cement and the aft magazine filled with 'furniture' from nearby spaces which were vacated to permit easy examination of the cement patch. Jim Brown recalled that:

> After repeated attacks by bombers whilst lying out in the harbour [Dockyard Creek] one very near miss holed the ship. This was later sealed by spreading concrete inside. We then went alongside and it wasn't long before we were covered in rubble from demolished buildings.[24]

That day, the C-in-C Mediterranean observed that it had not, as yet, been possible to get any oil out of *Breconshire*.[25]

The heavy and accurate air attacks of 4 April struck the Grand Harbour and aerodromes with the enemy seeming

to concentrate particularly on *Penelope* and *Lance* in dock
and *Havock* in Dockyard Creek at Floriana. At this time,
Vice-Admiral Malta hoped to be able to sail *Penelope* in
about a week and *Lance* as soon as the dock caisson could
be opened. He expected that *Havock* would be ready to
sail on 5 April. The air attacks of 4 April were particularly devastating and confirmed the wisdom of the earlier decision to get *Havock* away from Malta as soon as
practicable. Four air raids and an estimated 150 bombers further damaged the destroyer *Gallant* which had to
be beached and became a constructive total loss, while
Kingston was hit and pierced by a bomb which did not
explode. Furthermore, the 'L' class destroyer *Lance* had
her side blown in by a bomb and sank in the dock in which
she was being repaired. Sadly, *Kingston* was bombed and
sunk in dock on 11 April but the cruiser *Penelope* was able
to leave Malta on 8 April, passed Cape Bon early the following morning and survived frequent air attacks during
that day. She arrived at Gibraltar on 10 April with her
commanding officer, Captain A.D. Nicholl, wounded
and her hull riddled with holes from bomb splinters.
However, *Havock*, which was ordered to sail at 20.00 on 5
April, three days before *Penelope*, was not so lucky.[26]

Preparations to sail

Incredible as it might seem, Lieutenant Commander Watkins,
who must have been suffering from mental exhaustion by then,
was ordered by Vice Admiral Malta to undertake a demanding
operation the night before his ship was due to leave the Grand
Harbour. He recorded that:

> On the night immediately preceding our sailing [4/5
> April], I was ordered to take charge of a convoy of small
> ships by the Chief-of-Staff to V.A.M. with the object of tak-
> ing the last remaining 500-ton oil lighter round to Marsa
> Scirocco [Marsaxlokk] to unload the sunken *Breconshire*.
> This I accomplished not without difficulty and interfer-
> ence by enemy aircraft, and after a short sleep on one of
> the sofas at Calafrana [now Kalafrana] mess, returned to
> my ship by land.[27]

This was hardly ideal preparation for the dangerous voyage
through difficult waters that was to be attempted less than

twenty-four hours later and one cannot help wondering why Vice Admiral Malta had no suitably qualified supernumeraries on his staff that should have been capable of undertaking such an operation.

Jim Brown recalled that:

> One evening five of us were detailed to take the oil barge down to Kalafrana, where the *Breconshire* was towed after being hit, to try and get some oil out of the ship. We left Grand Harbour after dark with the barge towed by a small tug. Later when abreast the airfield of Hal Far we noticed flares on the runway which we thought were for a night landing. It turned out to be an air raid and minutes later the tug and the barge were being raked by cannon fire from I believe a Ju 88. They flew off leaving OS Carter dead. We made it to Kalafrana but did not get any oil that trip and returned to the ship about noon the next day.[28]

Having returned to his ship, Lieutenant Commander Watkins continued to get *Havoc* ready to sail:

> I went over to Lascaris [HQ in Valetta] to report to V.A.M. as soon as I could, But, owing to air raids I was unable to get transport across the harbour until about noon. Meanwhile, the ship was brought to four hours' notice for steam. I made a verbal report to V.A.M. and have since forwarded a list of recommendations for awards for the night's work. The V.A.M. told me that I was to sail that evening for the Eastward. I told V.A.M. that my ship was ready to sail in time but the cement in the magazine had had hardly time to set. I was already topped up with fuel and only had to ammunition. Not an easy job with constant air raids. But C-in-C Mediterranean signalled that I should sail to Westward.
>
> I got back on board about 13.00 and gave the necessary orders for sailing at 19.00 that night. There was still a lot to be done, many items were still in the Dockyard and there was hardly time to run up the gyro. I had been told to return by 1700 to the Admiral's office to get my sailing orders. I managed to get a broken sleep in a shelter for about an hour. Then I went to V.A.M.'s office with my navigator Sub Lieut. Lack R.N.V.R. a survivor from the *Southwold* sunk shortly before. He had been sent to replace Orpen as Navigating Officer (N.O.) and Gunnery Control Officer (G.C.O.) and I was informed by Chief of

Staff that he was recommended by his late commanding officer [Commander C.T. Jellicoe] to carry out these duties. He was a permanent service R.N.V.R. and had been three years at sea, but had only been in the ship a week so I was unable to form an opinion as to his efficiency. I took charts of the Western Mediterranean with me to get the latest corrections. I found my orders were to set my course from Malta swept channel to a point south of Kelibia Light, pass the latter at a distance of not more than 3,000 yards from the coast, and to continue at such a distance until past Cape Bon. I was to proceed at my maximum speed until past Galita Island and then to reduce speed in order to have sufficient fuel to reach Gibraltar. I corrected my charts up to date from the latest information in the Staff Office.

I had never been through this channel before and was not particularly enjoying the prospect under such conditions. I had originally requested to sail east as I knew the coast there extremely well, and should have been under air cover from Tobruk by dawn.

Owing to the air raids I did not get back on board until about 18.30. I found the current had been cut off the gyro on one occasion due to air raids but the N.A. said that it was running correctly. I had no Gunner (T). I found some passengers on board including Commander Jessel D.S.O., D.S.C. RN, the ex-commanding officer of *Legion* who I was pleased to see. I said so at the time, and asked him to come up on the bridge as he knew the coast of Tunisia well. Unfortunately, his broken foot was too bad to permit him.

I was feeling dead tired. I made out an intended track of the ship with the assistance of Sub Lieutenant Lack and Lieutenant Burfield my First Lieutenant, and checked the bearings of Kelibia Light when alterations should be made. I told Lack to work out the time-distance at 30 knots between the points I had drawn on the chart. Lieut. Burfield assisted him in this task, and discovered that Lack knew very little about navigation but this was not reported to me. By this time, I had hurriedly shifted into sea-going as it was time to sail. It was then about 19.15.

At this point I must describe the condition of my officers: Lieutenant J. Burfield D.S.C. RN was my First Lieutenant. His nerves seemed to have outwardly stood the strain and he had been G.C.O. of the ship – a very good one. Lieutenant M. Baillie-Grohman, my Second Lieutenant was in a very neurotic state. He had done extremely well in controlling fires, dealing with damage, and assisting generally in the Dockyard in addition to his other duties for which I have recommended him for an award. But his nerves were so bad that he could not sit in a Director. He was Tactical Control Officer (T.C.O.) and signal officer and was extremely busy getting his department ready for sea. He was acting Gunner as well and so I did not use him to navigate. I was anxious on the voyage to have him on the top line ready to fire torpedoes and not to have his hand under the chart table screen. In my opinion my greatest danger was in meeting some enemy force round the corner of Kelibia Light as other ships had done already done.

I had one Sub Lieutenant, R.C.N.V.R., and two midshipmen besides. All three, although young officers had very little sea experience. My more experienced Sub Lieutenant R.N.V.R. had been wounded and was in hospital. The only officer at the time that I could trust was Lieutenant Burfield the First Lieutenant. But I decided that he must go in the Director as G.C.O. for the dangerous period in the narrow channel, as Lack it appeared had never been inside a 4.7 in director or done any low angle firing. Incidentally, my Doctor's nerves and my Engineer Officers nerves were badly shaken.[29]

Disaster

Having offloaded any spare ammunition and stores and embarked passengers and just enough fuel to make the perilous passage to Gibraltar, *Havock* was ready to make her escape from Malta. For his night passage through Tunisian waters Watkins had been advised to (a) take soundings on approach to Kelibia Light, (b) note high ground N of Kelibia Light, (c) remember minefield to E and keep not more than two miles from shore and remember (d) the shoals off Ras el Mihr & Cape Bon. He was told to use his own discretion regarding speed when making landfall and be as far west as possible by dawn. Experience suggested that he could expect to meet enemy E-boats and minesweepers as well as Axis convoys carrying materiel to North Africa while making this passage past Cape Bon.

Although Watkins could not know it, in fact, on the night of 5/6 April, the Libyan convoy route was surprisingly quiet with only three convoys at sea. The first consisted of the Italian naval steamer *Una*, with four German minesweepers and the torpedo boat *Calliope* en route from Trapani to Tripoli which was well south of *Havock*'s track. Secondly, Italian tanker *Saturno* escorted by the destroyers *Folgore* and *Castore* were en route from Tripoli to Naples and passed Cape Bon before *Havock* arrived off Kelibia. Finally, the German steamer *Atlas*, with an escort of three German minesweepers plus the Italian torpedo boat *Perseo*, was en route from Trapani to Tripoli and well to the north of Cape Bon when *Havock* grounded.[30]

Havock's commanding officer decided to maintain thirty knots while rounding Cape Bon while at the same time maintaining a high level of gunnery preparedness just in case he encountered Italian MAS boats/German E-boats. In practice without remote power control his hand-trained 4.7-inch guns would have been useless in a short-range engagement with fast moving small craft while *Havock*'s close range automatic weapons lacked both range and stopping power. With the benefit of hindsight and the knowledge of what was to come, *Havock*'s experienced First Lieutenant would have been better employed in the Chart Room than in the 4.7-inch gun Director.

Lieutenant Commander Watkin's report of events that night continues:

> I let go at dusk (about 19.00) and proceeded down the creek. Luckily there was no raid at the time. The gyro appeared to be correct and Lack managed to get a check while I was conning the ship through the breakwater. I cannot tell whether this check was accurate. While navigating through the swept channel, I obtained fixes with St. Elmo Light and the R.A.F. beacon which was not satisfactory because the beacon is moved daily, and I was not absolutely certain of its position. I managed to get off the bridge for a couple of hours' very necessary rest leaving the First Lieut. there and came up when Pantelleria was sighted.
>
> The ship was in the second degree of readiness but I allowed half of my officers to sleep at their quarters at a time, in order to make them of some use if something happened. The First Lieutenant and Lieutenant Baillie-Grohman worked opposite each other as P.C.O. and Officer of the Watch (O.O.W.) with Sub Lieutenant Spearin R.C.N.V.R. or a Midshipman as assistant. Sub Lieutenant Lack was working independently as N.O. I

need hardly say that my magnetic compass could not be trusted in any respect.

I took over the ship shortly before she came to the first turning place and altered course to pass one and a half miles off Kelibia Light. Lack was on the chart by now. My range finder appeared to be correct although there had been no chance to check it. I glanced at the chart and saw we were being set in an altered course ten degrees or so away from the land. I cannot remember the exact courses. I was still doing thirty knots which I considered essential, (a) in order to carry out my orders which were to be as far as possible to the westward by daylight (b) in order to cross a superior force in the channel at the maximum rate of change of bearing. The night was clear, no moon but patches of mist over the land. I asked Lack whether we were being set in or out heading for my turning point. He replied that we were a little inside but quite alright. Midshipman Duncan heard this. I glanced at the chart again and considered it all right to steer in a bit and did so. I had instructed Lack to inform me when I was about to come on for bearing before making an alteration and then give me the time for each run. Everything had been tabulated on the chart previously to avoid error. There were some four alterations to make to round the corner of Kelibia Light. I did not dare to leave the Pellorus as I did not want to spoil my vision by the chart table light and also events were occurring at a speed of 30 knots. Again, my only real anxieties were the possibility of meeting an enemy and the minefield.

I went to the first degree of readiness before the first turn round the point. Lieutenant Burfield became T.C.O. and O.O.W. and I 'had' the ship. Lieutenant B-G had been asleep while we were in the second degree of readiness at the after end of the bridge and was not fully aware of what was happening. He was also in an extremely exhausted condition. I constantly asked Lack whether we were alright. To which he replied we were a 'bit' inside but were alright. Midshipman Duncan who was on the bridge heard this. I was still passing ranges and bearings which he was plotting. The last leg of the turn looked strange to me and I hung on a bit longer after he told me it was time to alter. The time was then 03.50. I saw what looked like a white wave ahead, and immediately altered out a little, then rushed to the chart table and ordered full speed astern and hard a starboard from there. But it was too late we had run on a sand spit and were hard and fast aground [at 03.58 hours on 6 April]. The chart in use was brought ashore but was destroyed owing to secret information on it.[31]

Jim Brown recalled that:

We left Malta under cover of darkness and made our way toward Gibraltar. I was on watch at the time when the ship ran aground in the early hours of the morning. I remember having just mentioned to a shipmate that there was something strange about the bow wave as though they had suddenly changed their form.[32]

Watkins' account continued:

There was nothing to be done. It was becoming light enough to see a little. The shore was a hundred yards off. I ordered all ammunition to be thrown over the side in an attempt to lighten the ship. But on going aft myself saw that it was futile and ordered all passengers to start going ashore, and preparations were made to destroy the ship. I also discovered from Engineer Andrewes that a valve box on the main steam line had burst in the engine room, killing one rating and badly burning five others, one of whom subsequently died in hospital.

All confidential books and secret papers were destroyed in No. 1 boiler room. All secret gear was completely destroyed; e.g. R.D.F. and aerials, V.C. and V.E., F.K.O. and A.F.G. Asdic Gear. All spaces were filled with cordite strips and oil fuel spread about them.

When every man had packed his needs and was ashore except the last whaler load (it was daylight by then) the cordite was ignited everywhere and when well started the T.G.M. lit the fuze of the depth charge in the Asdic Compartment. This blew out the entire side of the forecastle leaving the forecastle deck supported by the stem piece. The whaler was well clear by then. The ship was on fire fore and aft. We had

previously fired the torpedoes to seaward in case parts
of them were found by the enemy.[33]

Jim Brown recalled that:

> After an attempt had been made to get her off with
> engines the order prepare to abandon ship was given.
> I believe that a stoker was killed when the engines were
> put full astern because the impact had broken some sup-
> ports [in the boiler room]. This was after we had started
> to throw ammunition over the side the reduce weight.
> The torpedoes were fired out to sea. A fire was started in
> the boiler room to destroy documents etc. A charge was
> set and we made our way ashore by boat. I don't think
> that anybody got wet. We laid in the sand dunes in day-
> light waiting for the explosion and when it did come the
> air was full of flying metal. A Sunderland flying boat did
> a couple of circuits and then flew off unable to assist.[34]

The Commander-in-Chief Mediterranean's Diary records that at
04.15 hours on the 6th *Havock* reported having run aground in
position 20 degrees, two and a half miles from the Kelibia Light.
She had been routed close inshore at twenty-six knots. *Havock*
reported that the ship could not be re-floated and was being
destroyed. The crew were safely ashore except for one killed. It
was not possible to send any rescue craft in the circumstances
and the crew were interned. About 100 passengers had been
embarked in addition. Later air reconnaissance confirmed the
ship's position.[35]

Watkins account continues:

> On getting ashore I found that Commander Jessel had
> sent a Sub Lieutenant who spoke French (who was taking
> passage in the ship) to the fort at Kelibia light and had sur-
> rendered us and our arms to the French. In due course, we
> were marched off to the Coast Guard Barracks leaving our
> heavy luggage and stores under guard with the wounded.
> A Cant seaplane came over us at fifty feet. We scattered by
> French order but the Cant did not open fire, happily. I had
> decided to let some men have a chance of escape in the
> whaler and had navigational instruments and sails sent
> ashore for that purpose. But we found it impossible to col-
> lect the sailing gear once ashore and I consider it lucky
> that no one attempted to do so as there was no wind and
> Junkers 88s came over in quantity later on.

At about 14.00 when we were under guard and out
of sight of the ship, there was a colossal explosion from
the ship, and a column of smoke several hundred feet
high went up in the air. It was ascertained that the after
end of the ship had blown up. The depth charges had
been cooking in the sun and with the cordite fire beneath
had gone up. The after magazine may also have gone up.
There were frequent explosions all day from ready use
ammunition etc, and I am satisfied that nothing of value
was left for the French.[36]

The *Aradam* incident

Italian sources suggest that the submarine *Aradam* was responsible for the loss of *Havock*. For example:

Along the eastern coast of Tunisia there operated [in
April 1942], as we have mentioned earlier, several of our
submarines with the object to protect our traffic against
possible raids by light forces from Malta and to intercept
possible isolated enemy traffic.

On 5 April 1942, submarines *Turchese* and *Aradam* took
up watch, the first in the waters immediately north of Cape
Bon and the second a little eastward of Cape Kelibia. The
latter, commanded by Ten. Vasc. [Tenente di vascello –
Lieutenant] Oscar Gran scored a success on the 6th shortly
after having arrived in the area. Having in fact sighted at
03.12 a.m. a large enemy destroyer which headed to the
westward on course following the coast of the peninsular
of Cape Bon, she fired [03.17] a torpedo from 500 metres
range at the enemy ship. Having resurfaced after the short
engagement, she observed the enemy ship stopped on the
coast near Ras el Mirk, with a fire on board. In fact, this was
the English destroyer *Havock* which having left Malta on the
evening of the 5th, was heading for Gibraltar. On the ship,
brought to the beach on the coast there took place subsequently the magazine explosion that broke her in two.[37]

The key points when assessing the success or otherwise of
Aradam's attack, is the timeline relative to *Havock*'s narrative, coupled with the contemporaneous reports by the latter's crew.

As discussed in a later chapter, when *Havock* ran aground, the
engine room clock, which was keeping Malta Standard Time
(MST), stopped at 03.58 when she hit the shoal as she was

steaming at thirty knots. It is unclear what time *Aradam* was keeping but is most likely to have been Central European Time (CET) or daylight saving for the CET zone. If the two ships were using the same or similar time, then it is entirely possible that *Aradam* sighted *Havock* sailing along the coast and fired a torpedo that missed. Alternatively, *Aradam* came on the scene after *Havock* had grounded and fired a torpedo that either hit the seabed because of the shallow water or missed because *Havock* was stationary and the submarine assumed she was firing at a moving target.

Aradam's report claims that her torpedo caused the destroyer to be beached while at the same time causing a fire which triggered a magazine explosion observed by the submarine. There can be no doubt that *Havock*'s crew would have noticed if their ship had been hit by a torpedo just before she ran aground. They certainly noticed the explosion that occurred at 14.00 that broke the ship in two. It is inconceivable that *Aradam*, having 'torpedoed' *Havock* at 03.17 would have remained so close inshore during daylight hours in shallow water where she would have been very visible to patrolling aircraft. It therefore would appear that the Italian account is an attempt to reconcile *Aradam*'s report of firing a torpedo at a British destroyer with the wreck lying 300 metres from the shore near Kelibia. Another source suggests that the wrecked *Havock* was rendered unusable early 6th April by a torpedo from the *Aradam*. Once again, it is inconceivable that *Havock*'s crew, who were sitting on the nearby sand dunes in the early morning, would have failed to notice an explosion on the ship that they had just abandoned.

On night 7/8 April, an Italian commando troop commanded by Capitano di Fregata Ernesto Forza boarded the wreck from the salvage ship *Instancabile*, which was the former Yugoslav salvage tug *Spasilac* and apparently recovered secret information.[38] Whether or not the Vichy French knew about this clandestine violation of their 'neutrality' is unclear. The question also arises as to what they discovered when they boarded the wreck.

Havock after being wrecked

Although *Havock* had been destroyed, her wreck still remained in the war. Thus, on 15 June 1942 the destroyer *Ithuriel*, which was part of the escort to the *Harpoon* convoy to Malta, mistook the wreck of *Havock* for an Italian destroyer/torpedo boat and shelled it.[39]

Subsequently, during Operation *Pedestal* the Italian MAS boat *MS 16* accidentally ran aground at Ras el Mirh in the early hours of 13 August 1942 while escaping inshore after the torpedoing of the cruiser *Manchester*. Pursued by the gunfire of the British ships, the motosiluranti had turned around the half-sunken wreck of *Havock*, mistaking it for a unit of the convoy and then ran aground. The beached *MS 16* was re-floated with the assistance of the tug *Montecristo*.[40]

In April 1943, as the war in Tunisia was coming to an end, the Allies decided to insert a party of ten Corsican agents and saboteurs in civilian clothes with a wireless link into eastern Tunisia tasked with disrupting communications and destroying dumps and aircraft. The team, which was to be landed near Kelibia near the southern end of Cape Bon, was instructed to use the wreck of *Havock* as an unmistakable landmark. The operation was mounted from Malta using two Royal Navy MTBs on 6 April 1943 – twelve months to the day after the loss of *Havock*. The party was captured soon after landing having been the victim of a successful German counter-intelligence operation.[41]

When news of *Havock*'s loss was revealed by the Admiralty, the *Daily Mirror* of 8 April reported the news with the words:

> HAVOCK, Britain's No. 2 Destroyer of this war – second only in fame and glory to the COSSACK – has been wrecked off the coast of Tunisia … One of the Navy's most famous destroyers, a ship which survived bombs, torpedoes and full scale battles, has been wrecked.

The newspapers were right, because in two-and-a-half-years *Havock* had been awarded a staggering total of eleven battle honours. These honours (which excluded the Spanish Civil War) graphically track her progress through the war until her slow death in April 1942:

Atlantic	1939	Matapan	1941
Narvik	1940	Greece	1941
Norway	1940	Crete	1941
Cape Spada	1940	Libya	1941-42
Mediterranean	1940-41	Malta Convoys	1941-42
Sirte	1942		

The wreck of HMS *Havock* still lies approximately 300 yards from shore in about five metres of water.

Chapter 12

Prisoners of War in Laghouat (April – November 1942)

T he position in which *Havock*'s ship's company and their passengers now found themselves needs explaining. French
North Africa was as described, French, and the answer
to the question 'But I thought the French were on our side' the
official answer was that they were now neutral. The truthful
answer was that France in its Vichy guise was now a partner in
the German/Italian axis and, as has been seen in Syria, was prepared to use force to defend its territory. Thus, there were several
occasions during the period from the French Armistice in 1940 to
the North African landings in November 1942 when it seemed
as though Vichy France might re-join the war on the German
side. Fortunately, this never came to pass although, in practice,
the Vichy French government was distinctly collaborationist.
Thus, it is something of a misnomer to describe the incarceration
of *Havock*'s crew as internment. The reality was that they were
treated as prisoners of war under an enemy jurisdiction and in
some measure, apart from an age-old Anglophobia, this explains
the treatment they received and the attitude of their captors
towards them.

Havock's crew and 'passengers' were now on the dunes and
cognisant of the fact that the locals were watching them. Able
Seaman John Dodds remembered:

> We were half an hour ashore before Arab soldiers sur-
> rounded us. We were taken to Kelibia village and
> then off to Laghouat. The Commandant of the camp
> (Jeunechamps) was a pig. The French officers were tin
> gods. Our officers were held in their own block.[1]

ERA Maurice Cutler described camp life in the following terms:

> We lived on Pea Soup, Lentil Soup and Macaroni with a
> quarter of a litre of foul French Red Wine which we mixed
> with lemonade to make it more palatable. John Burfield

was in charge of the escape committee which I joined. We
dug a 70-yard tunnel three feet high, three feet wide and 12
feet down. We made oil lamps using wax. The spoil went
into a large basement under the hut. Twenty-four escaped,
I didn't go, but were all rounded up inside 24 hours and we
lost privileges like wireless, Red Cross Parcels and lighting.[2]

Whilst writing this history we were very fortunate to have access
to a unique diary of events written by an unidentified *Havock*
crew member or passenger. Below is the diary word for word.
The early pages describe the aftermath after the 6 April grounding. After these pages the story is taken up again on 25 May 1942:

The wounded ashore, we managed to get some tinned
food, cigarettes, bread and water before daylight came.
The ship was then blown up.
  We were now roughly a party of 250 officers and men
and we were soon spotted by Vichy France Army Officials.
Then our troubles started, after a trek of five or six miles
over sand and scrub we came to a village where we were
provided with a loaf of bread and two eggs each, no one ate
the bread, but the eggs came in useful. After being searched,
during which knives and such things were taken away
from us, we were packed into lorries and taken to the town
of Tunis. The journey took about 8 hours and we were thick
with dust on our arrival, with hardly anyone the means of
washing, I had neither soap nor towel. Here we were put
into army barracks and were well guarded for three days.[3]

Torpedoman Jack Surridge added:

We marched through Tunis to a French Army barracks,
which was really fairly clean, and the food quite good.
On the way, we gave the V sign to all and sundry and I
hope it upset them.[4]

The anonymous diarist continued:

The civil population here were very pro-British and
brought us beer. They also formed deputations to the
town Authorities and gave demonstrations in our
favour. However, nothing developed out of it, except
that we were almost mobbed by the young ladies when
we marched to the Railway Station.
  Next we had a train ride which took three nights
and two days over the Atlas Mountains. When we

disembarked, we found ourselves very dirty and tired in Laghouat, Algeria, washing and sleep were impossible on the train.[5]

At this point, John Burfield was about to start what was to be the first of multiple escape bids. He remembered:

To be suddenly ashore, and prisoners, must have been a bit disorienting for us as sailors because in a situation where we were not closely guarded, and in a seaport, instead of thinking about escape all I could think about, after making sure that the hands were fed and watered and as comfortable as circumstances allowed – was sleep. I am sure that with a bit of thought it would have been possible to talk one's way past the sentry at the gate. However, 'All Night In' does not happen often in the navy – especially on *Havock* where Four Hours On, Four Hours Off was the norm for most of us – and when it does happen one is liable to think of little else. We had certainly had a somewhat exhausting life recently, and for most of the two or three days we were in Tunis I was asleep.

The time came for us to move on and I paraded the ship's company ready to march off down to the railway station. A noisy little French Sergeant tried to push me into the ranks and conduct matters himself, but I told him as First Lieutenant I was in charge and that he could push off.

They packed us into a train, six officers in a compartment and we headed off westwards towards Algiers. By this time, Lieutenant Michael Baillie-Grohman and I had decided that we didn't like Frenchmen and that the sooner we took ourselves off, the better. We discovered that the bar across the single window could be removed and the window opened downwards to about halfway. We had no idea where we were, had no maps or any of the usual escape necessities but we did try to sort out the right kind of clothes and scrambled together little travelling packs.

In the navy you can't just push off without telling anybody, so we went along to see Commander Jessel, who had commanded *Legion* at Second Sirte, when he had been wounded during the battle. He was being sent to Gibraltar for treatment and was aboard *Havock* as a passenger. Now we were ashore he was the Senior Officer, so we went to ask his permission. Naturally he said yes, shook our hands and wished is luck.

Back in our compartment, we removed the bar, opened the window and climbed out. Michael was the first to go and I followed. As we rolled away from the track the Guards Van passed with the Guard standing in the open door. When you're up to something and you think you have been seen you feel twenty feet tall and brightly illuminated, but the train rattled on and we were on our own. In fact, our disappearance was not noticed until 9 o'clock the next morning.

The idea was to walk north, steering by the Pole Star, hit the sea and then, as sailors, we should be able to think of something.[6]

George Shuttleworth described the last part of the journey:

After Algiers, we changed trains to a narrow gauge railway which took us south over the Atlas Mountains and on into the desert. The railway ran about ten miles short of Laghouat at a town called Djelfa, and from there they packed us all into Lorries again before finally arriving at Laghouat.[7]

The anonymous diarist continued:

At Laghouat the people were mostly Arabs and were very anti-British. Their first action was to search us and take all our money. They then placed us in a corner of a Foreign Legion Outpost surrounded by four rows of barbed wire. This wire is 12-foot high and there are guards stationed all around with a double guard at the only entrance. Evidently, they were not going to let us escape easily, or otherwise.

Next day I ate and was glad of it. The following day turned out to be Sunday during which we had time to sort ourselves out a little. We found our food rations were a third of a loaf, a cup of macaroni and a cup of wine. This was divided into two meals a day.

We lived like this for a month, during which time we were supplied with beds and food utensils. These consisted of a bag of straw, two blankets and a rush mat. These were squeezed into the rooms as best we could. The utensils were, a spoon, fork, cup and a little tin bucket called a Gamel.

About this time our own cooks took over the Galley, the only difference being the food was cleaner, salt or sugar were never ours.

Have now sent 3 letters and 2 cablegrams home.

The heat here all this time was pretty terrific and it's only the beginning of Spring. Some of the lads have fainted several times. I myself have suffered the most awful stomach and headaches. This I put down to the food as well as the heat.

As I've said before, I had neither soap nor towel when I landed in this country and now after five weeks I still haven't any. Manage to keep clean by swilling myself down with cold water every day.

Clothes were treated the same. All I possessed in the way of garments was one undershirt, a Service Jersey, Battle Dress Jacket, trousers and a pair of Gym Shoes, not much to look after.

The French had now decided to make us pay for our keep. We were advised by the Officers to allot two pounds a month for this purpose. I found this a snag as I only had 36/- a month for myself, the rest of my pay being allotted home. There were various rumours about the Admiralty paying for it and so forth. However, having definitely decided not to alter the income back home, I let events take their course. Have heard no more about it.

They had also started a makeshift Canteen where by making a list of what you required, you sometimes got. Razor blades, sun glasses, tooth brushes, paste, spice, etc. If you got any of these articles you were more than lucky. We are not allowed to handle money. So I suppose they can charge us what they like. We can check our accounts each month if you can read French.

The food was now a little better. We sometimes got some turnip soup and a piece of meat. We were also given half a dozen dates to act as dessert. These dates were saved by my pal and myself together with bread, which I got in exchange for some wine when we had enough. I soaked the whole lot in water, mixed some spice in with it, put it into a bag that I made out of my pal's shirt, and boiled it for an hour or two. The result being a lump of 'Duff' weighing anything from 8 to 10 pounds. This we ate with relish. I expect the dog would turn his nose up at it at home.

We had now begun to organise sports amongst ourselves the favourites being Deck Tennis and 2High
Jimmy Knacker [a complex form of leapfrog]. We could
not play football or cricket owing to the lack of materials.
All kinds of foot races were included.

Whist Drives were also run and in spite of having to
sit on the floor while playing were quite good fun, especially when someone received a huge paper parcel with
a small tin of macaroni for the booby prize. The prizes
were usually cigarettes, which we were getting pretty
regularly from somewhere.

One of our great nuisances here are the flies. Same
kind as the common house fly in England only for everyone there, there are a thousand and one here. The both
sides of the room are always in a cloud of them.

There isn't any more I can add to this now except our
lavatories. These are open air trenches which we dig and
cover ourselves. Also the water, there are a dozen taps
between all of us.[8]

Meanwhile the train escapees, Burfield and Baillie-Grohman,
had been captured. This is best described in a letter home from
Michael Baillie-Grohman on 20 April 1942, who suggested that
the first thing to do on arriving somewhere new is to write home
and give them your new address:

Camp des Internees,
Laghoautte,
C/o American Consul
Algiers,

Dear All,

Is this not 'une affaire formidable?'. Interned by the
French of all people, in Algeria. We are situated about
250 miles south of Algiers, of which distance one half is
desert, and we are in a small oasis. This is not quite as
it sounds, for we occupy a wing of an enormous Spahi
barracks, all set about with barbed wire, not to mention
huge walls and sentries and what ho, and are on the out-
skirts of a fairly large Arab town. I have not been into the
camp proper yet, but am in prison and have been since
our arrival a week ago. I have a further three weeks to
do, but will let you know about that later.

We landed in Tunis, on Cape Bon, at about 08.00 a.m. on Monday, 6 April – Easter Monday, leaving the ship in 8 feet of water, and 250 yards from the land, burning merrily, with charges popping off at intervals. We knew nothing of the country in which we were landing, and it looked most deserted and barren, most of the space in the boats and rafts, journeying to and fro, was taken up with food and water. Before leaving finally No.1 [John Burfield] and I set the ship ablaze. It was the most heart-rending job as I had grown awfully fond of the old warrior. My cabin was the most pathetic sight. I had taken out all the clothes I could not put into a suitcase, piled them on the deck, with my books and letters and everything I had. And poured oil fuel on the lot.

We formed up – 250 of us – by a French Officer and a dozen soldiers and marched, carrying our gear, about 6kms to the nearest village. There we were given 'di vin et du pain' and they relieved me of my six shooter which I was keeping against emergencies. It gave the escort rather a shock as it burst out of my pocket and fell with a clatter at the feet of an astonished poilu. It was lucky it was not a Mills Bomb, or I would probably have been shot.

An incredibly long journey to Tunis followed and we arrived at a sort of barracks there at about 23.00. We had been at Action Stations all the night before, so we were all pretty tired by then. They were quite nice, and we were not at all sure what was going to happen to us. Great hopes of living in flats in Tunis until we were repatriated were quashed by the American Consul, when he eventually came to see us, who said that it was impossible even to think about it, and that as yet no arrangements had been put forward for exchanging the 90-odd people who were already at Laghouatte when we arrived. So the chances of a speedy return to England vanished, and we resigned ourselves to come here.

We stayed two nights in Tunis and then embarked on Wednesday evening in a train, en route to this place – the train was a special one, with six guards to a coach, and two officers in ours. Every station we stopped at had a couple of battalions round it, and the food was bad.

Thursday was a day of preparation, we collected food, water and a spare pair of socks, and at 01.00 on Friday the First Lieutenant and I slipped off the train and vanished into the mountains.

All that night we ran through the most fearful country, with the Pole Star always ahead, and at 05.30 in the morning found us on top of a foothill to the range of mountains in which the railway was running. Then we found a thorn bush, which we camouflaged with broom on the ground floor and there we lay all day. Maps we had, and a pair of binoculars and we 'fixed the ship' – or thought we had – before noon. The Arabs were passing right by us the whole day and never saw us. Most exciting.

Our plan had been to travel by night and lie up by day, and make for the coast. That night when we sailed forth from our hiding place was just as black as your hat. And climbing mountains in unknown country in these conditions was not child's play. We had been lucky in our rush the night before, and John Burfield, falling nastily, got away with a cut and bruised knee.

After three hours walking we were hopelessly lost. None of the tracks were where they ought to have been, and the path we were on was going southwards. We knocked at the door of an Arab village and asked to be put right. An enormous man answered, magnificently dressed, who was the Head Man of the village. He said he would put us on the road in the morning, but it would be stupid to go on that night. Would we like to stay with him for the night? Coffee was produced, and we accepted, for it was far too cold to sleep out, and in due course turned in with the Arab, his father, two sons and a daughter, his goats and his chickens, all in one bed. Oh, and I forgot to mention the fleas.

At 04.30 we trotted off with the Arab as a guide and to our amazement he took us over the same path as we had come, and said goodbye. Neither our French nor his was good enough for the task so we said goodbye and off we went.

In due course, we found that the only thing to do was to gain a really good point of vantage and there to study our maps and see where this elusive road really led, and where the blighter was. Accordingly, we climbed to the top of a mountain, and arrived there at 12.00. Then we sat down and ate some biscuits, pulled out our binoculars, and took a look at the country. To the north of us lay range after range of mountains going as far as we could see. We could not see a single stream or a single path. To the south and west was the railway and to the east were more mountains. The only thing to do was descend to the railway, hop on a train, clear out of the locality, and try again.

We reckoned that by this time every Frenchman and Arab in the neighbourhood would be searching for us, so we timed our arrival at the village for dusk. We thought it would be about five hours fast going to get down, and we wanted to gain a point of vantage so that we could descend on a train quickly should one arrive – for they were not awfully frequent.

The country in which we were was magnificent. Very like Austria except that the colouring was more drab and you did not get the vistas of endless peaks. A lot of the peaks we did see however were snow-capped and it was bitterly cold on the one we were on. The going was terrible, unless one managed to follow a path which did not lose itself in the stones. Landslides seemed to be common, and the paths we were on fre- quently blocked by them. They were so little used that it was difficult to discover where they emerged on the other side of the slide.

We timed our descent well and an hour before dusk we were prospecting for a point of vantage when we met an Arab. He was a revolting looking man and we made to pass him. He took one look at us and then sidled up to us and asked, in French, if we planned to escape on the train, we thought the game was up. However, he was a friendly bird, and from him we got the information they were expecting us on the railway and that it was hope- less to try. So we, who were very tired by then, said that we would buy tickets and travel like any ordinary bloke would. He would not help us there, so it was necessary for us to enlist the help of the French locals to procure us tickets and find out whether we had to change and what time the train went, and so on. To this end we produced 100 francs and told the old boy to lead us to a house sep- arated from the rest, where lived a Frenchman. This he did and he conducted us to *la maison du maitre d'ecole*, said *'voila'* and off he went. We arrived at the school building and all was dark and quiet, and there was no one in. So we said to ourselves that he must live away from the school, and spying a house a couple of hun- dred yards off, we knocked at the door and asked for the Maître. A tiny Arab boy came and said that the *Maître*

was away and that he lived over at the school. We asked
to be put on the road to Mausma to fool him and doubled
back, when he was gone, to the school garden. The time
was 21.00, we had been on foot since 04.30, and been half
way up and all the way down a good-sized mountain,
and were utterly done. So we broke a window, climbed
in and had a look around. The first thing we saw were
eggs, so we broke a pile of them into a saucepan and
made them scrambled over a fire that John had lit. He
cooked coffee and made some toast, and we had the best
meal I have ever had. Then we turned in the spare room
and flaked out.

I woke up at 10.00 and found the house surrounded by
gendarmes. Apparently, as I afterwards learned, the little
boy, damn his intelligence, thought we were thieves, and
they came up to the house expecting to find a couple of
louts who had been at large in the neighbourhood.

Anyway, we hid our gear, had a cold breakfast, and
set about hiding ourselves, praying meanwhile that the
Maître would return quickly, find his house empty, call
off the dogs of war, and then we could emerge and say
our piece. But the gendarmes got tired of waiting, broke
in, and with many explanations of surprise, pulled John
out first, and then yours truly.

We were handcuffed, taken down to the local jug, sat
on chairs, and there we were. They beamed on us, gave
us an enormous omelette, du vin et du pain, said 'Voila
les Anglais' and all was well. Cigarettes, soap and cigars
were presented to us and the Chief Gendarmes asked us
for coffee and liqueurs.

When they wanted to un-handcuff us, the gendarme
who was shackled onto John could not find the key. Not
a bit perturbed, he produced a pin from his tunic and
picked the lock. It amused us both awfully.

Then after more adventures, of which I can't write
here, we arrived here, were seen by the Commandant
and to the huge delight of the troops were given thirty
days' cells apiece.[9]

One of the first considerations on taking up new quarters is the
quality of the food. Prisoners of War, or Internees, are entitled to
be victualled on the same scale as are the soldiers of their captors.
The trouble with being held by the Vichy French Army in Algeria
was that the soldiers were Arabs and Muslim. Their diet suited

them, but not a European stomach. Baillie-Grohman continues his letter home:

> We are not badly off, and have all our gear, and are both in one cell. The food is filthy, but it is the same as everybody else gets. The place is fearfully rationed: there is little or no meat, and no potatoes or cabbage, or any of the things we get in England. Sugar is unknown, there is no petrol, cigarettes are local and obnoxious, chocolate or sweets are unheard of, there are no matches. Our diet consists of a few beans and lettuce at 11.00 washed down with wine, and a rather smaller quantity of the same at 17.30. Nothing else. They vary the beans by giving us macaroni, lentils or carrots. Occasionally a square meal is added. We get about 9 ounces of good wholesome bread each per day and that keeps body and soul attached. We are awfully hungry.[10]

John Burfield continued his recalcitrance on arrival at Laghouat and remembered well the hunger as he recalled:

> On our arrival we were put into cells – not the actual Punishment Block, that came later when we had been officially sentenced – quite a nice room with a couple of iron bedsteads, straw filled paillasses and canvas sheets, and we settled down to await the inevitable punishment for escaping. First, we started a calendar on the wall and then we devised a way of sharing the rations. We were fed on the same scale as the native troops and I got one cup of coffee in the morning – which wasn't too bad – a plate of stew and some vegetables at midday, with a hunk of bread and more coffee, or maybe some wine, in the evening. The trouble was the lack of utensils, and the problem of dividing the food fairly. The method hit on was 'You divide – I'll choose'. The peas for instance were carefully counted. We were forever hungry.
>
> Michael was next in seniority to me on *Havock* and we got on very well, which was all to the good as it needs a bit of give and take for two fellows to be shut up in a cell together for twenty-three hours a day for thirty days. For the other hour, we were let out for 'exercise'.
>
> When we were let out we crossed the parade ground to where there was a water trough for horses and camels and us. There we had a wash or a splash and a walk

around. This lasted for one hour only and then we were back inside. One day we were washing ourselves when one of the Trailleurs – who were always interested in European officers washing themselves in the camel trough – came along holding a handful of Couscous. This was a standard item of diet and is awful stuff even when you add things to it. On its own – dreadful. Nevertheless, I said to Michael 'Grab it – and run'; which he did – whilst I stood in the way of our Guard in what I suppose he thought was a threatening manner, although I never touched him. Not that that made any difference, because the Commandant weighed me off to another thirty days for assaulting a guard. I suppose I must be the only naval officer to be put away for thirty days for a handful of bloody couscous.[11]

Of his seven months in Laghouat, John Burfield spent three months in the cells.

Before the arrival of *Havock*, the population in Laghouat was relatively small and the inmates looked after themselves on a somewhat casual basis, a Fleet Air Arm pilot, Lieutenant Charles Lamb, volunteered to do the administrative legwork for them[12]. With *Havock* however, there came a more recognisable routine. Commander Jessel of *Legion* became the Senior British Officer (SBO) and a disciplined hierarchy was established which lasted to the end – the position of SBO eventually passing to Captain Drew, who had commanded the cruiser *Manchester,* after she was scuttled and the crew brought in to Laghouat.

There were also the crews of two British Motor Torpedo Boats (MTB) who had entered Tunis under the mistaken impression that France was neutral and that they would be afforded the usual courtesy of 24 hours in which to affect repairs. Sadly, they were now of the opinion that they would have had a more civilised reception if they had sailed into Hamburg. The same fate had overtaken Captain Montgomery who had lost touch with his regiment at Dunkirk and had 'successfully' made his way to Algiers, only to find that he had made the same mistake as those off the MTBs.

A mixed bag indeed. Shot-down pilots were common, mostly from Malta – indeed amongst *Havock*'s passengers there was a Fleet Air Arm squadron from the island who were unexpectedly re-united with one of their own pilots, Lieutenant Cliff Thornton, RN, who was already in residence. Operations in the Western Desert provided quite a few more aircrew. Then there were the soldiers. In addition to Captain Montgomery, there was Captain Adolph Cooper, a veteran of the First World War, an ex-Foreign Legion Sergeant and baiter of the Vichy French. He was sometimes something of a nuisance, something of a mystery at all times and one of the genuine characters, or eccentrics, which every community gathers unto to itself. In fact, an 'adventurer', and whether his stories were true or not he gave an entertaining lecture.

Jack Surridge addressed the issue of how to pass the time:

> Well, you can imagine we had a lot of talent around, and of all things we had an Ordinary Seaman who was a schoolmaster. He set exam papers to grade us – needless to say, the RAF boys came out on top. We had experts in their own field. The Engineer Officer taught us Maths, the Electrical Artificer Electricity and so on. We also had a Member of Parliament. Well, most matelots are not politically minded so we requested a lecture from him and he gave us a History of Parliament and how the House was run. Another pastime was sport, and Volley Ball was the favourite, with all that sand. We created a garden growing corn on the cob.[13]

Stoker Petty Officer George Shuttleworth remembered that:

> Our time was spent playing cards or Uckers [a game akin to Ludo but far, far more devious, being a naval specialty], although personally I was busy with my sewing machine. On one occasion, I helped to rig out two naval officers who thought they could escape dressed as Arabs. No luck, into the slammer they went for 14 days". [Burfield and Baillie-Grohman as usual!]

We can continue to follow day-to-day events in the camp through the diary of the anonymous *Havock* survivor:

> Tuesday, 26.5.42. 8th week. Marvel upon marvel, we actually got a tin of real English tobacco. Also, signed Parole Cards so that we might take a walk outside sometimes. Won't be allowed to go into town so I don't see what's of interest 100 miles in the Sahara Desert, still, may come in useful.
>
> Wednesday 27th. We were issued with a bottle of lemonade which we will pay for.
>
> Thursday 28th. Big day. Had some blades, toothpaste and soap powder from the canteen. Also, made another

'Duff'. Nearly everyone in our room had letters from home, except me. I suppose I shell [sic] get one someday.

Friday 29th. Instead of dates for dessert today we got some apricots. Ran about 12 a man. I boiled mine down and made some jam. Turned out very sour, but it gives a nice taste on dry bread. Also got another bottle of lemonade and two bottles of liquid soap between 32 men. Someone had the bright idea to start dancing classes. First one went alright although I am sure you would have had a good laugh to see a group of big tough guys, dressed in underpants, making elf like movements with their bare feet. It's much too hot to wear any clothes and bare feet slip over the stone floor easier.

Saturday 30th. French mustered all our gear today. Took about four hours to do it. Kept us hanging about in the hot sun. Ran in an obstacle race in the evening. Got up to the final and came in second. Won some cigarettes and barked my shins in the bargain. We had started a darts tournament, but someone bust the only set of darts we had so it was abandoned. No Mail.

Sunday 31st. Had church after Appel. I have forgotten to mention that we are mustered twice a day by the French. During these musters each man has to answer his name. They take place at 9 and 5 o'clock.

Monday June 1st. 9th Week. Our doctor gave us a lecture on various diseases, mainly typhus and typhoid, the latter seems to be a yearly occurrence in Laghouat. Two or three years ago it killed 6 per cent of the population. However, the M.O. is trying to get some medical stores, so that we may all be immunised.[14]

Under normal circumstances the French would have provided some level of medical care in cases of dire emergency, but day-to-day doctoring was in the hands of the in-house experts, namely the Sick Berth Attendants from *Havock* and *Manchester*, who worked with skill and dedication, but without much in the way of material assistance. However, at the forefront of the medical care available at Laghouat was Surgeon Lieutenant Robert Royds, RNVR, of *Havock*.

John Burfield describes Royds:

Royds was probably a bit older than the rest of us, late twenties I should imagine and maybe as a result he was a good friend to us all with whom one could talk with freely about matters outside the Service. He was a great friend of mine. Professionally, he looked after us extremely well, even periodically giving a fearsome illustrated lecture to the ship's company on the perils of Venereal Disease. Then, in Malta, he contracted polio – quite unknown to the rest of us. Think what that must have been like for a doctor – knowing and recognising all the symptoms. Then, only a few weeks before our release, he succumbed and they flew him out to Algiers where he died. Such a sad loss.[15]

The Commonwealth War Graves Commission informs us that Surgeon Lieutenant Robert Davies Royds RNVR, died during the night of 24/25 September 1942. Aged twenty-eight, he was subsequently buried in the Dely Ibrahim War Cemetery, ten kilometres south-west of Algiers, Algeria. His lasting resting place can be found at Grave 22, Row J, Plot 2.

The anonymous diarist continues:

Tuesday 2nd. Mail Day. Did not receive any, sent off another cable. The three have cost me over 300 Francs. I shall keep sending them until I get a letter. The Arabs are again cooking our food. Today's two meals were lousy macaroni.

Wednesday 3rd. The water has now been rationed. If we want to wash in the morning, we have to rise at 5.30. It is on for an hour four times a day. Went to the Whist Drive in the night. Scored 114, winner was 121.

Thursday 4th. Received a letter from home today. It was from Ella. Last letter I had was a Christmas Card. It was nice to read a letter again. Have been checking the hours between meals here. We get one at 12 mid-day and another at 6 meaning 18 hours between one and 6 the other.

Friday 5th. There is a rumour going round that there will be an escape tonight.

Saturday 6th. Nothing happened last night, but the escape is definitely going to be made tonight. So I shall have to look after this book in case there will be a search. Had a letter from Ma. Longest one I've ever had from her. Quite a lot of news.

Sunday 7th. The escape was made last night. 7 Officers [including Lieutenant John Burfield] and 22 Ratings went out by way of a tunnel, which took almost a year to dig.

The French Officer in charge of the Appel, nearly had a fit when he saw the Parade was not complete. However, his next action was to inform the Commandant who immediately turned the 'Spahis' out. Incidentally, the Spahis are the finest horse cavalry in the world. These mounted and went after the escapees. In less than 14 hour's freedom three ratings were brought in, during the day several more were caught. The tunnel they had dug had now been found. The Spahis found tracks leading from nowhere so they put two and two together and started to dig, almost immediately they found it and two of them were soon crawling through to see where it led. They came out in the Officer's cabin. This tunnel I believe is the longest dug to escape a place of imprisonment, being 180-foot long. There was one dug in Abyssinia, during the last war, which totalled 130-foot. Both being dug by hand. We had no food today.

Monday 8th. 10th week. More prisoners were brought in today. I feel terribly sorry for them. They worked hard for their freedom and now they will get at least 90 days' cells. We had one meal of macaroni today.

Tuesday 9th. Still more prisoners brought in. They have caught half of what originally went out. The French have cut off our electricity supply as a reprisal. Had a letter from Vi.

Wednesday 10th. All the escapees have been returned except for four officers, whom I hope will get away, then they can tell the outside world how we are being treated.

Thursday 11th. Have caught all escapees and now the French have threatened us with all sorts of reprisals. All this week the Arab guards have been most abusive. There have been several shootings; fortunately, no one has yet been hit.[16]

Jim 'Buster' Brown describes the killing of an escapee:

Apart from the tunnel escape attempt, one *Manchester* crewman tried to scale the wire but was shot dead and an American pilot managed to get out by hanging under a truck, but was captured and returned later.[17]

Able Seaman Alan Smith, of HMS *Manchester*, recalled that: 'We heard the shot and rushed outside to find Stoker Greaves lying dead under the wire.'[18] John Burfield was appalled at such an unnecessary loss of life: 'I was down there almost immediately afterwards – horrified at the callousness of it all.'[19]

The anonymous diarist continued his account:

> Friday 12th. While on food party today, I was marching second rank, the Arabs were marking points with their bayonets and passing remarks in French. The Duty Sergeant, who understood French, could not take this for long and slapped one of them on the jaw. This almost started a fight, but what chance would we have had. The sergeant has been given cells.
>
> Saturday 13th. A French General came to visit us today. But it was not what one would call a cordial one. His first action was to confiscate our Wireless, Piano and Gramophone. He has promised us still more reprisals. No Mail. Lights were given back.
>
> Sunday 14th. We had a treasure hunt today. Clues were hidden in various places over the camp. All was going well and was proving good fun until one of the guards turned a machine gun on us.
>
> Monday 15th. 11th Week. Nothing of importance today except that we were organised a game called 'Volley Ball' comprises of two teams of eight and a football. The rope which we use for a net is 7 to 8 feet high, the idea is to keep the ball in the air as long as possible, using both hands, no man being allowed to touch it twice.
>
> Tuesday 16th. Mail day. Only three letters between the whole camp.
>
> Wednesday 17th. Was terribly hot today. There was a breeze blowing from the desert and it was hard to bear being so hot. The ground is also too hot for bare feet.
>
> Thursday 18th. Quite a load of Red Cross parcels came today. A parcel a man. It could not be issued one each because the French pierce all the tinned food so that it must be eaten at once. We also got inoculated with Typhus which also came from the Red Cross. We were given a tin of corned beef between four and a tin of sardines between two this evening, made a decent supper. No Mail.
>
> Friday 19th. Big day. Received one cake of toilet soap, bar of chocolate, quarter pound tin of tea and sugar, tin of milk powder and a pound tin of butter between four. It's the first time we have had tea for over three months and boy did it go down well, I'll say it did. No bad effects after inoculation.

Saturday 20th. Hardly anyone had mail today. It is rumoured that the French are holding it back. Also, had biscuits, jam and tongue. Living like lords this week.

Sunday 21st. Nothing special happened today. Was no Red Cross issue it being Sunday. Today's meals were the usual.

Monday 22nd. Today's issue was salmon cheeses. Wood is very scarce, not a bit to be had anywhere.

Tuesday 23rd. Mail Day. Didn't get any. Cannot write home, writing paper all gone.

Wednesday 24th. Apart from the Red X gear nothing of interest. Mosquitos are getting plentiful. Am trying to procure nets for same.

Thursday 25th. No Mail. One of the lads woke up this morning and found a yellow scorpion in his bed. The sting of this kind is not fatal if the victim has a pretty good constitution. Whereas the sting of the black variety is deadly. I think either one would do us here.

Friday 26th. A representative of the Red Cross from Algiers arrived here today. He's a French Minister and a very decent chap. He has visited internment camps all over France and told us all the internees are receiving English Cigarettes and other Red Cross supplies regular. He cannot understand why we are not getting ours, however, he is going to look into the matter for us. He also wanted lists of books, musical instruments that we require. The camp as a whole has ordered a terrific amount of stuff. He's promised us to get them in a fortnight. The Canteen that had been closed was opened today. I had a half pint bottle of red ink and some razor blades.

Saturday 27th. Mail Day. None for me. Procured some straw hats from the canteen. They are like flowerpots with a rim six inches wide. Despite their appearance, they are cool.

Sunday 28th. French announced that they would return our wireless for one hour each evening., so that we may listen to the news. Have had French papers in the camp and theirs have various rumours about Libya and Sebastopol.

Monday 29th. The French went back on their word regarding the wireless, expect them to do a dirty trick like that. They also shot one of our dogs called 'Pluto'. It was exactly like Pluto of screen fame in movements of legs and body and was a great favourite amongst us.

Tuesday 30th. Post card from Ma. One of the lads had 9 letters. The wireless was returned. Wasn't working well so we missed half the news.

Wednesday 1/7/42. Wireless still in the camp. Heard today that Jerry is 70 miles from Abisi and still advancing. Seems I left the Mediterranean in time. Will be a bad thing for us all if they take Abisi.

Thursday 2nd. Mail Day. Letter from Margaret. Had mirror and shaving soap from canteen. Used soap for washing. Heard Jerry's been checked in Egypt.

Friday 3rd. French have organised walks for us. These take place at 6 o'clock in the morning. 30 to 40 men fall in and are escorted out by Spahis on horseback. Am unable to go myself owing to lack of footwear. Am tying my shoes on with wire. Had 2nd inoculation.

Saturday 4th. A third lot of Red Cross came today. If they keep coming like this we shall be pretty well off for food. We were issued with a block of Ghee, one a room. Don't feel too good after inoculation.

Sunday 5th. My shoes have finally worn out. Am now walking in bare feet.

Monday 6th. 13th week. Felt pretty … today, could hardly move my head and shoulders.

Tuesday 7th. Mail day. Cheers! Had a letter from Ken. Told me Ma was working. Had some terrible headaches. In a biscuit packet, I found an address belonging to a young lady in 'Canada'. Shan't be able to write from here.

Wednesday 8th. Felt terrible today. Almost fainted at Appel. Had permission to leave the parade in time. This inoculation has shaken us up considerably.

Thursday 9th. Mail Day. Did not get any. Effects of inoculation have worn off.

Friday 10th. No cigarettes in the camp. We did have a tin of Gold Flake last Saturday, but now they're gone. It's awful without a smoke.

Saturday 11th. The Admiralty sent us a pair of khaki shorts, a shirt, also a toothbrush. Nice to put clean clothes on again. No Mail.

Sunday 12th. Cut my right toe yesterday. Turned septic today.

Monday 13th. 14th Week. The French searched us all today. No one knew anything about it until it was too late. They employed over 300 guards for this purpose.

Absolutely turned the place inside out. Had a look at my diary but did not take it.

Tuesday 14th. Had letter from Nell. Said Irene Shears mother had died. Never expected that.

Wednesday 15th. The 4th lot of Red X parcels came today. Must say we are doing well. Be a bit bad going back to Arab food again. Still no cigs.

Thursday 16th. Had some Gold Flake from Red X.

Friday 17th. The Arabs seem to be building a Galley of sorts inside the camp.

Saturday 18th. Rumours about French cigarettes in the camp. No Mail.

Sunday 19th. Seems to be quite a lot of building going on in the camp. Had an issue of French cigs.

Monday 20th. Had an open razor from the canteen. Can shave alright with it too, although it isn't very good.

At this point the diarist seems to lose his way with dates and starts missing days. However, he continues:

Tuesday 24th. Had some more Red X representatives here today. This time they were two elderly ladies. Spoke with some of the lads and got some cigarettes for us.

Sunday 26th. French are erecting wooden huts, putting them up like lightning. Also, built some lavatories, true native style, better imagined than described.

Tuesday 28th. Received from Admiralty bar of soap and toothpaste. Am now walking about in bare feet.

Friday 31st. Had my third inoculation.

Saturday August 1st. Am being vittled from our own galley with our own cooks.

Friday 15th August. The French are now supplying us with beds. They stand 4ft high, made of wood and pretty shaky, but are better than sleeping on the deck.[20]

No account of Laghouat would be complete without mention of the 'Manchesters'. The cruiser HMS Manchester, part of the escort for the Operation Pedestal convoy to Malta, was torpedoed by an Italian MAS boat off Cape Bon on 13 August 1942. Unfortunately, her Captain's order 'Emergency Stations' had the effect of turning a damaged but still capable fighting unit into little more than a hulk manned by a disorganised rabble intent on abandoning their ship. Thanks to this faulty order no serious attempt was made to save the crippled cruiser although the engineering staff worked hard to restore power and correct the list. Eventually, Captain Drew decided, prematurely, that his ship could not be saved and gave the order to abandon ship at about 02.45 even though power had been restored and his ship would have been capable of thirteen knots. Eleven lives were lost when the torpedo struck, about 150 were evacuated by the destroyer *Pathfinder* and a similar number by the destroyers *Somali* and *Ashanti* which arrived on the scene soon after *Manchester* finally disappeared beneath the waves. But around 400 of the approximately 650 men who were in the boats or on Carley rafts and had been told to head for the flashing lighthouse at Cape Bon were interned in Laghouat.[21] The arrival of *Manchester*'s crew was recorded by the anonymous diarist:

> Thursday 20th. Most of the crew of the 'Manchester' arrived here today. Have enlarged the camp to twice the original size but have cut the Officers away from the ratings. The whole camp now consists of 82 officers and 800 ratings. We are now 48 in a room meant for 20. 14 double tier beds each side. Air's pretty smelly in the morning. Beds are also full of bugs.
>
> Saturday 29th. Had some British Red Cross parcels in today. Compared to the Canadian one's we have had, they're lousy, but better than nothing. Little tins of sugar, cheese containing two ounces, half a pound of marg, one two-ounce packet of Maypole tea and some uncooked sausages, bacon, etc, and last of all a bag of sweets. What a comparison, also got a small tin of Nestles milk.
>
> Monday 31st. Some of the lads had parcels today. One had a handkerchief and toothbrush, another the paper wrapping, hope mine doesn't arrive like that.
>
> Thursday 3rd, September. Can't understand where my letters are getting to. Every Mail Day the lads get their letters in batches of 5 and 10 or more. The most I've ever had on one day is two. I've a mate here … he's had 9 this week. I've had one so the post back home must be O.K.[22]

Jim 'Buster' Brown remembered a dog called Ozzy:

> When we were in Tewfik being repaired they were showing the film Wizard of Oz and you could stay out late if you went to see it. So everyone would go, pick up a ticket from the floor and go elsewhere. We picked up this dog which we called Oz or Ozzy. When we were in

Laghouat Ozzy was a great favourite. The Arabs kept rabbits in holes they had dug outside the wire. One day one of the rabbits escaped and another pet dog called Pluto, belonging to the *Manchesters* chased it. One of the guards shot Pluto dead. We caused a lot of trouble for a few days, but there was little we could do.[23]

Maybe the one thing a prisoner craves, apart from his freedom, is news from home. Technically, as Internees and not Prisoners of War, the inmates of Laghouat were entitled to send, and receive, as many letters and cablegrams as they wished – or could afford. That theory and practice differed when in the hands of the Vichy French is not to be wondered at. The wireless was connected to the camp's electricity supply. In times of stress, the French either removed the receiver or cut off the electricity. If they decided on confiscation, this did not represent a problem as a dummy receiver had been made for just such an emergency. Return, or reconnection, was always promised at their whim.

When the Allied forces began to make progress toward the camp, following the Operation *Torch* landings in November 1942, the conditions miraculously improved. The only news of the Allied landings in North Africa came from Alvar Liddell of the BBC over the wireless.

George Shuttleworth heard the announcement and remembered:

As soon as I heard this I ran to the Commander's cabin to tell him the news. He reported to the SBO, Captain Drew, who went to Jeunechamps (Camp Commandant) to ask for the wireless to be left on. Surprisingly he agreed: he too wanted to know what was going on. All day long we listened to what London was saying. At last it came – Algiers had fallen. At 22.00 hours off went the electricity, but at 06.00 the next morning we were up and about waiting for the switch-on and, low and behold, Alvar was on the air again, but it was three days before we knew what the outcome was to be.[24]

Jack Surridge recounted:

We generally had food, light and water shortages. We dug the tunnel for something to do. There was little expectation that we would escape as we were in the middle of the desert. We mainly had macaroni in olive oil with peppers or couscous in olive oil. Coffee was made with date stones. There were two cups of wine a day from the tenth press!! The senior French officer was anti-British because of our bombardment of Oran and Syria. When we were released we saw British troops in American uniform.[25]

Harry Jenkins: 'We burned our bunks as they were full of bugs and were shipped home on the [troopship] *Keren*.'[26] John Dodds commented: 'We weren't liberated as such. Nobody from our forces came. They just bussed us to the station.'[27]

Havock's First Lieutenant John Burfield summed up the release as follows:

> Jeunechamps had lost touch with any higher authority, but evidently the Allies' aim was to take over Algeria without upsetting the French too much; so he agreed to disarm the guards and we agreed to stay put for the time being without formally taking over the camp. Therefore, we didn't put Jeunechamps in the cells – much as we would have liked to.
>
> To get 800-odd of us away took a little time, but they rounded up some buses and I paraded my *Havocks* for the off. As First Lieutenant, this was my responsibility and nothing to do with captain, Lieutenant Commander Watkins, and we didn't see anything of him during the journey. First, we went by camion [a truck-based transport] to Djelfa, which was the railhead, and there, on the turntable, was a railway engine. Michael and I thought about taking matters into our own hands – there was plenty of steam raising ability amongst us all – but luckily wiser councils prevailed because if we had done anything silly to the engine we would have had a lot of very unhappy sailors on our hands. The train ran on wood and coal dust which didn't give a lot of power, so whenever we got to an incline it was a case of everybody off. We took watches on the footplate, to ensure the firemen did his best, and to brew tea.
>
> On arrival at Algiers we fell in on the platform and I started looking for someone to help with our baggage when that fearful oick Martin [French Officer] started insisting that we carried our own. Between a gap in the carriages we could see the White Ensign in the harbour. I let him have a good look and then asked him who was in command now.

We marched down to the harbour, a very ragged lot, but nonetheless in good order and a credit to the Navy. Just us *Havocks*.

Suddenly we found ourselves eating proper food; there was beer and cigarettes and not surprisingly people started flaking out. I did myself, but mine was jaundice. I found my way to a bunk on the transport and stayed there until we reached the UK. Then I remember standing on a bollard on the quayside and saying. 'Goodbye and Good Luck' to my *Havocks*, getting on a train and sleeping until London.

Unfortunately, we somehow got mixed up with a load of German prisoners – there we were, friend and foe alike, with hardly a scrap of uniform between us. My sister and my fiancée met me and I think had some difficulty picking me out. Before leaving London, I went to the Admiralty, just to let them know I was back, and they advised me to see a doctor and get myself to hospital – but I refused. Wouldn't you if it was the first time you had seen your fiancée for God knows how long.[28]

It is very curious to note that Burfield mentions virtually nothing about Watkins throughout his stay in Laghouat and the subsequent period up to and through the court martial. Their relationship seems to have been strained throughout Watkins' period as captain.

All inmates were released on 12 November, following the Allied landings in North Africa, and eventually shipped home to Greenock on the troopship *Keren*. They arrived at Greenock on 23 November, reaching Chatham by train on the 24th. According to ERA Maurice Cutler they were interrogated and then given seven weeks' leave.[29]

Jack Surridge found the whole process of release and return to Britain to be something of an anti-climax observing:

On our release, we made our way up north to catch one of the troopships going back to the UK. I must say they tried to kill us with kindness. First of all it was Tots all round then, although it was Friday 13th, we had the full Sunday lunch – soup, roast beef, plus a sweet. Well we were just not up to it. Once past the soup stage we were full up and ready for the Castor Oil. On arrival back at Chatham we were screened for identity, no medical, no counselling, nothing. Just kitted out and sent on Leave. It was as though nothing had happened.[30]

It is hard to know who should have the last word so let us give it to Ozzy the dog and let George Shuttleworth speak for him:

Some say Ozzy was shot, but he wasn't because I looked after him when the camp was blitzed for stray dogs. When we were released we were sent to Algiers to a liner for passage to the U.K. The dog was with me the whole time and slept in my bunk until we reached Greenock. Boarding the train had to be a little difficult. Poor Oz was in my kitbag from the boat to the train, but he soon settled down.

All aboard the train for Chatham dockyard. We were lined up in Barracks – can you imagine 150 sailors dressed in anything they could find? Some in bits of naval uniform, some khaki and all of it only fitting where it touched. Along came the Barracks Master at Arms.

'What's this lot then?'

'HMS *Havock* Master.'

'Then piss off out of it.'

So we did. We were marched into the Drill Hall where names and numbers were taken. All our belongings were brought into the Barracks and there was poor Ozzy wondering what was going on. I was lucky to find an old shipmate who was on duty taking men and baggage to the station. So who better to take my kit and Ozzy? Well I managed to get on board the Victoria-bound train ready for the home trip. A porter took my baggage to the train and Ozzy wondered where he was going next. My wife's uncle and his missus lived nearby, so he boarded there and remained with them in Croydon until the end.[31]

Havock's Battle Ensign was preserved throughout captivity by a crew member and finally laid up in St George's Church, Chatham, on 24 April 1951, in the presence of many shipmates and Commander Rafe Courage. But there was unfinished business, namely a Court Martial.

Chapter 13

Court Martial

Once back in the United Kingdom, Lieutenant Commander Watkins compiled his account[1] of the loss of his ship off Tunisia and forwarded it to the Admiralty on 1 December 1942, where it was studied by the Naval Law Department. Mr Lawson, the Head of Naval Law, decided that Watkins would be tried by Court Martial on a charge of negligently, or by default, losing HMS *Havock*. At about the same time, Commander Jessel, the former commanding officer of the destroyer *Legion,* which had been sunk in an air raid on Malta's Grand Harbour on 26 March 1942, submitted a report about the loss of *Havock* based upon his own experiences aboard the destroyer and on the verbal evidence that he had collected while a prisoner in Laghouat. Jessel was firmly of the opinion that the duty on which Watkins had been employed on the night preceding the sailing of *Havock* had been partly responsible for the extreme fatigue suffered by the destroyer's commanding officer during the night of 5/6 April.[2]

On 4 January 1943, Director of Operations Division (Foreign), Captain Angus Dacres Nicholl, who had commanded the light cruiser *Penelope* from 15 April 1941 to 15 June 1942, entered the fray on Watkin's behalf. Nicholl was eminently qualified to comment on the strain likely to be experienced by an officer commanding a ship in the Mediterranean in 1942 because his ship had been part of Force K based at Malta from 21 October 1941. He had been present when *Neptune* and *Kandahar* were sunk and *Aurora* and his own ship damaged by mines on 19 December 1941. Furthermore, he had been present at the Second Battle of Sirte on 22 March Sirte and experienced the incessant air raids on the Grand Harbour thereafter, until his splinter-damaged cruiser left Malta on 8 April en route for Gibraltar. He commented:

> I am able personally to corroborate Commander Jessel's remarks in his letter on the duty on which Lieutenant Commander Watkins was employed on the night

preceding the sailing of HMS HAVOCK. V.A.M. was very short of active service officers and found it necessary to call on the Commanding Officers of ships in dockyard hands. Lieutenant Commander Watkins was certainly subjected to great and uninterrupted strain in a most intense period from 21 March to 6 April, which was the culmination of long and arduous fighting service during the war. I would suggest that he deserves very generous treatment over the loss of his ship.[3]

On 5 January 1943, G.R. Hughes responded on behalf of the Head of Naval Law:

From the information available I concur with D.O.D. (F). Nevertheless, I consider that Lieutenant Commander Watkins should be tried by CM [Court Martial] for the loss of his ship – when should such a charge be proved, the Court will doubtless take into account all relevant factors in deciding the sentence. It would, in my opinion, be setting a dangerous precedent if extraneous circumstances were allowed to decide the issue of whether or not an Officer was to stand trial for the loss of his ship.[4]

A few days later, the Second Sea Lord, Vice-Admiral W.J. Whitworth, wrote to the Head of Naval Law saying that he had received a private letter from Admiral of Fleet Sir Andrew Cunningham who stated that Watkins had been under very considerable strain at the time of the loss of his ship and asking that the Court should take this into account should the matter be taken to trial. However, in his reply of 2 February Mr Lawson was insistent that the court martial would be held, pointing out that it was for the defence to highlight any mitigating circumstances.[5]

Lieutenant Commander "Robin" Watkins

Geoffrey Robert Gordon Watkins, who always known as Robin, was born on 2 September 1910, and was the son of Rear Admiral Geoffrey Watkins. He joined the Royal Navy as a cadet at *Britannia* in 1924 serving aboard the training cruiser *Frobisher* as a cadet and later midshipman from 14 January 1928 until 9 February 1930. He was promoted to Acting Sub Lieutenant on 1 January the following year and his rank became substantive on 12 March 1933. On 1 February 1934 Watkins was promoted to lieutenant subsequently serving as ADC to the Governor General of South Africa from 4 October 1938 until 31 August the following year. It was while in South Africa he met his future wife Daphne whom he married in 1941. With the outbreak of war imminent, Watkins was returned to more active duty being listed on the books of *Afrikander* until 12 September when he joined the newly-requisitioned Union Castle liner *Carnarvon Castle* which was in dock at Simon's Town being converted to an armed merchant cruiser. His service aboard *Carnarvon Castle* was short and ended on 30 September with Watkins being ordered to return to the United Kingdom. From 16 January 1940 to 24 February 1941, Watkins served as the First Lieutenant of the powerful and modern destroyer *Janus*. His performance aboard that ship was such that Vice Admiral H.D. Pridham-Wippell, then serving as Vice-Admiral Light Forces in the Mediterranean, personally recommended him to become the commanding officer of the destroyer *Havock* when that post became vacant. Watkins took up his appointment, as Lieutenant in Command, on 25 March 1941 just before the Battle of Matapan, where his ship torpedoed and sank the Italian destroyer *Carducci* and Watkins was awarded the DSC. Thereafter, he had commanded *Havock* during the evacuation of British and Commonwealth troops from Greece and Crete, the Syrian campaign and the Tobruk 'Run' in addition to miscellaneous convoy duties. Unsurprisingly, he had been promoted to Lieutenant Commander on 1 February 1942, and awarded a DSO for his part in the Second Battle of Sirte on 22 March 1942. Now, having spent just over seven months in the dreadful Vichy French internment camp at Laghouat, he had to explain how his ship had run aground at Ras el Mihr on 6 April 1942.

Court Martial

The court martial convened at Portsmouth on 9 and 10 March 1943 and Lieutenant Commander G.R.G. Watkins was charged with, that he did:

(1)   Negligently or by default hazard H.M.S. HAVOCK
(2)   Negligently or by default strand H.M.S. HAVOCK

The court consisted of Captain Philip Foster Glover, RN (President), Captain John Parrington Gornall RN, Captain Eric Paul Vivian RN (sitting as a Commander), Commander Charles Stuart Bell RN and Commander Eric George McGregor RN Paymaster Captain A.F. Cooper OBE, RN was the Deputy Judge-Advocate. The Prosecutor was Acting Commander Ronald

Earnest Cotton Dunbar RN Retired and the Accused's Friend was Commander John Anthony William Tothill DSC, RN[6] who had been Watkins commanding officer aboard the destroyer *Janus* during 1940-1941.

Prior to the court martial, Acting Commander Dunbar RN (Retd.) had compiled the circumstantial letter which was entered into court. In his summary, Dunbar recorded that all the times quoted were Malta Standard Time and that *Havock* had grounded about two miles to the northward of Kelibia Light and one-and-a-half cables to the southward of Ras el Mihr Point, and about 300 yards from the shore with the ship pointing northward.[7]

Thereafter, the Accused was asked how he pleaded and he answered, 'Not guilty'.[8] A total of eleven witnesses were called[9]:

> Lieutenant John Blackmore Burfield DSC, RN
> Commander Martin James Evans OBE, RN
> Temporary Lieutenant Royston Lack RNVR
> Lieutenant Michael Arthur Baillie-Grohman RN
> Petty Officer Reginald Arthur William Stopher
> Able Seaman John Edmund Dodds
> Engine Room Artificer 3rd Class Reginald Rose
> Electrical Artificer 3rd Class John Hurden Warner
> Lieutenant Commander Geoffrey Robert Gordon Watkins DSO, DSC, RN
> Lieutenant Commander William Wright Haddon Paine RN
> Chief Petty Officer Walter Henry Panrucker

After Lieutenant Burfield had confirmed the identity of Lieutenant Commander Watkins, the Prosecutor called witnesses in an order which provided a chronological account of the events as they unfolded.

Evidence of Commander Martin Evans, OBE, RN.

Commander Martin Evans had been Staff Officer Operations at Malta on the staff of Vice-Admiral Sir Ralph Leatham KCB (Vice Admiral Malta; VAM) from May 1941 until after *Havock* sailed on 5 April 1942. He confirmed that *Havock* had been taken in hand by Malta Dockyard on 23 March and that the island and the harbour were under very heavy and continuous air attack at the time. He said that ships which were not part of the local forces were sailed as soon as they could be made ready for sea or sailed in company depending on the circumstances. He remembered meeting the Accused on 5 April noting that *Havock* had completed temporary repairs and that a decision had been made by the C-in-C Mediterranean Fleet [Vice-Admiral Pridham-Wippell] to sail her westward. He said that the destroyer's captain and navigating officer were sent for and given their sailing orders.[10] Commander Evans recognised Exhibit 'C' as the sailing order which read:

HAVOCK R.A.S. MALTA X.D.O FROM V.A. MALTA. Have steam and be ready to slip by 1900 tonight Sunday [5 April].

(2) I will give you orders when to proceed which will probably be at about 20.00 unless absence of enemy aircraft allows sailing earlier.

(3) Route. Proceed as ordered by S.E. searched channel, keeping well clear of Q B B 241 and thence through

(A) 36 42.5N, 11.04E.

(B) 360 Cape Bon one mile. Between Kelibia and Cape Bon it is essential that you should keep within two miles of the shore to avoid minefield to seaward.

(C) South of Zembretta and Zembra.

(D) North of Cani Rock.

(E) Through Galita Channel thence, unless otherwise ordered by FOCNA through positions

(F) 37 29N, 06 29E

(G) 37 05N, 01 14E

(H) 180 Cape De. QTA 20 thence to Gibraltar.

(4) Navigational aids. The following lights have been reported lately as burning correctly Kelibia, Cape Bon, Sigli, Bengut Caxins.

(5) Own information. No friendly forces are at sea in vicinity of your route except submarines which are expected to be as follows:

(A) P35 in Kuriat Lampion area.

(B) URGE 36 25N, 14 10E at 2035/5, returning to Malta, expected to pass north but might return by south-east channel. Catalina aircraft may be met with anywhere west of 8 degrees east.

(6) Enemy information.

(A) E-boats may be encountered in vicinity of Malta and Pantellaria.

(B) Enemy air striking forces in Sardinia appear to consist mainly of Italian torpedo bombers.

(C) No enemy surface forces have been reported lately as based on west Sicilian ports except as convoy escorts. There are usually two or three torpedo boats or destroyers and may be met on the line Pantellaria and Kerkenah.

(7) Speed. Proceed at maximum speed possible until west of 4 deg E, thence best as fuel permits.

(8) Communications. Ships to Gibraltar broadcast at 2359B/2

Message timed at 1541 B/5/4/42[11]

Commander Evans said that details of his passage to Gibraltar were then gone into and included fully the question of the most difficult part of the passage through Tunisian territorial waters; the question of making the coast off Kelibia Light; soundings in the approaches thereto; the contours of the land in the vicinity of Kelibia and northward to Cape Bon; the question of the enemy minefields to the eastward of Tunisian coastal waters and the question of lights at Kelibia, Cape Bon and Cani Rocks which were expected to be burning in the vicinity, were fully discussed. Commander Evans stressed that recent prior experience [with *Aurora* and *Avon Vale* on 29/30 March 1942] suggested that it was very necessary to make as much ground as possible to the westward during the first night and following day but the question of actual speed through Tunisian waters was invariably left to the discretion of the commanding officers in verbal instructions given by VAM. Commander Evans said that the only offshore dangers were two shoals, one south of Cape Bon and one at Ras el Mihr.[12]

Commander Tothill cross-examined Commander Evans[13] on behalf of the Accused in an attempt to get more detail as to the instructions given to Watkins with regard to his passage through Tunisian waters. Commander Evans could not remember the exact details but stated that the rule was not more than two miles off shore but we told people to go as close as they dared. When questioned about the need for soundings, Commander Evans could not give a definite answer but said that soundings are of great value in helping one to ascertain one's position in the approaches to Kelibia Light.

Tothill then moved on to the date when *Havock* was ready to sail pointing out that she had been ready to sail four days earlier and had been damaged again by near misses while lying at buoy in the stream. He asked Evans to offer an explanation for the delay, who replied that we did not know whether she was to be sailed east or west or whether she was to be retained to sail as an escort to *Penelope*. Evans agreed that he had expected *Havock* to be sailed to the east because C-in-C Mediterranean was always short of destroyers and he expected her to be repaired fully at Alexandria.

Tothill then asked if it was appreciated that *Havock*'s high angle armament was considerably less than that of the first group of men of war [*Aurora* and *Avon Vale*] and *Penelope*, who had sailed westward a few days earlier than the destroyer to which Evans replied 'Naturally'. Commander Tothill then attempted to get Evans to speculate on whether *Havock* should have been sailed westward but he refused to be drawn merely reiterating that aircraft attacking Malta could be made available to attack ships sailing westward.

Tothill then addressed the issue of the other duties on which Lieutenant Commander Watkins was employed by VAM, to which Evans replied:

> He was placed in charge of a towing operation towing a lighter round from Grand Harbour to Calafrana harbour, which was required for holding oil from the sunken *Breconshire*. Owing to the enemy's complete air superiority this operation could only be carried out at night. The threat of E-boats and mines and the poor weather made it an unpleasant operation.

Evans could not remember if this operation took place on the night before *Havock* sailed or when it first became known when the destroyer was to be sailed to the westward but the signal arrived during 5 April.

Evidence of Temporary Lieutenant Royston Henry Lack, RNVR.

Temporary Lieutenant Royston Henry Lack RNVR confirmed that on 28 March 1942, he had been appointed to HMS *Havock* when still a sub lieutenant. Asked what occurred when he had arrived on *Havock* to take up his appointment he replied:

> I was introduced to the Captain and I was informed that my sole duties would be navigation. I informed the Captain that I did not feel competent about this position because I had not done any navigation for some time, but the Captain asked me whether I could take a sight and I replied 'Yes'

and he the said 'That is alright then, we will all give you a hand on the bridge'.

Lack said that he told the Captain that he had a full watch keeping certificate and then went off to the rest camp. He returned on 5 April to be told by the Captain that they would be sailing westward to Gibraltar later that day. At 19.00 on Sunday, 5 April he attended a conference with the Captain at the offices of VAM where Commander Evans gave them their sailing orders.[14] Lack remembered that it was stressed that they needed to be as far west as possible by 09.00 on 6 April and were warned about sandbanks off Cape Bon and Ras el Mihr. They were advised by Commander Evans to travel about one and a half miles from the shore while passing the coast between Kelibia and Cape Bon.

Lack said that we returned to the ship from VAM's office and within a half an hour *Havock* was underway. Lack remembered that:

> Just before leaving harbour I was about to check the gyro compass and the Captain told me not to stand in the way and asked me whether the courses had been laid off. I told him no because we had not had time to get this done, sailing directly after leaving the conference and I also informed the Captain that the compass had not been checked, neither the standard nor the gyro, but the Captain told me to go down to the Chart House and lay off the courses. I went down to the Chart House and from aposition south of Filfola Island I laid a course of about 293 degrees to Kelibia Light. I had only been down in the Chart House a short time when Lieutenant Burfield came down to assist me. From Kelibia Light I laid a course of 017 degrees one and a half miles from the shore to Ras el Mihr. I then laid a course of 1½ miles from Ras el Mihr to one and a half miles from Ras Idda. The Captain then came down to the Chart House to see how I was progressing. He approved the courses as laid as far as Ras el Mihr but told me that instead of a course from Ras el Mihr to Ras Idda he wanted to follow the indentation of the coast. After these courses had been laid I went down to the wardroom for supper and turned in. I was then called by the Officer of the Watch and when I went up to the bridge Kelibia Light was in sight and the high ground behind Kelibia could also be seen.[15]

Lack confirmed that the visibility was clear, the sea clam and there was no wind. The Captain then came on the bridge and took charge of the ship. Lack was informed that he was to remain on the bridge and plot all the bearings and ranges given to him by Watkins via Midshipman Duncan.

Lack said that when south of Kelibia Light the ship turned up to the north so as to arrive on a course of 017 degrees one and a half miles from Kelibia Light. He looked up from the chart table and could see the light approximately on the beam. After a while the Captain came down to the bridge chart table to see how we were going. We were slightly inside our course by about half a mile.

Dunbar then asked: 'What did you do as a result of this?'
Lack replied:

> I showed the Captain we were inside our course and the Captain then returned to the compass. Ranges and bearings were coming in fast and the dim red light on the chart table made the plotting very difficult. I heard Lieutenant Baillie-Grohman mention to the Captain that he thought we were near the coast, nearer than he thought we should have been. The Captain, in effect told him to shut up. The Captain then called out to me if it was time to alter course. I replied, 'Not yet, Sir, there is 5 minutes to go.' The Captain came and had a look at the chart a second time.

The Prosecutor then asked Lack to clarify what he meant by 'off your course' [sic] to which Lack replied, 'We were inside it. The Captain then came and had a second look at the chart and returned to the compass and a second time I heard Lieutenant Baillie-Grohman tell the Captain that we were very near the coast. The Captain in effect told him to shut up but also added that otherwise he would send him off the bridge. We were to alter course for Ras el Mihr when the Light was bearing about 238 degrees and then I told the Captain it was time to alter course. Lack told the Captain that we were still inside their course and then Watkins altered about 50 degrees to port [i.e. towards the shore].'Two more bearings and ranges came in and Lack realised that the destroyer was fast approaching the shore. Lack said that he shouted a warning to the Captain and simultaneously heard Lieutenant Baillie-Grohman shout something as well. Lack remembered:

> The next thing I heard was the Captain shout down the voice pipe 'starboard 20, hard a starboard, full astern both', but in a very few seconds afterwards we were

aground. Attempts were made to get the ship off, but the Captain decided it was impossible and all confidential matters with regard to navigation were destroyed by me, except charts which we were using, i.e. charts 250 and 165 and the large-scale chart of Malta. Charts 250 and 165 were taken ashore and the confidential matter on them was subsequently rubbed out. When aground I took the position of the ship from Kelibia Light and as far as I can remember it was 026 degrees 3,800 yards.

The Prosecutor then asked how this was obtained and Lack replied, 'By compass bearings which I took myself and the range from Kelibia Light from the rangefinder.' Lack said that the stranded destroyer was approximately 300 yards from the shore and heading up the coast with the compass showing a north-easterly direction. Lack added, 'The ship was then abandoned and when ashore the Captain told me not to worry because it was his fault and he would plead guilty'.[16]

Acting Commander Dunbar then asked Lieutenant Lack to look at, and read out, Article 1164 of King's Regulations and Admiralty Instructions (KR & AI):

Sounding on approaching land and in Pilotage waters. When approaching land or shoals the Captain is to see that soundings are always taken in good time and continued until the position of the ship is ascertained and her safety secured.

When in the vicinity of rocks or shoals and when the ship is in pilotage waters, he is to take care that soundings are invariably obtained by the hand lead or the best means available at the time, not only as a guide for securing the safe conduct of the ship, but also as a precaution against any mistake in navigation when a pilot is borne. Such sounds are to be obtained in the most frequented channels.

He is to take care that preparation has been made to anchor the ship at short notice.[17]

The witness was now cross-examined by Commander Tothill, the Accused's friend who was keen to learn what advice VAM had given about speed but Lack could not remember the details. When asked about his previous ship and his expectation of being returned to Alexandria. Lack replied that his previous ship was Southwold which had a struck a mine while going alongside Breconshire which had been bombed. He said that he had joined

Havock the day after *Southwold*'s commanding officer, Commander Jellicoe, had sailed in *Dulverton* en route to Alexandria. He added that the officers at St. Angelo told him that he would be returned to Alexandria in *Havock*.[18]

When questioned about the courses that he had laid in, Lack admitted that he could not remember the exact details but agreed that the sailing orders specified keeping not more than two miles from the shore and that Lieutenant Commander Watkins had wanted to follow the indentations of the coast while making the passage through Tunisian waters thereby avoiding the enemy minefield which was known to be in the area. Commander Tothill now explored the issue of whether or not Lieutenant Commander Watkins had asked if the ship was alright. Lack said that he did not remember the Captain asking if the ship was alright and when challenged with the statement that the Captain had asked him several times if the ship was alright he replied, 'I deny that'. There now followed an exchange in which the Prosecutor tried to get Lack to admit that range to Kelibia Light was 4,700 yards and not 3,800 yards. However, Lack was adamant that the range was 3,800 yards because 4,700 yards would have put *Havock* round the point of Ras el Mihr and furthermore he had plotted the stranded ship's position and shown it to the Captain.[19]

Tothill explored Lack's failure to check the gyro compass by transit. Lack said that he had reported this to the Captain but had been ordered off the bridge and told to go and lay off courses on the chart. Lack added that the Captain appeared on that occasion to be rather flustered. Tothill suggested that having missed his transit, it was only natural that the Navigator should be sent to prepare courses. To which Lack shot back:

> While the ship had only just come out of dock and it was more likely that these compasses were out, it was likely that the Captain would send me to go and lay off course, but in my own mind, I should have been allowed to check the compasses first of all.

Tothill then suggested that the Captain was angry with Lack, rather than flustered, because he had failed to get a transit. Lack replied:

> No, definitely not, because the Captain told me not to stand in the way. He was moving from one side of the bridge to the other and did not know that I was taking the transit, because he told me not to stand in the way and it was then I told the Captain what I was doing.

He told me to go down to the chart house and lay off courses. The Captain did not appear to be angry with me on the bridge because he was the same with everybody present.[20]

In response to a question about his difficulties in plotting, Lack admitted that he was:

A certain amount confused, particularly by Midshipman Duncan repeating the bearings and also the rate at which these bearings were coming in. It was almost impossible to plot due to the dimness and colour red of the light. Colours on the chart, such as lights, could not be seen due to the red light. I had beforehand asked the Captain if we could have a brighter light but he would not allow it.

Tothill now probed what had happened when Lack was first introduced to *Havock*'s Captain, asking 'Did he talk to you about doing the duties of Gunnery Control Officer?' Lack replied:

I told the Captain that had been my job in my previous ship [the Hunt class destroyer *Southwold*] and it was discussed, but then I was told that my sole duty would be navigation, to which I replied that I was not confident about this and asked him if either Lieutenant Baillie-Grohman or Lieutenant Burfield could do the job.[21]

Asked how long he had a watch keeping certificate Lack replied that it had been given to him by the commanding officer of HMS *Radiant*, a large armed yacht, in June or July 1941. There now followed an exchange in which Tothill tried to suggest that Lack's inability to obtain a transit had been caused by the fading light at dusk. However, the lieutenant was adamant that the light was more than adequate to obtain his intended transit and, had he not been sent below by the Captain he would have been able to obtain a transit using the breakwater and the light behind it.[22]

Commander Tothill now asked Lack how he knew when it was time to alter course, adding, 'Did you have a deck watch?' Lack replied 'We did not actually have a deck watch. Lieutenant Commander Watkins told me to use my own watch, which is a good one. I took it off and left it on the chart table.' At this point the Deputy Judge-Advocate asked, 'What sort of watch?' to which Lack replied "A Rolex wristwatch. I have not got it now. It was left on the chart table and after the ship had gone aground it was missing.'[23]

Evidence of Lieutenant Michael Arthur Baillie-Grohman R.N.

The next witness was Lieutenant Michael Baillie-Grohman who had served as Confidential Book Officer, Anti-submarine Control Officer, Torpedo Control Officer and R.D.F. and Signals Officer aboard *Havock*. He confirmed that after the destroyer had left harbour he went up to the bridge as Officer of the Watch and was able to obtain good fixes on the island of Pantellaria which was on the starboard bow at about midnight. He gave the bearings to Lieutenant Burfield shortly after the latter relieved him as Officer of the Watch and then turned in on the after side of the forebridge. He said that he was shaken awake at 03.50 and went up on the bridge as Torpedo Control Officer. He saw the Captain was leaning over the compass and passing bearing of a bright occulting light on the port quarter to Sub Lieutenant Lack at the chart table via Midshipman Duncan. There was also a Signalman on the bridge. Asked what if could see anything Baillie-Grohman replied, 'Yes, I could see trees or shrubs, I could not make out which they were', and asked the Captain 'Are we not close to the beach?' Watkins replied, 'We are 3,000 yards.' Baillie-Grohman described what happened next:

> I then started to clean my binoculars and started to sweep with them from the starboard beam. When I came round ahead I saw a sandbank right ahead and I shouted to the Captain 'Sandbank ahead', jumped to the voice pipe and passed the order simultaneously with the Captain who had been in the chart table, 'Hard a starboard, stop starboard'. I heard the gyro compass clicking in and the ship began to heel, then there was a bump and several more bumps. After that the Captain ordered 'full speed astern'. I do not know what other orders the Captain gave.
>
> Lieutenant Burfield came on the bridge and the Captain said, 'We are aground Number One' and suggested throwing ready use ammunition overboard. I said that if we threw all our ammunition overboard and depth charges and torpedoes we might lighten her about a foot. I received an order to jettison ammunition aft and I went aft and took soundings abreast 'Y' gun. The depth was 8 feet. It was exactly 04.00 then.

Baillie-Grohman said that, at the time of her grounding *Havock* was drawing fifteen feet aft and was approximately on Ras el

Mihr point, about a cable from the beach and parallel to it and heading northwards. Upon receipt of the order to prepare to abandon ship Baillie-Grohman set about destroying confidential material as well as ensuring that *Havock*'s radar equipment was thoroughly wrecked.

After the Prosecutor had finished his examination, Commander Tothill tried to get more detail from Baillie-Grohman but he could add nothing more, although he did confirm that *Havock* was not equipped for echo sounding.[24]

Evidence of Lieutenant John Blackmore Burfield D.S.C., R.N.[25]

The next witness was Lieutenant John Burfield who had joined Havock as a Sub Lieutenant on 21 January 1939 and been promoted to Lieutenant in February 1940. While serving in the destroyer, Burfield had acted as Gunnery Control Officer, Navigating Officer and First Lieutenant being awarded a D.S.C. for his work during the Battle of Matapan.[26]

Lieutenant Burfield confirmed that *Havock* was carrying about fifty survivors from *Breconshire* and *Legion* including the latter's captain, Commander Jessel. Burfield said that before the ship sailed he had asked about the officers' duties suggesting that either he or Lieutenant Baillie-Grohman should do it. The Captain replied that Sub Lieutenant Lack, who had been Gunnery Control Officer in *Southwold*, would do the navigation and that Burfield would be the Gunnery Control Officer because Lack had no experience in a low-angle director and low angle firing. Watkins also made it clear that *Havock* would remain at full speed while rounding the coast of Tunisia in case the enemy was encountered. Burfield confirmed that the course intended would mean that the destroyer would be one and a half miles off the coast when passing Kelibia Light, Ras el Mihr and Cape Bon.

Burfield said that he then showed Sub Lieutenant Lack how to make out his notebook for the alterations of course round the Tunisian coast after which he checked the aft magazine which had been damaged in Malta and then turned in as he was due to go on watch at midnight. Upon relieving Lieutenant Baillie-Grohman at about midnight he used the fixes obtained off Pantellaria to confirm that the gyro compass was correct. Thereafter he remained in the director until the ship grounded. He said that the shore looked very close because the ship struck the sandbank and was able to confirm Baillie-Grohman's account of the grounding and subsequent destruction of the abandoned destroyer.

The Accused's friend, Commander Tothill, questioned Burfield about the damage to the starboard side of the after magazine asking if the ship had a cement patch on it. Burfield replied that near misses had blown in some of the ship's side causing some rivets to come out and a cement box was placed over the damaged area inside. This had necessitated the removal of the some of the aft magazine's ammunition stowage racks which meant that the ship had a reduced outfit of ammunition.

Tothill now asked why Burfield had suggested to the Captain that either Lieutenant Baillie-Grohman or himself should do the navigating and was told that Burfield felt that navigation through these difficult waters would require someone fully competent. Unfortunately, Watkins was not convinced. Tothill then asked, 'Why did you lay off the courses?' to which Burfield responded:

> I had been to assist Sub Lieutenant Lack in laying off the courses and assisted him by actually laying off myself and then explaining to him how to make out his notebook.

The President of the Court asked, 'Did you form the opinion that Sub Lieutenant Lack was not competent to make out his own notebook?', and Burfield replied 'I don't think he knew how to do it, he had no experience'. At this point the Prosecutor asked, 'Did you tell the Captain this fact?' to which Burfield replied, 'No'.

Commander Tothill resumed his cross-examination, asking if Burfield had at any time been the navigating officer of *Havock*. He replied, 'Yes, during the Crete evacuation, the Greek evacuation and at Matapan'. Burfield then went on to describe navigation in Greek waters as very difficult but despite this neither he nor Watkins had got into any difficulty.[27]

Evidence of Petty Officer Reginald Arthur William Stopher

Petty Officer Stopher, whose action station was on the 12-foot HA Director Rangefinder, confirmed that he had been asked by the Captain to range on a white light which was about 19,000 yards away. Thereafter he ranged at regular intervals on the Captain's orders down to about 5,000 yards until the ship grounded. He told the Court that the least ranges he obtained were 4,500 yards before grounding and 4,700 yards after grounding.[28]

Evidence of Able Seaman John Edmund Dodds

Able Seaman John Edmund Dodds, whose action station was in the wheelhouse, confirmed that after leaving Malta orders were given for 300 revolutions and this remained unchanged until the grounding. He said that at 03.50 we got a sudden order hard a starboard followed by stop both which was followed immediately by full astern.[29]

Evidence of Engine Room Artificer 3rd Class Reginald Rose

Engine Room Artificer 3rd Class Rose confirmed that both engines were doing 300 revolutions ahead and the state of the engines was not altered until after *Havock* had grounded. The Prosecutor asked what occurred during his watch and he replied:

> Nothing happened until 03.58 when there was a terrific vibration and after that the telegraphs were altered to stop both and full astern. I managed to get the starboard ahead throttle shut and it was getting very hot and the high-pressure boxes burnt out. I shut the starboard ahead throttle and got the astern throttle half open. Thereafter they were scalded rather badly and had to evacuate the engine room.

Asked how he knew the time was 03.58, Rose replied that he took the time from the engine room clock immediately he felt the first bump.[30]

Evidence of Electrical Artificer 3rd Class Sydney John Hurden Warne

Electrical Artificer 3rd Class Warne, who had been in charge of *Havock*'s electrical systems including the gyro compass, the fire control system and the high-pressure system, explained that orders for air raids at Malta were that that the boiler room was shut down. This meant that the dynamo had to be stopped and, after each air raid he had to restart the dynamo and the gyro compass. He said that he had told the Captain that once the gyro compass had been given two hours to run up it would be correct to with a degree and half.[31]

Warne was the last witness for the Prosecution and Commander
Tothill now called Lieutenant Commander Geoffrey Robert
Gordon Watkins to give evidence in his own defence.

Evidence of Lieutenant Command Geoffrey Robert Gordon Watkins, D.S.O., D.S.C., R.N.

Watkins related how he had contacted Vice-Admiral Malta
by signal requesting a replacement for Sub Lieutenant Orpen,
who had been killed on 22 March, specifying that the officer
would not only be a Qualified Gunnery Control Officer but
would also be competent to navigate a destroyer and, needless
to say, would hold a watch keeping certificate. Watkins said that
he had spoken personally to the Chief of Staff and the latter
had promised that this would be done. Asked what happened
when he had interviewed Sub Lieutenant Lack after he had
joined *Havock*, Watkins had enquired as to his capabilities as
a Gunnery Control Officer and navigator. Lack replied that he
had only experience of high-angle Directors as fitted in Hunt
class destroyers but that he had a full watch keeping certificate and that he had been R.N.V.R. proper, gone through his
full midshipman's time, namely two years at sea followed by a
year as a sub lieutenant. Watkins maintained that Lack had told
him that although he had not been navigating officer aboard
Southwold he was confident that he could undertake the duties
of navigating officer aboard *Havock*.

Tothill then asked Watkins to explain his reasons for not
employing any of his other officers as that navigator. The
Accused replied that his primary anxiety was the danger of
meeting enemy forces on this particular trip and consequently
he was more concerned about Lack's inexperience of low-angle
firing than his navigational short-comings. Watkins remarked
that Lieutenant Baillie-Grohman appeared to be too overwrought
to serve either as navigator or Gunnery Control Officer which
left Lieutenant Burfield as the only officer competent to man the
low-angle Director because Sub Lieutenant Spearin R.C.N.V.R
and the two midshipmen had little or no sea experience. The only
executive officer amongst the passengers aboard the destroyer
was Commander Jessel who had a broken foot and so could not
go on the bridge.

Tothill now turned his attention to the conference in Vice-
Admiral Malta's office before asking whether Watkins whether he

had any previous experience of ships entering an area of mined waters. The latter replied:

> I had been aboard *Janus* when *Hyperion* was mined on the northern edge of the same minefield which we referred to between Kelibia and Cape Bon and I was also present when *Neptune* was sunk; two other cruisers [*Aurora* and *Penelope*] damaged and *Kandahar* lost off Tripoli by going into a minefield. The experience was very vivid in my memory.

Thereafter Tothill took Watkins through the events of the night of 5/6 April allowing him to expand on the points made in his account, submitted on 1 December 1942, of the loss of *Havock*. The Accused was particularly dismissive of Lack's failure to get a transit but said that the fixes obtained off Pantellaria satisfied him that the gyro compass was correct – unlike the magnetic compass which must have been affected by the concussive effects of near misses while in harbour. Furthermore, there had been no time to check the magnetic compass by swinging the ship before she sailed. [32]

Watkins then gave a detailed account of the passage past Kelibia Light saying that:

> I had ranges taken at intervals approaching Kelibia Light and I was taking bearings myself and passing ranges and bearings to Lack. I glanced at the chart and found that we had been set in a little and I was surprised at there being no mention of this in the Pilot [House]. I altered course some 10 degrees in order to allow for this. I glanced at the chart later and found that we were on the correct line and resumed my original course. When it was time to turn, I asked Lack whether we were alright and he replied, 'Yes, but we are a little inside'.

Watkins said that he considered this was in order, altered to his new course and continued to pass ranges and bearings to Lack asking if we were alright to which he invariable replied 'Yes'. Watkins said that he had drawn courses to pass one and a half miles of the coast for the whole passage from Kelibia to Cape Bon and that this involved two or three alterations. He went on:

> The final alteration was the turn to port of 40 to 50 degrees when we turned onto this course I noticed what appeared to be wash of a ship ahead going right across

my course. I sensed something was wrong, went to the
chart table, saw the last plotted positions were heading
us straight for the land and sung out to Duncan, 'Hard a
starboard', following shortly afterwards by 'Full astern'.

He remembered that Lieutenant Baillie-Grohman had also seen
the danger shortly after he had and also gave some order which
Watkins did not remember. *Havock* struck as he was saying 'Full
astern'. Watkins added that he didn't think that any good was
ever done by going full astern because he discovered on looking at the screws over the side later that the blades had wrapped
themselves round the shaft.

Asked to describe the position of the ship at daylight on 6
April he said that he could see Cape Bon quite distinctly across
the Bay adding that, 'We were just clear of the sand spit of Ras
el Mihr and another twenty yards we would have been in deep
water'. Finally, Watkins denied that he could not recollect what
was said at that time but was emphatic that: 'I had made no mention to Lack of the possibilities of a Court Martial or whether I
should prove innocent or guilty.'[33]

In his cross examination, the Prosecutor asked why he had
then chosen Sub Lieutenant Lack to be the navigator despite his
lack of confidence and experience. Watkins merely re-iterated that
he had given his reasons to the Court already. The Deputy Judge-
Advocate told Watkins that he must answer the question and was
told: 'I employed him because there was no-one else to do so.'

The Prosecutor was not convinced and went onto explore the
decision in detail, questioning why, if Watkins had been confident
of Lack's competence, did he ask Lieutenant Burfield to assist
him. The Accused replied that he did so because he had already
given Lack an assurance that he would be assisted. Tothill then
turned to the discussion between Lieutenant Burfield and his
Commanding Officer regarding the duties of *Havock*'s officers
when the destroyer left Malta. Watkins remembered that Burfield
had suggested that either himself or Baillie-Grohman should
undertake the navigation duties in preference to a newly joined
Sub Lieutenant R.N.V.R. He added that he had made it clear to his
First Lieutenant that he had decided that he must have a reliable
Gunnery Control Officer in preference to a reliable navigator. The
Prosecutor now invited Watkins to look at page 860 of the *Navy
List* for December 1942 and asked him to tell the Court Lack's
rank at the time of joining *Havock*. Watkins expressed his surprise
upon discovering that Lack was a Temporary Sub Lieutenant
R.N.V.R. rather than regular R.N.V.R.[34]

When questioned about the need to take sounding during the approach to Kelibia Light because of shoals off Ras el Mihr and Cape Bon Watkins replied that he did not want to reduce to twelve knots if he used his Kelvin sounding machine. He remembered that the Mediterranean Pilot said that the shoals off Ras el Mihr and Cape Bon were the only navigational dangers when passing through these Tunisian waters.[35] He also remembered a conversation with Lieutenant Burfield during which the latter had asked if speed should be reduced on approaching Kelibia Light. He told Burfield that he intended to stay at full speed in case he encountered the enemy. The Prosecutor now asked if it was the case that having decided to maintain full speed, Watkins had also decided not to take soundings and received the reply:

You cannot go at full speed according to my sailing orders and take soundings and I had decided to take the risk unless bad weather or no lights prevented it.

He also admitted that he did not take soundings from the time he left Malta until the ship grounded and went on to confirm that Sub Lieutenant Lack was fully occupied receiving bearing and ranges from Midshipman Duncan and then plotting them on the chart. He remembered that Petty Officer Stopher was passing ranges to Kelibia Light but not that the range was under 2,000 yards. He agreed that if the range had been less than 2,000 yards he would have been considerably to the north of his intended course.[36]

Commander Dunbar asked if Sub Lieutenant Lack had informed him shortly after passing Kelibia Light that the ship was about half a mile from her intended course to which Watkins replied: 'No. I did not know. He said nothing of the sort. I looked at the chart and decided that the ship was about one tenth of a mile inside the intended course.'

Watkins remembered Lieutenant Baillie-Grohman saying to him, 'Are we not too close, Sir?' He went on to say that he was not unduly perturbed because he looked at the coast and it appeared to be about 3,000 yards and told Baillie-Grohman just that. He did not remember Lack telling him that the ship was inside his intended course but he did agree that the ranges and bearings were being passed to the Sub Lieutenant very rapidly.[37]

With regard to visibility at the time Watkins said that it was light and clear with a haze over the land and admitted that he was not looking out for the high sand hill at Ras el Mihr but looking at the shore frequently and could see the shore line clearly. The following exchanges[38] addressed the critical issue:

Destroyer at War

Dunbar: How did the coast appear to you?

Watkins: There were very marked features of the land up to a certain distance where it tailed off into what I think was a slight mist and looked like a bay ahead

Dunbar: Could you plainly see the shore line?

Watkins: Only as far as I said. Up to a certain point you could see clearly the high headlands and after that the land tailed off

Dunbar: Can you say on what approximate bearing relative to the ships' head that the land tailed off?

Watkins: Port bow as far as I can remember.

Dunbar: Why then did you alter course 50 degrees to port at the time?

Watkins: I don't think that it was exactly 50 degrees. My alteration still made me clear of the land I could see.

Dunbar: Then how was it that the ship went aground?

Watkins: I think that the coast ended as far as I could see at the time, while on my port bow, but this sandbank on which I think there was a slight mist merged into the bay behind.

Dunbar: Were you entirely satisfied with your position before you made your final alteration of course?

Watkins: I was.

Dunbar: You stated before that you had not checked the position of the ship yourself.

Watkins: Is that so. At what stage?

Dunbar: Immediately before final alteration of course.

Watkins: To the best of my recollection, no.

Dunbar: Would it be fair to suggest therefore that the moment you altered course to port, i.e. towards the land, you did so at thirty knots without ascertaining the position of your ship, without maintaining proper lookout, relying on the calculations of Lieutenant Lack who had informed you that he was not competent to carry out navigational duties?

Watkins: No, it would not be, because the ship was at Action Stations. All guns' crews looking out, all lookouts were correctly placed, the Signalman was on the bridge keeping a lookout. Lieutenant Baillie-Grohman was on the bridge, also keeping a look out, I myself was regarding the land. Furthermore, Lieutenant Lack by his evidence on page 85 had assured me that he was capable of

carrying out his duties. He did not warn me we were in
danger contrary to his evidence. This I will say, I did rely
on his work and this was a mistake.

Watkins, who said that he had no knowledge of what Lieutenant
Baillie-Grohman was observing, reiterated that he had never
heard Lack say anything to him just before the ship grounded adding that when he had last looked at the chart we were alright. He
added that, unfortunately, his only witness to that, Midshipman
Duncan, was in South Africa.

The Accused had no recollection of the interval between giving the order 'Hard a starboard' and the ship running aground
but agreed that this was under a minute. He estimated that, as
Havock had a clean bottom at the time and was in shallow water
she would have been doing about twenty-eight knots. After
the destroyer had grounded, he gave the order for *Havock* to be
abandoned and destroyed once Lieutenant Baillie-Grohman had
reported a sounding aft of eight feet.

In his penultimate question[39] Dunbar asked Watkins if he
could account for the fact that *Havock* went aground and the
Accused replied:

> I have had eleven months to consider this problem and
> my recollections are extremely vague on the whole
> set-up, but should say we must have turned inside prob-
> ably on to the wrong course, and nobody remembers
> what the ship's head I turned to – I don't know nor does
> anybody else – and that I must have continued to turn
> inside.
>
> Dunbar: Do you agree that at the high speed you were
> steaming it was impossible to plot ranges and bearing
> efficiently?
>
> Watkins: No, but I do agree that it was impossible to plot
> all ranges and bearings. I expected, and in fact told Lack,
> to write them down and then pick out the latest one for
> plotting.

Evidence of Lieutenant Commander Geoffrey William Haddon Paine R.N.

The witness, who was attached to HMS *Dryad*, the Navigation
School, told the President of the Court that he had been asked
by the Court to prepare two tracks on Chart 250 showing the
intended and most probable tracks of *Havock* from Fratelli Rocks

to Mahedia. Paine said that from the evidence of the Accused and the ranges given by the rangetaker the position of the grounding appeared to be approximately 027.5 degrees Kelibia Light, 2.35 miles. Unfortunately, the evidence that he had heard subsequently was insufficient to enable him to plot the approximate course from the time of leaving Malta but was able to mark out an area of probability on the chart which should contain the actual track of the destroyer.[40]

In his summing-up, Dunbar noted the conflict in the evidence given by Lieutenant Commander Watkins and Lieutenant Lack and the extreme difficulty under which the latter must have been working including the necessity of using his own watch for timing of alteration of courses. The evidence presented to the Court also suggested that as a result of the continuous strain to which he had been subjected, Watkins had become difficult to work with. For example, Lack may have felt himself pressurised into undertaking a task for which he knew lacked the necessary experience while Burfield neglected to pass on evidence of Lack's inexperience. Finally, the Prosecutor said that the Accused had hazarded his ship for the following reasons:

(a) That he omitted to cause soundings to be taken on the approaches to land in accordance with K.R. & A.I. Article 1164.

(b) That when causing H.M.S. *Havock* to alter course at a speed of thirty knots in a channel in close proximity to the land and an enemy minefield, he relied on and failed to check the calculations of Lieutenant Lack as to the position of the ship although that officer to his knowledge had little experience of navigation.

(c) That when in charge of the handling of H.M.S. *Havock* he failed to maintain a proper look-out and consequently to see that that ship standing into danger and that his negligence or default in these respects resulted in the stranding of that ship.

The Prosecutor then argued that the weight of evidence presented to the Court was more than sufficient to prove both charges beyond reasonable doubt.[41]

The Case for the Defence

Commander Tothill now presented the Accused's defence[42] saying that had *Havock* been equipped with echo sounding gear she could have made the passage at twenty-five knots without the necessity of reducing his speed to twelve knots so as to operate the Kelvin sounding machine. He argued that a reduction to twelve knots would have been at variance with Watkins' sailing orders which specified the need to use maximum speed so as to get as far west as possible by dawn. This was especially relevant because *Havock* had the weakest high AA armament of any of the three warships which had run the gauntlet during this period of maximum Axis air capability. He went on to argue that Watkins could reasonably expect to encounter E-boats in the vicinity of Pantellaria. The passage close to the Tunisian coast had been used on 29/30 March by the cruiser *Aurora*, seven days before and the Italians must have been made aware of this by their intelligence in Tunisia. Tothill said that the Accused had also decided that in the event of meeting Italian cruisers and destroyers off Tunisia, his greatest chance of safety lay in high speed.

He explained that, as Lieutenant Commander Watkins approached the land, he had to choose between either reducing speed to take soundings in accordance with K.R. & A.I. Article 1164 or attempt the passage at high speed without the aid of soundings. Bearing in mind the need to be as far west as possible by daybreak emphasised in his sailing orders and the prospect of encountering enemy forces in confined waters it was not unreasonable for Watkins to opt for a high-speed passage. Thus, he decided, that because he could take bearings and ranges from a charted light, the navigational dangers were outweighed by the prospect of enemy action. Thus, reducing speed to facilitate soundings was unjustified because accurate navigation was possible in the Kelibia-Cape Bon passage.

Having explained why Watkins had elected not to take soundings, Tothill addressed the issue of the replacement for Sub Lieutenant Orpen who had been killed in action on 22 March. Vice-Admiral Malta's Chief of Staff, Captain Wadham had provided a replacement from one of the ships that had been sunk, namely Sub Lieutenant Lack from *Southwold*. Tothill said that despite Lack's concerns at becoming *Havock*'s navigating officer, Watkins was convinced of the Sub Lieutenant's competency because of his possession of a full watch-keeping certificate and Wadham's assurance that he was competent to navigate. At this stage, it had been expected that *Havock* would be sailed eastward to Alexandria which would have been an easy passage which Watkins knew well. Consequently, *Havock*'s commanding officer had concentrated on getting his destroyer seaworthy rather than exploring the capabilities of his navigating officer – which was reasonable in view of the ease the eastward passage could be navigated.

Tothill reminded the Court that the order to sail west was only received during the forenoon of the day she sailed. As there was so little time before sailing, Watkins didn't have time to lay off courses and so had to ask Lack to do it with the assistance from Lieutenant Burfield. The former's lack of experience soon became apparent but, evidently, no one told the Accused. The Court was told that Lieutenant Commander Watkins had had more than a year's experience in the Mediterranean in command of a Fleet destroyer including some very intricate and danger-ous navigation during the evacuation from Greece. Hence it was inconceivable that with his previous experience in command he would have deliberately risked his ship in the hands of an offi-cer who had little or no experience of navigation. Unfortunately, force of circumstance had led the Accused to believe that Lack was competent.

Because Watkins had a high expectation of meeting the enemy it was essential that he should be in actual charge of the ship and not spend a large portion of his time checking navigation or have his head in the chart table. Tothill continued, saying that as Watkins had no reason to doubt the competence of Sub Lieutenant Lack there was no point in telling off another offi-cer to check his calculations and, in point of fact, the ranges and bearings were plotted correctly. On the last course before ground-ing the Accused asked Lack if the ship was alright and received the reply 'Yes, quite alright'. This could have been confirmed by Midshipman Duncan who was in South Africa. Apparently, Sub Lieutenant Lack's reply was made in spite of the fact that the last two positions plotted on this new course indicated that *Havock* was steering for shoal water.

The third statement on which the charges were based was that the Accused failed to maintain a proper lookout and consequently to see his ship was standing into danger. Commander Tothill reminded the Court that the sandbank was difficult to see in the moonlight in a flat calm. Full action lookouts had been placed in accordance with the orders made out by the First Lieutenant. The Accused's friend also wondered about the statements of the wit-nesses questioning their reliability after months of imprisonment under unhealthy and unpleasant conditions. Thus, he speculated that those concerned with the grounding may well have begun to reconstruct the circumstances to portray in their own minds everything that happened so as to exonerate themselves from blame. In such a scenario, their evidence would be at variance from reality in their subsequent meditations which may well have led them to give an unintentionally false account of events.

Finally, the Court was reminded that Watkins had won his command of a Fleet destroyer when serving as First Lieutenant of the large, modern Fleet destroyer *Janus* in the Mediterranean Fleet and, at the time he was selected, Watkins was the most junior officer to be given command of such a ship. Furthermore, for over a year he had held that command under conditions of the most arduous and dangerous service, and that when assessing the value of the evidence, Tothill asked the Court to bear in mind that with his record and experience Watkins was not likely to have committed the offences of negligence which were imputed.

Verdict

Despite Tothill's well-argued case, the Court found that the charge against the Accused of negligently, or by default hazarding and stranding HMS *Havock,* was proved and that the hazarding and stranding were due to the following reasons:

> When causing His Majesty's Ship HAVOCK to alter course at a speed of thirty knots in a channel in close proximity to the shore and an enemy minefield he failed (a) to verify the position of his ship (b) to ensure that the bearing and distance of Kelibia Light showed that it was safe for this alteration of course (c) to have the calculations of Temporary Sub Lieutenant Royston Henry Lack R.N.V.R. checked as to the position of the ship, even though he had little knowledge of this officer's capabilities in navigation.[43]

Pleas for Mitigation of Punishment

After the verdict had been delivered, Commander Tothill read out testimonials supporting Lieutenant Commander Watkins from:

> Rear Admiral P.J. Mack (23/1/1943): Lieutenant Commander Robin Watkins D.S.C. R.N. was executive officer of H.M.S. JANUS in my flotilla from the commencement of the war until about February 1941. Both during his time in JANUS and HAVOCK I had considerable experience of him and formed a high opinion of his capabilities as a leader of men.

The whole of his war service up to the time he was taken prisoner was, from my personal experience, of a very arduous and gallant nature.

Captain H. St. L. Nicholson, late Captain (D), DF2 Mediterranean Flee (13/1/43): Lieutenant G.R.G. Watkins D.S.O., D.S.C., R.N. served under my command in the Second Destroyer Flotilla, Mediterranean Fleet, as Lieutenant in command of H.M.S. HAVOCK from February 1941 to February 1942.

Throughout this time, which was his first experience in command, he showed himself to be a capable destroyer Captain, handling his ship with determination and judgement in many difficult circumstances. He specially distinguished himself at the Battle of Matapan, the evacuation of Greece and Crete, the Syrian campaign and the supply of Tobruk.

Although he was one of my junior Captains my personal knowledge of his ability and enthusiasm gave me confidence that he could do all that was required of him and not fail to act on his own initiative should circumstances demand it.[44]

Rear Admiral Irvine Glennie (17/2/43): Lieutenant Commander G.R.G. Watkins D.S.O., D.S.C., R.N. served with me in the Eastern Mediterranean from the date of my hoisting my flag as Rear Admiral (D) on 12 May, until he had the misfortune to lose his ship H.M.S. HAVOCK by grounding.

After a period of service as First Lieutenant of H.M.S. JANUS in the Eastern Mediterranean he won his own command in February 1941 upon the same station, and retained it with distinction throughout a period of some fourteen months of almost continuous active operations commencing with the Battle of Matapan for which he was awarded the D.S.C., followed by the evacuation of Greece (mentioned in Despatches), the evacuation of Crete, the Syrian Campaign, the Tobruk siege supply line and finally the remarkable convoy action of 22 March 1942 for which he was awarded the D.S.O. Throughout this arduous period as a young Commanding Officer he was ever resolute and willing.

Vice-Admiral H.D. Pridham-Wippell (27/1/1943): Lieutenant Commander G.R.G. Watkins D.S.O., D.S.C., R.N. served under my direct notice in the

Mediterranean from May 1940 onwards while I was Rear Admiral commanding 1st Battle Squadron, Vice-Admiral Light Forces and Vice-Admiral Commanding 1st Battle Squadron.

I had, and have the highest opinion of his capabilities and it was through my recommendation that he was selected for a command on the station in a vacancy which occurred while he was First Lieutenant of the JANUS, a selection which he fully justified by his subsequent conduct in command.

His ship, the HAVOCK, was badly damaged when escorting the March 1942 convoy to Malta. At the time that sufficient repairs had been completed for her to be reported as fit to be sailed I was Commander-in-Chief. It was appreciated that conditions in Malta at that period were such that little chance existed for the rest necessary for the personnel of the HAVOCK nor any likelihood of the replacement of casualties, but the probability of further final damage to the ship by remaining there, necessitated her sailing at the earliest possible date.[45]

Admiral of the Fleet Sir Andrew Cunningham (via the Second Sea Lord Vice Admiral W.J. Whitworth 17/2/43): In a letter I received from Admiral of the Fleet Sir Andrew Cunningham a month or two ago he told me that Lieutenant Commander Watkins, the Commanding Officer of H.M.S. HAVOCK, had been through an extremely trying time prior to going to Malta and while he was at Malta and Admiral Cunningham expressed the hope that this might be taken into account by members of the Court in the event of a Court Martial taking place.

Admiral Cunningham also said in his letter that after Lieutenant Commander Watkins had had a good rest he would be glad to have him as Commanding Officer of a destroyer in his command.[46]

Clearly, despite his youth and short time in command of *Havock*, Lieutenant Commander Watkins had made a considerable impression on his superiors including Sir Andrew Cunningham. Commander Tothill then made a plea for mitigation of punishment arguing that the extreme strain to which Watkins and his crew had been subjected to in the months leading up to the stranding had been a contributory cause of the ships' loss. He noted that Chief Petty Officer Panrucker could give an account of the operation on which the Accused was employed the previous night to sailing and which accounted for the condition of extreme fatigue. By permission of the Court, Panrucker was allowed to give his evidence and this was granted. The Chief Petty Officer said that:

> Approximately 18.30 on the Saturday evening before we sailed, a party was detailed to take an oiling lighter to Calafrana. We left the ship approximately 18.30 to 19.00 and got away from the Harbour about 22.00. We arrived at Calafrana between 05.00 and 06.00 the following morning. On the way, we were attacked by enemy aircraft. We arrived at Calafrana to rejoin the ship at about 08.00. During that time raids were still on and were continuous during the whole day. The ship sailed at 20.00 that night.

When asked what opportunities there were for rest and sleep during this night before sailing, Panrucker replied, 'None at all'.[47]

The Sentence and beyond

Lieutenant Commander Geoffrey Robert Gordon Watkins, D.S.O., D.S.C., R.N. was sentenced to be reprimanded[48] despite support received from luminaries such as Sir Andrew Cunningham. The sentence was not particularly severe and would not necessarily have precluded a further period in command. However, there can be little doubt that the court martial and its outcome must have been a severe emotional blow and Watkins never had another command. After time at the Admiralty's Operations Division, Watkins joined the staff of Rear Admiral McGrigor commanding the 1st Cruiser Squadron and flying his flag in the 8-inch gun cruiser *Norfolk*.

On 11/12th January 1945, the cruisers *Norfolk* and *Bellona* and the destroyers *Onslow*, *Orwell* and *Onslaught* encountered a German convoy off Egersund, Norway, sinking the merchant ships *Bahia Camarones* (8,551 grt) and *Charlotte* (4,404 grt) and the minesweeper *M 273*. McGrigor's squadron withdrew under fighter cover from the escort carriers *Trumpeter* and *Premier* which frustrated an attack by torpedo carrying Ju 88s from II./KG 26. For his part in this successful operation Watkins was mentioned in Despatches.

Watkins served a post-war commission aboard the cruiser *Leander* in the Mediterranean and retired from the Navy in 1948 after twenty-five years' service. His wife Daphne predeceased him in 1989 and he crossed the bar in 1993 then aged eighty-ywo. They had three sons.[49]

What if *Havock* had escaped to Gibraltar?

At the time of her stranding, *Havock* was one of just four remaining Hero class destroyers afloat. Thus, on 10 April 1940 the flotilla leader *Hardy* had been damaged by 5-inch shellfire from German destroyers in Ofotfjord and beached in position 68°23'N, 17°06'E. A little later that morning *Hunter*, which had also been damaged by German destroyers' 5-inch gunfire, sank after collision with *Hotspur* in position 68°20'N, 17°04'E. During the early summer the seven survivors returned to the Mediterranean only for *Hostile* to be mined and sunk, in position 36°53'N, 11°19'E at 0317 on 23 August 1940 when eighteen miles south-east of Cape Bon, Tunisia. The next to go was *Hyperion* which was torpedoed at 01.56 on 22 December 1940, when twenty-four miles east of Cape Bon in position 37°40'N, 11°31'E by Italian submarine *Serpente*. *Hyperion* was taken in tow and later scuttled by *Janus* aboard which Watkins was serving as First Lieutenant.

The heavy air attacks experienced during the evacuation of Crete and Greece were particularly dangerous for these destroyers with their inadequate HA armaments and, unsurprisingly, at 06.25 on 29 May1941, *Hereward* was sunk five miles south of Crete, in position 35°20'N, 26°20'E by German air attack during an operation to evacuate Commonwealth troops from Heraklion. By now it was clear that, like all surviving A to I class destroyers, *Havock* and her sisters had become outmoded because of their poor AA capability. Furthermore, neither she nor her three surviving sisters had been properly refitted since completion and consequently they were becoming mechanically unreliable. In addition, the rivets popped and plating dished by the concussive effects of too many near misses meant that these ships were in urgent need of dockyard attention with *Hero* being in a particularly poor condition.

As related above, *Havock* was badly damaged during the Second Battle of Sirte, and the question remains as to why, with her weak AA armament, she was sailed westward at a time when Axis air power was particularly rampant. One possible answer is that, by 5 April it was clear that the inadequately maintained destroyer had accumulated so much damage that it could only be fully repaired in a British shipyard. Assuming this to be the case, it is interesting to speculate as to the future career of *Havock* had she managed to escape to Gibraltar and been repaired instead of becoming stranded off Kelibia in position 36°48'N, 11°08'E on 6 April 1942. *Hasty*, the final unit of the class to be lost during the war, was damaged by a torpedo from the German E-boat *S.55* at

05.25 hours south-east of Crete, when in position 34°10′N, 22°00′E, while escorting the *Vigorous* convoy. Her sister *Hotspur* had the melancholy task of scuttling the crippled destroyer.

Two Hero class destroyers, *Hero* and *Hotspur*, survived the war and their employment after leaving the Mediterranean gives an insight into *Havock*'s role had she survived the journey westward in April 1942. During 1943, both of these obsolete and outmoded Fleet destroyers were converted to escort destroyers with improved weaponry and increased depth charge throwers and depth charge stowage. The DCT and Rangefinder on the bridge were replaced with a lantern housing Type 271 surface warning. The AA armament was upgraded to six single 20mm guns, with two fitted in the bridge wings, two between the funnels and two abreast the former searchlight platform. A tall vertical HF/DF mast was added aft which necessitated the removal of the 12-pounder AA gun installed in lieu of the after set of torpedo tubes. Had she survived, *Havock* would undoubtedly have been converted to an escort destroyer along the lines of *Hero* and *Hotspur* and would have been employed escorting North Atlantic convoys. In 1943, *Hero* was gifted to the R.C.N., being renamed *Chaudiere*, and was in such bad shape by 1945 that she was paid off for disposal in August of that year and broken up in 1950.

Hotspur remained operational as a training ship after 1945 but was slated for demolition in 1948. However, on 23 November of that year she was sold to the Dominican Republic being renamed *Trujillo* in honour of the Dictator who ruled that nation from 1930. General Trujillo was assassinated in 1961 and the following year *Trujillo* was renamed *Duarte* and as such remained on the Dominican Navy list until 1972 when she was sold for demolition. The career of the last of *Havock*'s sisters was finally at an end after thirty-five years afloat.[50]

Particulars of HMS *Havock*

Ordered:	13 December 1934
Laid down:	15 May 1935, by William Denny & Brothers, Dumbarton
Launched:	7 July 1936
Completed:	16 January 1937
Displacement:	1,350 tons standard
	1,860 tons full load
Dimensions:	323 feet (overall) x 32 feet 3 inches x 8 feet 6 inches/10 feet 9 inches full load
Machinery:	Two-shaft geared turbines, 34,000 shaft horse power = 35.5 knots as designed/31.5 knots full load
Oil Fuel:	455 tons
Endurance:	5,300 miles at 15 knots
Armament:	As completed: Four 4.7-inch (4 x 1, 200 rounds per gun); eight 0.5-inch AA (2 x 4, 10,000 rounds per mounting); four 0.303-inch Lewis (2,000 rounds per gun) guns; eight 21-inch (2 x 4, 8 torpedoes) torpedo tubes; two depth charge throwers and one depth charge rail, 20 depth charges
	In mid-June 1941 her armament had been modified to: Four 4.7-inch (4 x 1); one 3-inch AA (in lieu of after torpedo tubes); two 20mm Breda AA (2 x 1; one on either side of the flag deck); two 20mm Oerlikon AA (2 x 1; one on either side of the searchlight platform); eight 0.5-inch AA (2 x 4; to port and starboard between funnels) and three twin 0.303-inch Lewis guns (abaft the 3-inch gun) and four 21-inch (1 x 4) torpedo tubes; two depth charge throwers and one depth charge rail, 20 depth charges
Complement:	137 peace/146 war

Appendix II

Report of Proceedings of HMS *Havock* during the Action off Narvik, 10 April 1940

N arvik was a baptism of fire for the crew of *Havock*, very many of whom were 'Hostilities Only' sailors and many had not even been to sea when they joined the ship after her Chatham refit. Eye-witness accounts are many and varied in history, but some are more valid than others – and so it is with Lieutenant Commander Courage's official report (ADM199/473, pp.77-80) of the first battle, submitted to Rear Admiral (D), HMS *Woolwich* and dated 27 April 1940:

REPORT OF PROCEEDINGS OF H.M.S. *"HAVOCK"* DURING THE ACTION OFF NARVIK 10 APRIL 1940

(1)   H.M.S. *Havock* was in company with Captain D.2 in *Hardy*, *Hotspur*, *Hostile* and *Hunter* during the night of April 9th-10th and was the fourth ship in line.

(2)   The weather was overcast, with frequent squalls of snow and the visibility varied between 5 and 2 cables.

(3)   The passage up the fjord was without incident except that touch was lost once due to a sudden alteration of course, but was regained by the use of Asdics.

(4)   At 0426 the snowstorm cleared and the south side of the harbour of Narvik and some merchant ships were disclosed.

(5)   Captain D. entered the harbour between the British SS *North Cornwall* and the remainder of the merchant ships, and opened fire with guns and torpedoes. *Hunter* followed and as soon as she was clear *Havock* followed her. Fire was opened with the guns at a destroyer alongside a merchant ship whose gun-flashes could be seen, and with torpedoes at merchant ships and a destroyer at anchor. Three torpedoes only were fired as *Hunter* appeared to have hit all the merchant ships in sight, and a second destroyer was not

seen until the sights were past. All torpedoes were heard to hit and the destroyer vanished. As the enemy gun-fire was getting hot and they had the advantage of light I increased speed and cleared out.

(6)   Just before entering the harbour two columns of water were seen ascending just inshore of the *Hunter* and it is thought that they were caused by badly aimed torpedoes from an enemy destroyer.

(7)   While leaving the harbour I passed close to *North Cornwall*, and one of the guards there fired on the bridge with a revolver. He was silenced by a Lewis gun.

(8)   Firing now increased from the harbour and *Havock* was straddled but not hit. Fire was returned by the after group and an explosion seen in an enemy ship, while the foremost group bombarded the shore with H.E. Shell from which quarter a hot fire from rifles and machine guns was arriving.

(9)   Once clear of the harbour *Havock* passed backwards and forwards across the entrance engaging ships inside with gunfire at 3,000 to 4,000 yards. Spotting was almost impossible owing to smoke but blind ladders were used and success hoped for.

(10) At 0.507 a number of torpedoes were seen approaching from the harbour and were avoided by going full speed ahead or astern. One torpedo appeared to pass underneath the ship, and if it was fitted with a magnetic pistol the de-gaussing circuit undoubtedly saved the ship. I then withdrew out of torpedo range and as ships were interfering with each other's fire formed astern of Captain D, who made a signal 'Follow Round' at 05.14. By this time, we were 6,000 yards from the harbour.

(11) At 05.35 we passed the harbour for a second time but were not fired at and then *Hardy* led towards Rombaks Fjord.

(12) At 05.40 Three German destroyers were sighted bearing 350 degrees apparently coming from Herjangs Fjord. Captain D. ordered 30 knots and "Withdraw" to the westward at the same time opening fire on the second ship. I turned to follow him and engaged the leading ship at 10,000 yards. *Hardy* made an enemy report of a cruiser and two destroyers and in the bad light this looked possible. The enemy however appeared to turn away under our fire.

(13) At 05.58 two more enemy destroyers appeared ahead and opened fire. *Havock* was slightly to port of *Hardy* and I

engaged the left-hand ship but as soon as I saw the leader was not fired at shifted to her. The range was about 3,000 yards, and fire soon took effect, the third salvo hitting aft and caused a violent explosion. She ceased fire with her main armament but continued to fire machine guns, an incendiary bullet of which set fire to ready-use cordite locker at A Gun.

(14)   As we passed her I ordered the remaining torpedoes to be fired but they unfortunately passed astern due to an under-estimation of the enemy speed.

(15)   Just before *Havock* fired torpedoes enemy torpedoes were seen approaching on the surface and easily avoided by combing the tracks. *Hardy* however which was steering more to port appeared to be hit by one as there was a high column of smoke from her after boiler room and much flame from the funnel. Actually from accounts afterwards this was a salvo of shell, and she rapidly lost way and passed astern.

(16)   As I was now at the head of the line and no enemy appeared to be to the westward of us. I turned to Starboard 180 degrees and closed the enemy astern, opening fire at 10,000 yards.

(17)   During this run I passed *Hunter* who was on fire and losing speed and *Hotspur* whose steering gear seemed to be out of action.

(18)   Unfortunately the order to open fire could not be complied with as both the foremost guns were out of action, and having no torpedoes I decided that it would be folly to close the range any further, and I turned to starboard passing close astern of *Hostile* who was making smoke.

(19)   At this moment the two leading enemy appeared to be unhit and were firing well placed salvoes, while two in the rear were very ragged. *Havock* was again straddled but not hit except by splinters. While withdrawing the after group continued the engagement, until the enemy was lost in smoke.

(20)   While running to the west *Hotspur* was observed to collide with *Hunter* who appeared to be in a bad way, but the former got clear.

(21)   Once clear of the smoke I drew up alongside *Hostile*, and both foremost guns being reported again in use, followed her back into the action to relieve the pressure on *Hotspur*. Fire was opened at 10,000 yards and continued until *Hotspur* was out of range when all ships withdrew. The leading enemy appeared to be still untouched and were straddling

effectively while we were turning. They made no attempt however to close the range, after we had slowed to *Hotspur's* speed.

(22) On the way down the fjord a merchant ship was sighted which proved to be the German SS *Rauenfels*, and *Hostile* stopped her with a shot and ordered me to examine her. I fired another round into her bow and she stopped and the crew hurriedly abandoned ship. I stopped and picked them up while the ship slowly drifted to the beach. I sent an armed boat over but she was burning furiously and I was uncertain as to whether she had used her W/T to call her friends. I decided not to risk the loss of my party and ordered their return. When the boat was hoisted I fired two H.E. into her to hasten the fire and went ahead. The result was certainly startling, as the German literally erupted and a column of flame and debris rose over 3,000 feet as testified both by *Hostile* and *Hardy's* survivors to the west who saw it over the mountains that height. Fortunately, no damage was sustained in *Havock* but some damage to the hull was done. Judging from the fragments picked up she contained all the reserve ammunition and torpedoes for the destroyer flotilla, and also the Narvik minefield.

(23) *Havock* then joined *Hostile* off Tranøy Light.

A later post-war attachment to *Courage's* report contains extracts from B.R. 1840 (1) German Naval History Series and lays out the situation of the German destroyers on 10 April and their subsequent fate and damage after the action of that day. Time differences are caused by use of German time as opposed to Greenwich Mean Time.

German Destroyers at dawn 10 April:
Lüdemann and *Künne* oiling alongside Jan Wellem
Heidkamp (Cmdre Bonte) & *Schmitt* at anchor in the inner harbour
Roeder inner harbour
Roeder diary states 'am relieving *Schmitt* from 04.00 as AJS Patrol in the harbour entrance until dawn'. *Roeder* entered harbour at about 05.00.
At 05.30 *Heidkamp* and *Schmitt* were torpedoed in the inner harbour. *Roeder* was hit and set on fire and abandoned ship.

Lüdemann hit and had to flood after magazine. *Künne* engines temporarily out of action owing to concussion from torpedo which hit *Schmitt*.

Ballangen Group. *Thiele* and *Arnim* 1st D.F.

Herjangs Group. *Zenker, Koellner* and *Giese*

Damage and casualties.

Schmitt	Sunk 50 dead
Heidkamp	Sinking 81 dead
Roeder	5 hits unseaworthy, 13 dead
Lüdemann	2 hits unseaworthy, 13 dead, magazine partly flooded
Künne	Splinter damage, engines usable
Thiele	Several hits, 2 guns out of action, fire, magazine flooded, 2 dead
Arnim	5 hits, boiler out of action, barely seaworthy
Zenker, Koellner and Giese	undamaged, half ammunition gone

German destroyers had planned to return to Germany on the 11th

Copy of W/T (Wireless Transmission) Log of HMS *Havock*, Communications during the First Battle of Narvik, 10 April 1940

D2 is HMS *Hardy* (2nd DF Leader). There is darkness, a considerable snowstorm, very poor visibility with ships following stern light of line ahead, tension mounts.

UK Time	To	From	Signal
0044	2nd DF	D2	Proceed at 12 knots
0057	2nd DF	D2	Turn in succession to 044 degrees
0106	2nd DF	D2	Proceed at 20 knots
0131	2nd DF	D2	Turn in succession to 060 degrees
0146	2nd DF	D2	Proceed at 12 knots
0215	*Hotspur*	D2	Are you alright
0216	D2	*Hotspur*	Yes, you are just out of sight
0221	2nd DF	D2	My course and speed 075 degrees, 12 knots
0232	*Hotspur*	D2	I am about to pass Hamnes Holm abeam to starboard
0233	D2	*Hotspur*	In touch
0234	2nd DF	D2	Turn in succession to 095 degrees
0239	*Hotspur*	D2	Are you in touch
0240	D2	*Hotspur*	Yes
0242	2nd DF	D2	Good luck, let them have it
0249	2nd DF	D2	Make your call signs if in touch

Appendix III *(Continued)*

Appendix III *(Continued)*

UK Time	To	From	Signal
0250			Call Signs
0330	2nd DF	D2	Turn in succession to 080 degrees
0342	2nd DF	D2	Turn in succession to 110 degrees
0344	2nd DF	D2	Am steering for entrance of Narvik harbour
0346	2nd DF	D2	Form on a line of bearing 280 degrees
0350	2nd DF	D2	Proceed at 6 knots
0352	2nd DF	D2	Turn together 20 degrees to starboard
0356	2nd DF	D2	Hostile in touch
0359	2nd DF	D2	Turn together 30 degrees to port
0405	2nd DF	D2	Stop engines
0406	2nd DF	D2	Proceed at 10 knots turn together 40 degrees to port
0408	2nd DF	D2	Stop engines
0410	2nd DF	D2	Go astern
0411	2nd DF	D2	Stop engines
0412	2nd DF	D2	Turn together to 010 degrees proceed at 10 knots
0413	2nd DF	D2	Point ship to 010 degrees
0415	2nd DF	D2	Turn together to 010 degrees proceed at 10 knots
0416	2nd DF	D2	Proceed at 6 knots
0418	2nd DF	D2	Turn together to 090 degrees
0422	2nd DF	D2	Am entering south side of harbour
0423	2nd DF	D2	Am turning to port follow me round
0424	2nd DF	D2	Proceed at 12 knots
0426	2nd DF	D2	Alarm bearing 010 degrees
0428	2nd DF	D2	Am turing to port, stand by to fire, torpedoes starboard side
0429	2nd DF	D2	Near ship is British

Appendix III *(Continued)*

UK Time	To	From	Signal
0439	2nd DF	D2	Am turning to northward
0431	2nd DF	D2	Am going astern
0441	*Havock*	D2	Come and fire torpedoes
0442	D2	*Hotspur*	Nothing to northward
0444	*Hotspur*	D2	Fire your torpedoes into the harbour
0448	*Hotspur*	D2	Stop making smoke
0456	2nd DF	D2	Report number of torpedoes fired
	D2	*Hotspur*	Four
	D2	*Hunter*	Five
	D2	*Havock*	Five [Actually 3 with 5 left]
0459	D2	*Hostile*	None
0501	2nd DF	D2	Report damage to enemy seen
0503	D2	*Hotspur*	Two merchant ships sinking
0504	D2	*Hostile*	Merchant ship and Destroyer observed to be hit by 4.7 shell
0505	D2	*Hunter*	Five torpedoes hit, damage to enemy destroyer not observed
0506	D2	*Havock*	Destroyer hit by 4.7 shell
0507	*Hostile*	D2	If you can find a suitable warship target, send four torpedoes in
0509	2nd DF	D2	Look out for torpedo tracks
0514	2nd DF	D2	Stand by to follow round again, keep a sharp lookout for torpedoes
0515	2nd DF	D2	Stop making smoke
0520	*Hostile*	D2	Have you fired any torpedoes yet
0521	2nd DF	D2	Proceed at 20 knots
0522	D2	*Hostile*	Intend to fire torpedoes when going round this time
0531			All ships made call signs
0533	*Hostile*	D2	Follow round, don't go wrong way each time

Appendix III *(Continued)*

Appendix III *(Continued)*

UK Time	To	From	Signal
0535	2nd DF	D2	Proceed at 12 knots
0537	2nd DF	D2	Proceed at 15 knots
0541	D2	*Hotspur*	Look out for floating torpedo to the westward of the shoal
0545	2nd DF	D2	Proceed at 20 knots
0550	2nd DF	D2	Proceed at 30 knots
0553	2nd DF	D2	Withdraw
0556	2nd DF	D2	Keep on engaging the enemy
			[This was the last signal made by D2]
0558	D2	*Hostile*	Three Destroyers leaving harbour
0559			Signal passed in by *Hunter*. No reply from Hardy Only *Hostile* and *Havock* make call signs

Source: Frank Hall, Leading Signaller of *Havock*, who copied the W/T Log and sent it to David Goodey on 20 January 1987.

Appendix IV

HMS *Havock* Ship Movements

January 26, 1937	At Chatham
February 7, 1937	Arrived Portland
February 8, 1937	Left Portland (2nd DF Med. Fleet)
February 12, 1937	Arrived Gibraltar to Refuel before continuing to Malta
March 5, 1937	Arrived Gibraltar
March 25, 1937	Arrived Tunis
April 1, 1937	Arrived Malta
April 14, 1937	Malta
May 3, 1937	Left Malta-Nyon Patrols
May 7, 1937	Arrived Gibraltar
May 14, 1937	Arrived Cadiz
May 24, 1937	Arrived Gibraltar
May 31, 1937	Off Malaga
June 8, 1937	Off Malaga
June 12, 1937	Departed Gibraltar for patrol off Malaga
June 19, 1937	Arrived Malta. Docked June 22 to July 2
July 17, 1937	At Malta
August 12, 1937	Departed Malta
August 14, 1937	Arrived Valencia
August 20, 1937	Barcelona and Marseilles
August 22, 1937	Barcelona and Palma
August 28, 1937	Valencia
August 31, 1937	Departed Valencia
September 1, 1937	Reported. 'Attacked by S/M in 38.46N, 00.31E; am hunting S/M'
September 2, 1937	Arrived Gibraltar
September 8, 1937	Arrived Gibraltar. Left Sept 10, Valencia 11, Barcelona 12, Palma 14
September 20, 1937	Arrived Malta. There to October 12
October 14, 1937	Departed Malta for Gibraltar
October 17, 1937	Arrived Gibraltar
Oct 19-Nov 13, 1937	Remained at Gibraltar for refit
November 17-20, 1937	Departed Gibraltar following refit on 17th, returned 20th

December 13, 1937	Departed Gibraltar
December 18, 1937	Arrived at Oran on the North Mediterranean Coast of Africa
December 23, 1937	Arrived back at Malta for Christmas
January 1, 1938	Departed Malta for Skyros
January 2, 1938	Arrived at Port Vatika
January 6, 1938	Arrived at Port Trebuki
January 7, 1938	Arrived at Mudros
January 9, 1938	Arrived at Port Trebuki
January 12, 193	Arrived at Malta
Feb 18-March 10, 1938	Docked for three weeks
March 11, 1938	Departed Malta
March 13, 1938	Arrived Port Kalloni
March 15, 1938	Departed Port Kalloni
March 17, 1938	Arrived Malta
March 19, 1938	Departed Malta
March 29, 1938	Arrived Gibraltar
April 12, 1938	Departed Gibraltar on patrol
April 16, 1938	Arrived at Gibraltar. When berthing fouled corner of wharf sustaining damage. Docked for three weeks.
May 6-9, 1938	Departed Gibraltar on the 6th returned 9th
May 24, 1938	Departed Malta on patrol (with *Hotspur* to relieve *Hereward* and *Hyperion* on 27th)
June 3-9, 1938	Arrived Gibraltar on the 3rd and left again on the 9th.
June 12, 1938	Arrived Malta.
July 5, 1938	Departed Malta for exercises.
July 7, 1938	Arrived Navarin until Jul 14
July 28, 1938	Arrived Hvar
July 30, 1938	Arrived Malta
August 7, 1938	Arrived Gibraltar
August 16, 1938	At Gibraltar
August 24-27, 1938	Escorted HM submarine *Snapper* from Gibraltar to Malta
September 15, 1938	Departed Malta for autumn cruise
September 17, 1938	Arrived Phalerum Bay
September 22, 1938	Arrived Alexandria, Egypt
October 24, 1938	Departed Alexandria
October 27, 1938	Arrived Malta
November 8-14, 1938	Docking for defect repairs. Stayed until December 27, 1938
February 6, 1939	Arrived Palma

February 7, 1939	Arrived Gandia
February 8, 1939	Arrived Barcelona
February 9, 1939	Arrived Marselles
February 12, 1939	Arrived Barcelona
February 13, 1939	Arrived Palma
February 21, 1939	Arrived Gandia
February 22, 1939	Arrived Marseilles. A.O. of 22.2 stated 'All visits to Barcelona are cancelled until further orders'
February 24, 1939	Arrived Palma
February 26, 1939	Arrived Gibraltar
February 28, 1939	Departed Gibraltar for exercises, returned 10.3
March 20, 1939	Departed Gibraltar
March 23, 1939	Arrived Ajaccio
March 31, 1939	Arrived Sorrento
April 4, 1939	Arrived Malta. Ordered, 'To proceed to Haifa to assist in prevention of illicit immigration of Jews'
April 26, 1939	Departed Malta
April 29, 1939	Arrived Haifa
May 13, 1939	Departed Haifa
May 14, 1939	Arrived Alexandria
June 17, 1939	Departed Alexandria
June 29, 1939	Arrived Poros
July 5, 1939	Departed Poros
July 10, 1939	Departed Mykoni
July 12, 1939	Arrived Alexandria
July 31, 1939	Departed Alexandria for Malta
August 3, 1939	Arrived Malta
August 9, 1939	Arrived Gibraltar
August 13, 1939	Arrived Sheerness for Chatham.
August 15, 1939	Chatham refit to August 22
August 26, 1939	Departed Sheerness
August 29, 1939	Arrived Gibraltar. Ordered to Freetown with *Hotspur, Hunter* and *Hyperion*
August 30, 1939	Departed Gibraltar for Freetown (S Atlantic Command)
September 4, 1939	Arrived Freetown
September 5, 1939	Departed Freetown for Rio de Janeiro with *Hotspur*
September 13, 1939	Arrived Rio de Janeiro
September 21, 1939	Departed Rio de Janeiro
October 12, 1939	Arrived Montevideo, River Plate

October 14, 1939	Departed Montevideo
October 23, 1939	Arrived Buenos Aires
October 25, 1939	Departed Buenos Aires for Trinidad (America and West Indies Command)
October 31, 1939	Arrived Pernambuco
November 1, 1939	Departed Pernambuco and reported port engine out of action on passage to Trinidad
November 9, 1939	Arrived Freetown
November 16, 1939	Departed Freetown
November 27, 1939	Arrived Gibraltar
December 12, 1939	Departed Gibraltar for Chatham. Defects repair estimated two months
December 16, 1939	Arrived Sheerness
December 19, 1939	Chatham refit, completed March 16, 1940, ready March 18
March 25, 1940	Arrived Plymouth
March 27, 1940	Arrived Scapa
April 2, 1940	Departed for Sollum Voe
April 29, 1940	Arrived Leith
May 4, 1940	At Rosyth
May 9, 1940	Departed Rosyth
May 13, 1940	Based Harwich
May 16, 1940	Arrived Plymouth (15th DF, Med Fleet)
May 20, 1940	Departed Gibraltar
May 26, 1940	Arrived Alexandria (2nd DF Med) – June 11 Boom Patrols
June 11, 1940	To July 20 Alexandria area
July 11, 1940:	Departed Alexandria MF1 to Malta
July 13, 1940	Arrived Malta, immediately departed for Alexandria
July 19, 1940	Battle of Cape Spada. Sinking of the *Bartolomeo Colleoni*. Bomb damage
July 27, 1940	Arrived Suez, docked there August 7, completed September 15
September 19, 1940	Departed Port Said. In and out of Alexandria until November 6
September 28, 1940	Operation MB5 to Malta and return for October 1
October 2, 1940	Sank Italian submarine *Berillo*
October 8, 1940	MF3 to Malta. Remained until October 16
October 24, 1940	Departed Alexandria with AN5 to Aegean. Operation *MAQ2*

November 6, 1940	Departed Alexandria with MW3 to Malta. Operation *MB8*
November 10, 1940	Departed Malta with fleet as screen for Swordfish attack on Taranto
November 14, 1940	Arrived Alexandria. Remained in that area until December 16
November 25, 1940	ME3 from Malta. Convoy also to Greece
December 13, 1940	In collision with battleship *Valiant*
December 22, 1940	Arrived Malta, repairs to February 11, 1941
February 19, 1941	Departed Malta with MC8 to Alexandria
February 23, 1941	Departed Alexandria. In and out of Alexandria until December 1941
March 29, 1941	Battle of Cape Matapan Action. Sank *Carducci*
April 1, 1941	Departed Alexandria with troopships to Piraeus, Greece and other islands activity
April 11, 1941	Arrived Alexandria
April 18, 1941	Departed Alexandria for Suda Bay, Crete
April 21, 1941	Shelling of Tripoli. Returned Alexandria April 23
April 24+, 1941	Evacuation of Greece. Suda Bay, Greek mainland and islands
May 2, 1941	Arrived Port Said
May 6, 1941	Operation *Tiger* to May 12
May 8, 1941	Bombarded Benghazi
May 9, 1941	Arrived Malta
May 15, 1941	Arrived Alexandria
May 20, 1941	Arrived Alexandria after patrol off Greece
May 22, 1941	Departed Alexandria for evacuation of troops from Crete
May 23, 1941	Bombed and badly damaged returned to Alexandria for repair to June 16
June 21, 1941	Arrived Haifa for Syrian Operations on coast of Palestine and Syria to July 13
July 15, 1941	Arrived Alexandria
July-September, 1941	Supply runs to and from Tobruk
September 20, 1941	Grounded. Starboard propeller damage
October 21, 1941	Shaft damage repair at Alexandria to December 4
December 15, 1941	Cover *Breconshire* to Malta and return cover for *Aurora* to Alexandria

December 21, 1941	At Malta, repairs to January 3, 1942
January 5, 1942	Departed for Alexandria. In and out of Alexandria until February 20
January 6, 1942	Cover *Breconshire* to Alexandria
January 9, 1942	Arrived Alexandria
January 16, 1942	Convoy MW8 to January 20
February 13, 1942	Convoy MW9
February 20, 1942	Departed Haifa (now 22nd DF)
February 27, 1942	At Alexandria
February 28, 1942	Departed Port Said
March 6, 1942	In and out of Alexandria to March 20
March 13, 1942	Support for Cruiser bombardment of Rhodes
March 20, 1942	Convoy MW10 to Malta
March 22, 1942	Second Battle of Sirte. Serious damage from 15-inch shell near miss
March 23, 1942	Arrived at Malta
April 2, 1942	Bombed at Malta while repairing
April 5, 1942	Departed Malta for Gibraltar
April 6, 1942	Grounded at speed off Kelibia, Tunisia. Total loss

The above is an incomplete list of HMS *Havock*'s ship movements primarily based on Admiralty Movement Lists (Pink Lists) plus data from other independent sources. The wartime log books were lost with the ship.

Appendix V

Two Speed Destroyer Sweep[1]

In the mid-1920s, it was believed that the antidote to mines laid in the path of the oncoming battlefleet was the Two-Speed Destroyer Sweep (TSDS) while the antidote to the submarine was the ASDIC-equipped armed with depth charges. However, in view of the likely congestion on the quarterdeck it was felt that a destroyer could be equipped with either but not both unless there was an increase in the size of such ships. Therefore, it was envisaged that flotillas of destroyers would be equipped with either ASDIC or TSDS. By 1928 it had been agreed that all destroyers would be fitted with trunks and offices so that they could be fitted with ASDIC even if completed as TSDS ships.

The TSDS, which replaced the earlier high-speed sweep mine sweep, consisted of a paravane right astern from which were towed the two sweep paravanes, which could be set to any depth between twenty and sixty feet, on either side. TSDS enabled the sweeping for and cutting of mine moorings at high and low speeds respectively and the shift from one speed to the other was automatic. At low speed, the outboard paravanes maintained maximum spread of 320 yards but as speed increased at the pre-set value the spread angle was automatically reduced to 150 yards. The maximum speed at which TSDS could be operated was twenty-five knots. The serrated sweep wire was expected to cut through most mooring cables but was supplemented by cutters about four feet from the paravanes. The minimum effective speed was about eight knots on the low-speed setting while at the high-speed setting TSDS was effective against simple moored mines at twelve knots and above and against anti-sweep devices at eighteen knots and above. The TSDS, which could be used to search ahead of an oncoming fleet, as a protective sweep, or as a clearance sweep, was heartily detested by the destroyer crews, that operated the device.

Cablegram from Lieutenant Commander G.R.G. Watkins to his Wife, 13 April 1942

ADM 358/506 (cablegram 13.4.42)
From Lt Cdr G.R.G. Watkins DSC RN,
Camp des Internees Britannique,
Laghouat

To: Mrs G.R.G. Watkins,
The Ivy,
Chippenham,
Wilts

I would not have believed so many misfortunes could have overtaken me since we left home[1] three weeks ago. I got clouted by the largest type of enemy and very nearly sank, came to a standstill and had ten minutes on my own with a lot of firing going on in local control. The Director Officer was killed. We just got the old boiler going and got away and had a nightmare of the night following. Very rough and quarter sea. We very nearly capsized. Staggered into harbour and had to be held up by dockyard wires. Our time in harbour was hell … Mary Tothill's[2] home.I had to do a special job before I sailed which entailed no sleep and was quite done in when we sailed. Got a few hours sleep – we were travelling at high speed, but not enough and through sheer lack of reaction ran aground with a whacking great light in sight. My helpful subordinates had all been killed and a new Sub … did not give me enough help poor lad … We landed at Kelibia near Tunis. I had hoped to sail off in a whaler but felt responsible for my lads. Lucky I didn't as Ju 88s appeared later. I was interviewed by Captain de Corvette Martin.

Appendix VII

Report of Commanding Officer of HMS *Havock*, Lieutenant Commander Watkins, on the Loss of his Command

SECRET
> The Ivy,
> Chippenham,
> Wilts,
> England

TO THE SECRETARY OF THE ADMIRALTY

Sir,

It is with profound regret at the loss of His Majesty's Ship most fortunate ship of war that I am forwarding for the information of their Lordships this report of the circumstances under which His Majesty's Ship HAVOCK, then under my command was lost off the coast of Tunisia on the night of 5–6 of April 1942.

(2)   I must crave their Lordships indulgence for submitting what at first sight must appear to be irrelevant details of the conditions and the occurrences preceding the disaster and more particularly of my own condition but, these were in fact the primary source of the disaster.

(3)   H.M.S. HAVOCK had taken part in Rear Admiral Vian's action on 22 March 1942 in which she had been severely damaged and just managed to make Valetta [now Valletta] harbour. Sub lieutenant Orpen my trained gunnery control officer (G.C.O.) and navigator had been killed; Mr Thompson my Gunner (T) was lost over the side and the remaining officers, including for the first time myself, were

severely shaken. Conditions in Malta at the time were not conducive to a speedy recovery of nerves. On the contrary, the reverse was the case.

The island was being subjected to the most severe pounding yet from the Luftwaffe. Life in the Dockyard narrowly approximated to the Biblical conception of Hell. And what little rest there was obtainable was to be found in the underground dressing stations. It was futile to even man the guns in the berth the ship occupied in, or close by No. 1 dock, Dockyard Creek as the view on all sides was obscured by buildings. Fire watchers only remained on board, and after each lull in the bombing I rushed out of my shelter to see if the ship had survived the attack and to deal with the damage in and near her.

(4)   The ordeal was nerve-wracking. In the shelter, every big explosion seemed to be striking my ship. But she survived, although everything round her was devastated and she herself was constantly covered in masonry and dust from the surrounding ruins. No direct hits were received and it was only when she was fit for sea and in stream some four days before she sailed on her last voyage that important damage was done. The after magazine and shell room were holed and roughly repaired with cement which had hardly set on our departure.

(5)   The morale of my officers and men remained high. Although my doctor Surgeon Lieutenant Royds R.N.V.R., who has since died in internment, was of the opinion that it was on the point of cracking. As a result of this sequence of events, the situation was extracting more from our constitutions than we could stand. I myself, although I did not realise it at the time, was deeply affected. I did not report my nervous condition to Vice-Admiral Malta, as there was no one to relieve me, and my brother officers were no fitter than myself. But it was my intention on the advice of my medical officer to demand fourteen days leave immediately the ship reached any other port. I considered that I was able to do my duty efficiently until such time was the case.

(6)   On the night immediately preceding our sailing, I was ordered to take charge of a convoy of small ships by the Chief-of-Staff to V.A.M. with the object of taking the last remaining 500-ton oil lighter round to Marsa Scirocco (Marsaxlokh) to unload the sunken BRECONSHIRE. This

I accomplished not without difficulty and interference by enemy aircraft, and after a short sleep on one of the sofas at Calafrana [now Kalafrana] mess, returned to my ship by land.

(7)   I went over to Lascaris to report to V.A.M. as soon as I could, But, owing to air raids I was unable to get transport across the harbour until about noon. Meanwhile, the ship was brought to four hours' notice for steam. I made a verbal report to V.A.M. and have since forwarded a list of recommendations for awards for the night's work. The V.A.M. told me that I was to sail that evening for the Eastward. I told V.A.M. that my ship was ready to sail in time but the cement in the magazine had had hardly time to set. I was already topped up with fuel and only had to ammunition. Not an easy job with constant air raids. But C-in-C Mediterranean signalled that I should sail to Westward. I got back on board about 13.00 and gave the necessary orders for sailing at 19.00 that night. There was still a lot to be done, many items were still in the Dockyard and there was hardly time to run up the gyro. I had been told to return by 17.00 to the Admiral's office to get my sailing orders. I managed to get a broken sleep in a shelter for about an hour. Then I went to V.A.M.'s office with my navigator Sub Lieutenant Lack R.N.V.R. a survivor from the *Southwold* sunk shortly before. He had been sent to replace Orpen as Navigating Officer (N.O.) and Gunnery Control Officer (G.C.O.) and I was informed by Chief of Staff that he was recommended by his late commanding officer [Commander C.T. Jellicoe] to carry out these duties. He was a permanent service R.N.V.R. and had been three years at sea, but had only been in the ship a week so I was unable to form an opinion as to his efficiency.

I took charts of the Western Mediterranean with me to get the latest corrections. I found my orders were to set my course from Malta swept channel to a point south of Kelibia Light, pass the latter at a distance of not more than 3,000 yards from the coast, and to continue at such a distance until past Cape Bon. I was to proceed at my maximum speed until past Galita Island and then to reduce speed in order to have sufficient fuel to reach Gibraltar. I corrected my charts up to date from the latest information in the Staff Office. I had never been through this channel before and was not particularly enjoying the prospect under such conditions. I had originally requested to sail east as I knew the coast there extremely well, and should have been under air cover from Tobruk by dawn.

(8)   Owing to the air raids I did not get back on board until about 18.30. I found the current had been cut off the gyro one occasion due to air raids but the N.A. said that it was running correctly. I had no Gunner (T). I found some passengers on board including Commander Jessel D.S.O., D.S.C. RN, the ex-commanding officer of *Legion* who I was pleased to see. I said so at the time, and asked him to come up on the bridge as he knew the coast of Tunisia well. Unfortunately, his broken foot was too bad to permit him.

(9)   I was feeling dead tired. I made out an intended track of the ship with the assistance of Sub Lieutenant Lack and Lieutenant Burfield my First Lieutenant And checked the bearings of Kelibia Light when alterations should be made. I told Lack to work out the time-distance at thirty knots between the points I had drawn on the chart. Lieutenant Burfield assisted him in this task, and discovered that Lack knew very little about navigation but this was not reported to me. By this time, I had hurriedly shifted into sea-going gear it was time to sail. It was then about 19.15.

(10) At this point I must describe the condition of my officers: Lieutenant J. Burfield D.S.C. RN was my First Lieutenant. His nerves seemed to have outwardly stood the strain and he had been G.C.O. of the ship – a very good one. Lieutenant M. Baillie-Grohman, my Second Lieutenant, was in a very neurotic state. He had done extremely well in controlling fires, dealing with damage, and assisting generally in the Dockyard in addition to his other duties for which I have recommended him for an award. But his nerves were so bad that he could not sit in a Director. He was Tactical Control Officer (T.C.O.) and signal officer and was extremely busy getting his department ready for sea. He was acting Gunner as well and so I did not use him to navigate. I was anxious on the voyage to have him on the top line ready to fire torpedoes and not to have his hand under the chart table screen.

In my opinion my greatest danger was in meeting some enemy force round the corner of Kelibia Light as other ships had done already done. I had one Sub Lieutenant R.C.N.V.R. and two midshipmen besides. All three, although young officers had very little sea experience. My more experienced Sub Lieutenant R.N.V.R. had been wounded and was in hospital. The only officer at the time that I could trust was Lieutenant Burfield the First Lieutenant. But, I decided that he must go in the Director as G.C.O. for the dangerous period in the narrow channel, as Lack it appeared had never been inside a 4.7 in director or done any low angle firing. Incidentally, my Doctor's nerves and my Engineer Officers nerves were badly shaken.

(11)   To continue with the history of events; I let go at dusk (about 19.00) and proceeded down the creek. Luckily there was no raid at the time. The gyro appeared to be correct and Lack managed to get a check while I was conning the ship through the breakwater. I cannot tell whether this check was accurate. While navigating through the swept channel, I obtained fixes with St. Elmo Light and the R.A.F. beacon which was not satisfactory because the beacon is moved daily, and I was not absolutely certain of its position. I managed to get off the bridge for a couple of hours' very necessary rest leaving the First Lieutenant there and came up when Pantellaria was sighted. The ship was in the second degree of readiness but I allowed half of my officers to sleep at their quarters at a time, in order to make them of some use if something happened. The First Lieutenant and Lieutenant Baillie-Grohman worked opposite each other as P.C.O. and Officer of the Watch (O.O.W.) with Sub Lieutenant Spearin R.C.N.V.R. or a Midshipman as assistant. Sub Lieutenant Lack was working independently as N.O. I need hardly say that my magnetic compass could not be trusted in any respect.

(12)   I took over the ship shortly before she came to the first turning place and altered course to pass one and a half miles off Kelibia Light. Lack was on the chart by now. My range finder appeared to be correct although there had been no chance to check it. I glanced at the chart and saw we were being set in an altered course 10 degrees or so away from the land. I cannot remember the exact courses. I was still doing 30 knots which I considered essential, (a) in order to carry out my orders which were to be as far as possible to the westward by daylight (b) in order to cross a superior force in the channel at the maximum rate of change of bearing. The night was clear, no moon but patches of mist over

the land. I asked Lack whether we were being set in or out heading for my turning point. He replied that we were a little inside but quite alright. Midshipman Duncan heard this. I glanced at the chart again and considered it all right to steer in a bit and did so. I had instructed Lack to inform me when I was about to come on for bearing before making an alteration and then give me the time for each run. Everything had been tabulated on the chart previously to avoid error. There were some four alterations to make to round the corner of Kelibia Light. I did not dare to leave the Pelorus as I did not want to spoil my vision by the chart table light and also events were occurring at a speed of 30 knots. Again my only real anxieties were the possibility of meeting an enemy and the minefield.

(13) I went to the first degree of readiness before the first turn round the point. Lieutenant Burfield became T.C.O. and O.O.W. and I 'had' the ship. Lieutenant B-G had been asleep while we were in the second degree of readiness at the after end of the bridge and was not fully aware of what was happening. He was also in an extremely exhausted condition. I constantly asked Lack whether we were alright. To which he replied we were a 'bit' inside but were alright. Midshipman Duncan who was on the bridge heard this. I was still passing ranges and bearings which he was plotting. The last leg of the turn looked strange to me and I hung on a bit longer after he told me it was time to alter. The time was then 0350. I saw what looked like a white wave ahead, and immediately altered out a little, then rushed to the chart table and ordered full speed astern and hard a starboard from there. But it was too late we had run on a sand spit and were hard and fast aground. The chart in use was brought ashore but was destroyed owing to secret information on it.

(14) There was nothing to be done. It was becoming light enough to see a little. The shore was a hundred yards off. I ordered all ammunition to be thrown over the side in an attempt to lighten the ship. But on going aft myself saw that it was futile and ordered all passengers to start going ashore, and preparations were made to destroy the ship. I also discovered from Engineer Andrewes that a valve box on the main steam line had burst in the engine room, killing one rating and badly burning five others, one of whom subsequently died in hospital.

(15) All confidential books and secret papers were destroyed in No, 1 boiler room. All secret gear was completely destroyed; e.g. R.D.F. and aerials, V.C. and V.E., F.K.O. and A.F.G. Asdic Gear. All spaces were filled with cordite strips and oil fuel spread about them.

(16) When every man had packed his needs and was ashore except the last whaler load (it was daylight by then) the cordite was ignited everywhere and when well started the T.G.M. lit the fuze of the depth charge in the Asdic Compartment. This blew out the entire side of the forecastle leaving the forecastle deck supported by the stem piece. The whaler was well clear by then. The ship was on fire fore and aft. We had previously fired the torpedoes to seaward in case parts of them were found by the enemy.

(17) On getting ashore I found that Commander Jessel had sent a Sub Lieutenant who spoke French (who was taking passage in the ship) to the fort at Kelibia light and had surrendered us and our arms to the French. In due course we were marched off to the Coast Guard Barracks leaving our heavy luggage and stores under guard with the wounded. A Cant seaplane came over us at fifty feet. We scattered by French order but the Cant did not open fire, happily. I had decided to let some men have a chance of escape in the whaler and had navigational instruments and sails sent ashore for that purpose. But we found it impossible to collect the sailing gear once ashore and I consider it lucky that no one attempted to do so as there was no wind and Junkers 88s came over in quantity later on.

(18) At about 14.00 when we were under guard and out of sight of the ship, there was a colossal explosion from the ship, and a column of smoke several hundred feet high went up in the air. It was ascertained that the after end of the ship had blown up. The depth charges had been cooking in the sun and with the cordite fire beneath had gone up. The after magazine may also have gone up. There were frequent explosions all day from ready use ammunition etc, and I am satisfied that nothing of value was left for the French.

(19) The French Guards were very civil to us and we were fed, and then taken by lorry to Tunis where we were housed in the local Barracks. After three days we were moved by train to Laghouat in Algeria. While in Barracks we were interrogated by French Naval Officers in plain clothes. I had

previously warned the crew not to say anything beyond giving their names and next of kin. If asked for more they were to say, 'I don't know, ask the Captain'. This they did, to the annoyance of the Interrogating Officers. My officers searched amongst the men's personal gear in case they had brought items of military value ashore. I am convinced that nothing was given away to the enemy of any importance.

(20) I consider that had I been mentally and physically fit my reactions would have been sufficiently quick and alert to have prevented this dreadful disaster to one of His Majesty's Ships. Sub Lieutenant Lack had been subjected to comparable strain as myself and this must have affected his efficiency at plotting in addition to his lack of experience of which I was at the time unaware. I had debated taking Benzedrine tablets [amphetamine, a potent central nervous system stimulant] but had decided that it might make me act peculiarly, and I knew should the enemy be sighted my weariness would leave me. My chief concern was not navigating – for once there was a light – but for the mine-field and the possibility of an enemy force being encoun-tered which it would have been my pleasure to engage. Commander Jessel carried out a verbal enquiry at Laghouat on the grounding.

HMS *Havock* Roll of Honour

Every effort has been made to ensure the accuracy and completeness of this appendix. However, the sources are few and this must be accepted as an incomplete list.

We apologise for any inaccuracy or omissions.

Surname	Christian Names	Age	Rank	Date	Fate	Action/Comments	Source
						Narvik	
Carter	George William Clarke	n/k	CPO Torp Inst	10/04/40	WIA	Transferred to Gravdal (Shrapnel wounds).	Don Kindell
Dulieu	Robert Stewart	n/k	Ordinary Seaman	10/04/40	WIA	Transferred to Gravdal Hospital near Skjelfjord	Don Kindell
Goddard	Ronald	n/k	Able Seaman	10/04/40	WIA	Transferred to Gravdal Hospital near Skjelfjord	Don Kindell

Appendix VIII (*Continued*)

Appendix VIII (Continued)

Surname	Name	Age	Rank	Date	Status	Notes	Source
Smith	Hugh Aldridge	n/k	Lieutenant	10/04/40	WIA	Transferred to Gravdal. Mention in Desp, London Gazette 7/6/40	Gravdal List
Sutton	Albert Breisford	23	Able Seaman	29/05/40	Drowned	HMS Cavalier Website. Chatham Naval Memorial.	Don Kindell
Harflett	Alan Jack	25	Stoker 1 Class	01/08/40	Died	HMS Cavalier Website. Alexandria (Chatby) War Memorial. Bombing during Crete Evacuation	Don Kindell
Abnett	Albert Ernest	40	Ord Artificer 1	23/05/41	MPK	Cavalier Web. Bombing. DSM, London Gazette 7/6/40. MID	Ian McLeod/DK
Allen	Ronald Victor	18	Able Seaman	23/05/41	MPK	HMS Cavalier Website. Bombing	Ian McLeod/DK
Forsyth	Edward James 'Lofty'	31	Leading Seaman	23/05/41	MPK	HMS Cavalier Website. Bombing. DSM and MID	Ian McLeod/DK

Appendix VIII (Continued)

Appendix VIII (*Continued*)

Surname	First Name	Age	Rank	Date	Status	Details	Source
Glenister	Donald Gordon 'Ginger'	21	Able Seaman	23/05/41	Killed	Cavalier Website. Bombing. Alexandria (Chatby) War Memorial	Ian McLeod/DK
Green	Gordon Geoffrey	23	Ordinary Seaman	23/05/41	MPK	HMS Cavalier Website. Bombing. Portsmouth Naval Memorial	Ian McLeod/DK
Sinclair	George	34	Elect. Art. 1.	23/05/41	MPK	HMS Cavalier Website. Bombing. Chatham Naval Memorial	Ian McLeod/DK
Bridge	Rodney	n/k	AB 'A' Gun Layer	23/05/41	WIA	CGM Awarded. Stayed at gun whilst severely wounded	Napper/Gazette
Daniels	Cecil William	n/k	Gunner (T)	23/05/41	WIA	DSC	
Chawner	Archibald	25	Stoker 2nd Class	23/08/41	Accident	HMS Cavalier Website. Alexandria Cemetary 2.C.10. (Hadra)	Don Kindell
Bagnall	William	23	Able Seaman	28/10/41	Accident	Cavalier Website. Alexandria Cemetary War Memorial (Hadra) Bombing Malta Harbour	Don Kindell

Appendix VIII (*Continued*)

Appendix VIII (*Continued*)

Surname	First name(s)	Age	Rank	Date	Cause	Notes	Source
Bidmade	William Ernest	n/k	Able Seaman	04/01/42	Killed	Cavalier Website. Bombing. Malta Naval Cemetary Capuccini	Ian McLeod/DK
Godman	Thomas Ellison	26	Act. Lieutenant	04/01/42	Killed	Cavalier Website. Bombing. Awarded DSC. Malta Capuccini	Ian McLeod/DK
Morehen	Walter	25	Stoker 1 Class	04/01/42	Killed	Cavalier Website. Bombing. Malta Capuccini Cemetery	Ian McLeod/DK
						Second Battle of Sirte	
Brown	Claude Ronald	27	Ord. Sig.	22/03/42	DOW	Cavalier Website. 2nd Battle of Sirte. Malta Capuccini Cemetery	ADM 358/458
Crane	Arthur Charles Gordon	30	Ord. Sig.	22/03/42	Killed	Cavalier Website. 2nd Battle of Sirte. Malta Capuccini Cemetery	ADM 358/458
Gimblett	Alexander Ernest Samuel	29	Supply Asst	22/03/42	MPK	Cavalier Website. 2nd Battle of Sirte. Portsmouth Memorial	ADM 358/458
Orpen	Walter David	21	Sub-Lt GCO Nav	22/03/42	Killed	Cavalier Website. 2nd Battle of Sirte. Malta Capuccini Cemetery	ADM 358/458

Appendix VIII (*Continued*)

Appendix VIII (*Continued*)

Surname	First name	Age	Rank	Date	Status	Notes	Source
Reid	Frederick Albert	41	Able Seaman	22/03/42	MPK	Cavalier Website. 2nd Battle of Sirte. Chatham Naval Memorial	ADM 358/458
Thompson	James William	n/k	Gunner (T)	22/03/42	MPK	Lost Overboard. 2nd Battle of Sirte. Portsmouth Naval Memorial	ADM 358/458
Hulme	James William	n/k	Able Seaman	22/03/42	Killed	Cavalier Website. 2nd Battle of Sirte. Malta Capuccini Cemetery	ADM 358/458
Douglas	Maurice	n/k	Ordinary Seaman	22/03/42	WIA	Confirmed by Maurice Douglas at crew reunion.	ADM 358/458
Carter	George Gordon Frederick	20	Able Seaman	05/04/42	DOW	Cavalier. 2nd Sirte. Imtarfa Military Cemetary Malta Grounding and Ship Loss	Cav/ IMcL/DK
Robinson	James Russell	21	Leading Stoker	06/04/42	Killed	HMS Cavalier Website. Chatham Naval Memorial	Cav/ IMcL/DK
Rose	Reginald 'Lofty'	n/k	ERA 3rd Class	06/04/42	WIA	Severely scalded by super-heated steam on grounding.	Maurice Cutler
Woods	Bertram	n/k	Leading Stoker	25/04/42	Died	Died in Tunis hospital. Medjez-el-Bab Cemetery, Tunisia. DSM Laghouat Internment Camp	Cavalier/ IM/DK

Appendix VIII (*Continued*)

Appendix VIII (*Continued*)

Royds	Robert Davies	28	Surgeon Lt.	24/09/42	Died	Polio In Algiers while (POW). Dely Ibrahim War Cemetery, Algeria	Cav/McLeod/DK
Hastings	Norman Grenfell	32	Able Seaman	18/10/42	Died	Natural causes. Sec 5 C of E Grave 86. Liverpool Cemetery.	Cavalier/IM/DK

WIA — Wounded in Action
MPK — Missing Presumed Killed
DOW — Died of Wounds
MID — Mention in Despatches

Appendix IX

HMS *Havock* Decorations, Medals and Awards

NAME		RANK	COMMENTS	SOURCE
Conspicuous Gallantry Medal				
Bridge	Rodney	Able Seaman	Crete Evacuation/ Bombing of ship.	LG 8/1/42
			'Who stood to his gun, though grievously	
			wounded by an enemy bomb, and went	
			on firing without thought for his injury'	
Distinguished Serrvice Order				
Courage	Rafe Edward	Lt Commander	Narvik 10/4/40	LG 7/6/40
Millns	Frederick Leslie	Gunner (T)	Sinking of Italian sub-marine *Berillo*	ADM 1/11655
Distinguished Service Cross				
Bruce	Michael Alastair Mitchell	Lieutenant	Narvik 10/4/40	LG 7/6/40
Courage	Rafe Edward	Lt Commander	Holland	LG 11/7/40
Courage	Rafe Edward	Lt Commander	Bar for sink-ing of Italian submarine *Berillo*	ADM 1/11655

Appendix IX (*Continued*)

Destroyer at War

Appendix IX *(Continued)*

NAME		RANK	COMMENTS	SOURCE
Watkins	Geoffrey Robert Gordon	Lieutenant	Matapan	LG 29/7/41
Burfield	John Blackmore	Lieutenant	Matapan	LG 30/1/42
Daniels	Cecil William	Gunner (T)	Matapan	LG 30/1/42
Godman	Thomas Ellison	Acting Lieutenant	Bombing in Malta Harbour	FWR

Distinguished Service Medal

Kemp	Frederick Richard	CPO G.I.	Narvik 10/4/40	LG 7/6/40
Brickell	William Joseph	Able Seaman	Narvik 10/4/40	LG 7/6/40
Baker	William George 'Pash'	Ordinary Seaman	Narvik 10/4/40 RNVR	LG 7/6/40
Abnett	Albert Ernest	Ordnance Artificer	Narvik 10/4/40 Killed 23/5/41	LG 7/6/40
Cauchi	Vincent	Leading Cook	Narvik 10/4/40	LG 7/6/40
McDonald	J	Marine *(Renown)*	Narvik 10/4/40 Threw shell overboard	LG 7/6/40
Forsyth	Edward James 'Lofty'	Leading Seaman	Sinking *Berillo. Havock* not *Hasty* in LG	ADM 1/11655
Langton	Hugh 'Bob'	Able Seaman	Sinking *Berillo. Havock* not *Hasty* in LG	ADM 1/11655
Isden	James John 'Lofty'	Petty Officer	Matapan. Bar to previous DSM	LG 30/1/42

Appendix IX *(Continued)*

Appendix IX *(Continued)*

NAME		RANK	COMMENTS	SOURCE
Surridge	Alfred John 'Jack'	Temp Act L Seaman	Matapan	LG 30/1/42
Panrucker	Walter Henry	Chief Petty Officer	April 1942	IWM
Mentioned in Despatches				
Smith	Hugh Aldridge	Lieutenant	Narvik 10/4/40 Wounded	LG 7/6/40
Pevler	Albert Victor	Able Seaman	Narvik 10/4/40	LG 7/6/40
Walley	Leslie George	ERA 2C		LG 13/1/41
Bean	Albert Edward	Stoker Petty Officer		LG 13/1/41
Hope	Reginald Symes	Stoker Petty Officer		LG 13/1/41
Burfield	John Blackmore	First Lieutenant	Sinking of Italian submarine *Berillo*	ADM 1/11655
Chapman	Arthur Robert	Able Seaman	Sinking *Berillo*. *Havock* not *Hasty* in LG	ADM 1/11655
Miles	Frederick Francis Turner	Chief Petty Officer	Sinking *Berillo*. *Havock* not *Hasty* in LG	ADM 1/11655
Addison	John	Stoker Petty Officer	Second Battle of Sirte 22/3/42	LG 10/1/41
Abnett	Albert Ernest	Ordnance Artificer	Posthumous. Crete Evac./ Bombing of ship	LG 8/1/42
Golby OBE	John Edward	Lt Commander (E)	Crete Evacuation/ Bombing of ship	LG 8/1/42

Appendix IX *(Continued)*

Appendix IX *(Continued)*

NAME		RANK	COMMENTS	SOURCE
Elliott	Robert Gravett	Stoker Petty Officer	Crete Evacuation/ Bombing of ship	LG 8/1/42
Hope	Reginald Symes	Stoker Petty Officer	Crete Evacuation/ Bombing of ship	LG 8/1/42
Napper	Derek William	Midshipman	Matapan	LG 30/1/42
Starkey	John Henry	Able Seaman	Matapan	LG 30/1/42
Forsyth	Edward James 'Lofty'	Leading Seaman		LG 11/11/41
Gaynor	John Albert	Temp Act L Seaman		LG 11/11/41
Marjoram	Sidney George Baker	Temp Act L Seaman		LG 11/11/41
Brickell	William Joseph	Able Seaman	Also DSM. Took bomb away in lorry, Malta	LG 11/11/41
Bruce	Michael Alastair Mitchell	Lieutenant	Also holder of DSC	LG 11/11/41, 1/1/42
Kemp	Frederick Richard	Chief Petty Officer	Also holder of DSM	LG 11/11/41
Watkins	Geoffrey Robert Gordon	Lt Commander	Greece Evacuation. Also holder of DSC	LG 27/1/42
Rowe	Maurice	Stoker 2nd Class	Second Battle of Sirte 22/3/42	LG 8/9/42

Information is from available sources; list is not guaranteed to be complete.

Key:

ADM   Admiralty files

FWR   Forces War Records

IWM   Imperial War Museum archives

LG   *The London Gazette*

Notes and References

Chapter 1: A Ship is Born

1. Sir Bolton Eyres-Monsell (22/2/1881 – 21/3/1969), First Lord of the Admiralty, 1931–1936.
2. ADM 167/88, *Admiralty Board Minutes 3104 of 9th October and 3106 of 1st November 1933.*
3. Norman Friedman, *British Destroyers From the Earliest Days to the Second World War*, (Seaforth Publishing 2009), p. 77. The Assistant Director of torpedoes Captain, later Admiral, Bernard Currey (11/5/1862 – 2/6/1936) 'remarked in December 1908 that the threat a fleet could fire a torpedo broadside into the centre of the opposing fleet could force the latter to maintain longer ranges favouring the British (who had superior fire control)'.
4. These 'browning' shots were apparently named after the use of shotguns to 'brown' a covey of birds.
5. *Destroyers and Flotilla Leaders 1914 – 1920*, p.10 (DNC Department, Copy No.127); Author's archive.
6. ibid.
7. ibid, p.6.
8. ibid, p.7.
9. ibid, p.11.
10. David K. Brown, *Nelson to Vanguard: Warship Development 1923 – 1945* (Seaforth Publishing 2000), pp.86–7.

Chapter 2: Spanish Civil War (January 1937 to March 1939)

1. Often known as Nyon markings, the Nyon Conference (10-14 September 1937) took place after *Havock* had been attacked on 30 August 1937.
2. ADM 116/3534, *Spanish Civil War: Attack by Government and Insurgent Arcraft on HMS Blanche, HMS Royal Oak, HMS Gipsy, HMS Havock and HMS Hardy. Submarine Attack on HMS Havock.*
3. John Thomson, personal communication to DG, 30 May 1987.
4. Frank Hall, personal communication to DG, 20 January 1987.
5. Griff Gleed-Owen, personal communication to DG, 12-15 February 1937.

6. The cruiser was *Libertad*, her sister *Miguel de Cervantes* having been put out of action by a torpedo hit on 21.11.1936.

7. The infamous red light district.

8. ADM 116/3534.

9. *Iride* was ceded for several months to the Spanish Nationalist Navy as *Gonzales Lopez*. In 1940. *Iride* was transformed to carry SLC assault craft, the deck gun was removed and four watertight containers were mounted fore and aft of the conning tower. On 21 or 22 August *Iride* was sunk in the Gulf of Bomba, Cyrenaica, by Fairey Swordfish torpedo bombers from HMS *Eagle* while preparing for a human torpedo attack on Alexandria.

10. Junio Valerio Borghese (1906-1974), was a prominent hard-line fascist politician, nicknamed the 'Black Prince'. The second son of the 11th Prince of Sulmona, he is often incorrectly styled 'Prince' instead of 'Don' in Anglo-Saxon literature. Borghese thought that he was engaging a Republican destroyer on 31 August/1 September 1937. In the Second World War, he commanded the Italian Navy's famous underwater assault team unit during 1940-43, and then led a notorious group of Fascists diehards on land in 1943-45. In 1970, he took part in planning a neo-fascist coup that was aborted once the Italian press discovered it and fled to Spain.

11. The Republican fleet operated sixteen Churruca class destroyers which were virtually repeats of the British Scott class flotilla leaders and therefore could be mistaken easily for any of the Royal Navy's A to I class destroyers.

12. See Appendix VII for the mundane nature of this work.

13. John Burfield, personal account of his service aboard HMS *Havock* 10.2.1939 – 6.4.1942.

14. ibid.

15. ibid.

Chapter 3: Run Up to War (March 1939 – March 1940)

1. Burfield.

2. Fred Buckingham, *The Strife is O'er*, unpublished undated personal reminiscences. Copy held by David Goodey.

3. Burfield.

4. Because of its poor performance during the night phase of the Battle of Jutland on 31 May 1916, during the inter-war period the Royal Navy undertook numerous night exercises in which light forces attacked a well-defended battlefleet. The resultant proficiency in night fighting paid dividends during the Second World War.

5. John Burt, personal communication with David Goodey.

6. Thomson.

7. ibid.

8. Known by the crew as 'Nutty' Courage, not because of his behaviour but because of his full head of ginger hair.

9. Hall.
10. Thomson.
11. The Hamburg South America Line ship *Monte Olivia* (13,750/1925) successfully ran the blockade back to Germany. On 3.4.1945 she was bombed by aircraft of the 8th USAAF and burnt out while under repair at Kiel. Raised on 12.6.46, she was scrapped in 1948.
12. *Reader's Digest, Time* etc.
13. Thomson.
14. Burfield.
15. J.A. Brown, personal correspondence with David Goodey, 7 March 1987.

Chapter 4: The Battle for Narvik (April 1940)

1. Alex 'Bugs' Levene, personal dictation with David Goodey in 1984 and 1985.
2. Freddie Kemp, Imperial War Museum, Sound Archives number 10503, 13 December 1988.
3. Geirr Haarr, *The German Invasion of Norway April 1940*, (Seaforth Publishing 2009), p.87.
4. ibid. See pp 90-7 for details.
5. Albert Goodey, personal communication.
6. Jim 'Buster' Brown, Imperial War Museum, Sound Archives number 10504, 15 December 1988.
7. Geirr Haarr, *The German Invasion of Norway April 1940*, (Seaforth Publishing 2009), p.87.
8. ibid. See pp. 307-314 for details.
9. ADM 199/474, *Reports of proceedings, Norway*, 4.6.1940.
10. ibid.
11. Haarr, p.338.
12. ibid. p.339.
13. ibid. p.340.
14. ibid. p.445.
15. Levene.
16. ibid.
17. Haarr, p.342.
18. John Dodds, Imperial War Museum, Sound Archives number 13148 April 22. 1993.
19. Harry Jenkins, Imperial War Museum, Sound Archives number 10490 November 23, 1988.
20. Haarr, p.342.
21. ADM 199/473, *Narvik* & ADM 199/474, *Reports of proceedings, Norway*, 4-6.1940.
22. Haarr, p.345.
23. Ibid, p.346.
24. Kemp.
25. George Carter, communication from nephew Mike Harris with David Goodey August 2015.

26. Kemp.
27. Dodds.
28. Brown.
29. Levene.
30. Haarr, p.347.
31. ADM 199/473, *Narvik*.
32. Dodds.
33. Albert Goodey, personal records and memorabila.
34. ibid.
35. Kemp.
36. Leslie Millns, personal communication with David Goodey.
37. Maurice Cutler. Imperial War Museum, Sound Archives number 11328, 30 May 1990.
38. Frank E. Hall, personal communications with David Goodey 1987.
39. Dodds.
40. Axel Niestlé, *German U-boat losses during World War II: details of destruction*, (Frontline Books, 2014), p.117.
41. Haarr, pp. 358-74 for details of Second Battle of Narvik.
42. A 'puffer' is the name given to coal-burning small coasters that plied their trade in inshore waters around Scotland – some were sent to Harstad to support the ships and men based there during the Norwegian campaign.
43. ADM 199/361, *Home Fleet Diaries 1940*, p.75.
44. ibid. pp.78-9.
45. Burfield.
46. Levene.
47. Commander Rafe E. Courage D.S.O., D.S.C., with bar, who commanded the destroyer *Maori* in the Mediterranean action in which three British destroyers and a Dutch destroyer severely damaged a much heavier Italian force, married Lance Corporal Nancy Petersen W.T.S.

Chapter 5: The Invasion of Holland (May 1940)

1. ADM 199/361, *Home Fleet War Diary 1940*, p.31
2. ADM 1/10607, *HMS* Havock, *Report of Proceedings off Dutch Coast 9th to 15th May 1940*, p.12.
3. ibid.
4. ibid.
5. ibid.
6. ibid.
7. ADM 1/10607.
8. Brown, personal communication with David Goodey March 1987.
9. ADM 1/10607.
10. ibid.
11. Levene.
12. ADM 1/10607, p.13.
13. Thomson.

14. ADM 1/10607, p.13.
15. Levene.

Chapter 6: Mediterranean Maelstrom (May 1940 – February 1941)

1. ADM 199/386, *War Diary, Mediterranean 10/6/40 – 6/9/40*, p.100.
2. ibid, p.106.
3. ibid. p.132.
4. *Naval Staff History Second World War Selected Operations (Mediterranean) 1940*, p.25, Historical Section Admiralty, 1957.
5. Times are Zone minus three hours.
6. *Naval Staff History*, p.26.
7. ibid, p.28.
8. ibid. pp.29–30.
9. 'Buster' Brown, Imperial War Museum, Sound Archives 10504, 15 December 1988.
10. *Naval Staff History*, p.30.
11. ibid, p.31.
12. ibid, pp.32-3.
13. 'Buster' Brown, IWM.
14. *Naval Staff History*, p.33.
15. ADM 234/444, *HM Ships Damaged or Sunk by Enemy Action 3rd Sept 1939 – 2nd Sept. 1945*, p. 140
16. ADM 199/386, pp.181-2.
17. ADM 199/387, *War Diary, Mediterranean 6/9/40 – 20/12/1940*, p.10.
18. ibid, p.13.
19. ibid, pp.19-20.
20. ibid, p.24.
21. ibid, p.33.
22. ibid, p.31.
23. ibid, p.36.
24. ibid, p.34.
25. Burfield.
26. ADM 199/387, p.34.
27. ibid, p.36.
28. ibid, p.34.
29. ibid, p.40.
30. ibid, p.43.
31. ibid, pp.46-7.
32. ibid, p.50.
33. ibid, p.60.
34. ibid, pp.78-9.
35. ibid, pp.80-2.
36. Burfield.
37. ADM 199/387, p.95.
38. ibid. p.115.
39. Stoker Albert Goodey, personal communication with David Goodey.

40. Frank 'Nobby' Hall, personal communication with David Goodey, January 20, 1987.
41. Hugh 'Bob' Langton, personal communication between Kim Langton (son) and David Goodey July 11, 2012.
42. Burfield.
43. 'Buster' Brown, IWM.

Chapter 7: The Battle of Matapan (27 – 30 March 1941)

1. ADM 199/445, *Mediterranean Operations*, 1940-41.
2. For convenience, we have adopted S.W.C. Pack's designation of the Italian forces as X, Y and Z. British reports of the period routinely refer to the Mediterranean Fleet as Force A, Force B etc., as found in his *Night Action off Cape Matapan*, Ian Allan, 1972.
3. The Italian movement had been detected by a Bletchley Park decrypt but, as always with Enigma, the intelligence break-through was concealed from the Italians by ensuring there was a plausible reason for the Allies to have detected and intercepted their fleet. In this case, it was a carefully directed reconnaissance plane. Interestingly, the report in the official Admiralty publication of 1943, *East of Malta, West of Suez: The Admiralty Account of the Naval War in the Mediterranean* (HMSO, 1943) credits the detection of the Italian force to 'one of *Formidable's* aircraft on reconnaissance', p.56.
4. S.W.C. Pack, *Night Action off Cape Matapan*, p.19.
5. ibid, p.17.
6. ibid, pp.25-6.
7. ibid, pp.31-4.
8. ibid, pp.42-3.
9. ibid, p.45.
10. ibid, pp.54-6.
11. ibid, p.61.
12. ibid, pp.68-70.
13. ibid, p.77.
14. ibid, p.73.
15. Burfield.
16. Pack, pp.78-91.
17. ibid, pp.94-5.
18. Freddie Kemp, Imperial War Museum Sound Archives 10503, 13 December 1988.
19. Pack, p.95.
20. Jack Surridge, Imperial War Museum, Sound Archives 11455, 9 August 1990.
21. Pack, pp.95-6.
22. Surridge.
23. Pack, p.97.
24. ibid, p.100, Cunningham actually thought that he had fired on *Hasty*.

25. Derek Napper, copy of his actual Midshipman's Log provided to David Goodey.
26. Surridge.
27. Napper.

Chapter 8: Convoys and the Tripoli Bombardment (April – May 1941)

1. Napper.
2. Brown.
3. *Bonaventure* was torpedoed and sunk, while escorting convoy GA-8 from Greece to Alexandria, by the Italian submarine *Ambra* about 100 nautical miles south-south-east of Crete in position. There were 310 survivors.
4. *York* was crippled by an Italian explosive motor boat in Suda Bay on 26 March 1941, and further damaged by German bombing during the invasion of Crete. Her main guns were destroyed by explosive charges before the wreck was captured by German troops.
5. During an abortive attempt to attack Port Sudan the Italian destroyers *Nazario Sauro* and *Daniele Manin* were bombed and sunk by Swordfish aircraft from HMS *Eagle* on 3 April. Two more destroyers *Tigre* and *Pantera* were scuttled on the Arabian coast after being attacked by RAF aircraft on 3 April 1941.
6. *Mohawk* was torpedoed by the Italian destroyer *Tarigo* on night of 15/16 April 1941 off Cape Bon.
7. Naval Staff History Second World War, *Selected Bombardments (Mediterranean), 1940-1941*, Historical Section Admiralty 1954, p.38.
8. ibid, p.39.
9. ibid, p.40.
10. ibid, p.41.
11. ibid, p.43.
12. ibid, p.46.
13. ibid, p.46.
14. ibid, p.47.
15. Napper.
16. Brown.
17. Naval Staff History Second World War, *Selected Bombardments*, p.47.
18. Napper.
19. Naval Staff History Second World War, *Selected Bombardments*, p.48.
20. ibid, p.70.
21. ibid, p.51.
22. ibid, p.52.
23. ibid, p.73.
24. ibid.

25. ibid.
26. Napper.
27. ibid.

Chapter 9: Evacuation of Greece and Crete (April – June 1941)

1. *Admiral Sir Andrew Cunningham's despatch to the Admiralty sent on 7 July 1941*, published in the Supplement to *The London Gazette* 18 May 1948 (HMSO), p.3050.
2. ibid, p.3047.
3. ibid, p.3051.
4. ibid, p.3052.
5. ibid, p.3050.
6. ibid, p.3051.
7. ibid, pp.3051-2.
8. Napper.
9. ibid.
10. *Admiral Sir Andrew Cunningham's despatch*, p.3053.
11. Napper.
12. Surridge.
13. Albert Goodey.
14. *Admiral Sir Andrew Cunningham's despatch*, p.3054.
15. Napper.
16. *The Sun* (Sydney), 16 May 1979.
17. *Admiral Sir Andrew Cunningham's despatch*, p.3055.
18. Napper.
19. ibid.
20. ibid.
21. Peter C. Smith and Edwin Walker, *The Battles of the Malta Striking Forces* (Ian Allen, 1974), p.35.
22. Napper.
23. ibid.
24. Smith & Walker, p.36.
25. *Admiral Sir Andrew Cunningham's despatch*, p.3105.
26. Naval Staff History Second World War, *Naval Operations in the Battle of Crete 28th May-1st June 1941*, Historical Section Admiralty 1960, p.8.
27. Napper.
28. ibid.
29. Naval Staff History Second World War, *Naval Operations in the Battle of Crete*, p.15.
30. ADM 234/444, *HM Ships Damaged or Sunk by Enemy Action 3rd Sept 1939-2nd Sept. 1945*, p.167.
31. Napper.
32. Surridge.
33. Jim 'Buster' Brown.
34. Albert Goodey.

35. This was the very popular 'Ginger' Glenister who is remembered at the Chatby War Memorial in Alexandria.
36. C-in-C Med 1234C/14 to CS 15.

Chapter 10: No Rest for the Wicked: Syria, Tobruk, Groundings and More Convoys (June 1941 – February 1942)

1. ADM 199/679, *Naval Support for the Syrian Campaign*, p.8.
2. Napper.
3. ADM 199/679, p.8.
4. Kim Langton son of Hugh 'Bob' Langton various communications with David Goodey in 2012/2015.
5. Napper; ADM 199/679, pp.9-11.
6. Burfield.
7. Napper.
8. ADM 199/679, pp.12-3.
9. Napper.
10. ibid.
11. ADM 199/679, p.15.
12. Midshipman Derek Napper (later Captain Derek Napper CBE), was in *Havock* from 18 March to 16 July 1941. Derek Napper died on 26 December 2007, at the age of eighty-six.
13. Naval Staff History Second World War, *The Tobruk Run June 1940 to January 1943*, Historical Section Admiralty 1956, p.14.
14. Napper.
15. Brown.
16. Surridge.
17. Harry Jenkins Imperial War Museum, Sound Archives, 10490, 23 November 1988.
18. ibid.
19. The Australian Government's position is discussed in detail in Arthur Nicholson's, *Very Special Ships: Abdiel Class Fast Minelayers of World War Two* (Seaforth Publishing, 2015), pp.45-51.
20. ADM 199/799.
21. NL 19666 3/10/41.
22. ADM 199/799
23. Brown.
24. Norma Hudson, *Sole Survivor, One Man's Journey, the biography of John Norman Walton – Sole Survivor of HMS Neptune*, The Memoir Club, 2007.
25. Peter C. Smith & Edwin Walker, *The Battles of the Malta Striking Forces* (Ian Allan, 1974), pp.89-91.
26. ADM 199/650, *Mediterranean Fleet Diary, January to July 1942*, p.9.
27. ibid, pp.10-3.
28. Surridge.
29. Brown.
30. ADM 199/650, p.20.
31. ibid, p.21.

32. ibid, p.22.
33. ibid, p.23.
34. Brown.
35. ADM 199/650, p.29.
36. ibid, pp.45-7.
37. ibid. p.54.
38. ibid, p.77.
39. ibid, pp.86-7.
40. ibid, pp.89-92.
41. David Masterman Ellis's personal notes dated February 8, 1988. Provided to David Goodey by Ellis's nephew Richard Gleed-Owen.

Chapter 11: The Slow Death of HMS *Havock*: The Second Battle of Sirte and Beyond (March – April 1942)

1. S.W.C. Pack, *The Battle of Sirte* (Ian Allan, 1975), pp.32-5 for full discussion.
2. ibid. p.28.
3. ibid.
4. ibid. p.29.
5. ADM 199/650, *War Diary of C-in-C Mediterranean January-July 1942*, p.96.
6. ibid. p.98.
7. Pack, pp.42-73 for full details.
8. John Dodds. Imperial War Museum, Sound Archives, 13148, 22 April 1993.
9. David Masterman Ellis's personal notes dated 8 February 1988. Provided to David Goodey by Ellis's nephew Richard Gleed-Owen.
10. ADM 358/506, Cablegram from Lieutenant Commander G.R.G. Watkins to his wife sent 13/4/1942.
11. S.W.C. Pack, pp.72-3.
12. ibid. p.74.
13. ADM 199/650, pp.99-100.
14. ibid. p.102.
15. British contemporary documents from the Mediterranean routinely misname *Avon Vale* as *Avonvale*.
16. ADM 358/458, *Damage suffered by RN destroyers at Second Battle of Sirte*.
17. ADM 199/650, p.100.
18. ibid. pp.104-5.
19. ibid, p.105.
20. ibid. p.107.
21. ADM 1/12040, *Loss of HMS Havock 5/6-4/42. Report of Commanding Officer Lt. Cmdr. Watkins*. p.1.
22. ADM 199/650, p.112.
23. Brown.
24. ADM 234/444, p.195.

25. ADM 199/650, p.120.
26. ibid. p.125
27. ADM 1/12040, p.2.
28. Brown.
29. ADM 1/12040, p.2.
30. Aldo Cochia, *La Marina italiana nella seconda Guerra mondiale, Vol. VII, La difesa del traffic con l'Africa settentrionale dal 1° ottobre 1941 al 20 settembre 1942* (Ufficio Storico della Marina Militare, 2nd ed. 1976); Translated for the authors by Andrew Smith.
31. ADM 1/12040, pp.2-4.
32. Jim Brown. Letters to David Goodey dated 1987/88.
33. ADM 1/12040, p. 4.
34. Brown.
35. ADM 199/650, p.129.
36. ADM 1/12040, p.4.
37. Marcello Bertini. *La Marina italiana nella seconda Guerra mondiale, Vol.XIII, I Sommergibili nel Mediterraneo*, Tomo II (Ufficio Storico della Marina Militare, 1968), pp.23-4; Translated for the authors by Andrew Smith.
38. See http://www.wlb-stuttgart.de/seekrieg/42-04.htm.
39. Vincent P. O'Hara, *In Passage Perilous: Malta and the Convoy Battles of June 1942* (Indiana University Press, 2013), p.140.
40. Erminio Bagnasco, *I MAS e le motosiluranti italiane 1906-1968* (Ufficio Storico della Marina Militare, 2nd ed. 1968), pp.440-3. Translated for the authors by Andrew Smith.
41. Brooks Richards, *Secret Flotillas: Clandestine Sea Operations in the Western Mediterranean, North African & the Adriatic 1940 – 1944* (Pen & Sword, 2013), p.218.

Chapter 12: Prisoners of War in Laghouat
(April – November 1942)

1. Dodds.
2. Maurice Cutler. Imperial War Museum, Sound Archives, 11328, 30 May 1990.
3. Anonymous diarist. This diary, in typed form, was provided to David Goodey in the 1980s and is most likely that of Midshipman David Masterman Ellis. The authors have been unable to confirm this and therefore the author of this original evidence must remain as anonymous.
4. Surridge.
5. Anonymous diarist.
6. Burfield.
7. George Shuttleworth included in John Burfield's unpublished memoirs.
8. Anonymous diarist.
9. Michael Baillie-Grohman included in John Burfield's unpublished memoirs.

10. ibid.
11. Burfield.
12. Charles Lamb, *War in a Stringbag: The Classic Second World War Fleet Air Arm Autobiography* (Bantam Books, 1980).
13. Surridge.
14. Anonymous diarist.
15. Burfield.
16. Anonymous diarist.
17. Brown.
18. Alan Smith included in John Burfield's unpublished memoirs.
19. Burfield.
20. Anonymous diarist.
21. Richard Osborne, *The Watery Grave: The Life and Death of HMS Manchester* (Frontline Books, 2015) provides a detailed account of the loss of this cruiser.
22. Anonymous diarist.
23. Brown.
24. Shuttleworth.
25. Surridge.
26. Harry Jenkins. Imperial War Museum, Sound Archives, 1490, 23 November 1988.
27. Dodds.
28. Burfield.
29. Cutler.
30. Surridge.
31. Shuttleworth.

Chapter 13: Court Martial

1. ADM 1/12040, *Loss of HMS Havock 5/6-4/42, Report of Commanding Officer HMS Havock Lt Cdr GRG Watkins to be tried by Court Martial.* See Chapter 11 for Watkins' account of the loss of his ship.
2. ibid.
3. ibid.
4. ibid.
5. ibid.
6. ADM 156/252, *HMS HAVOCK Report of Grounding on Tunisian Coast 6/4/42; Lt Cdr. G.R.G. Watkins DSO, DSC, RN tried by Court Martial at Portsmouth 9 – 10/3/1943*, p.1.
7. ibid. pp.7-10.
8. ibid. p.11.
9. ibid. p.12.
10. ibid. p.18.
11. ibid. p.19.
12. ibid. p.20
13. ibid. pp.21-5.
14. ibid. p.29.
15. ibid. p. 30.

16. ibid. p.31.
17. ibid. p.32.
18. ibid. p.33.
19. ibid. pp.34-6.
20. ibid. p.37.
21. ibid. p.38.
22. ibid. p.39.
23. ibid. p.40.
24. ibid. pp.42-6.
25. John Blackmore Burfield 31/05/1917–13/11/1998. First Lieutenant of destroyer *Faulknor* during Normandy landings June 1944; Lieutenant in Command of frigate *Byron* December 1944; Acting Lieutenant Commander 1 November 1945; Lieutenant Commander 1 July 1945; Commander 30 June 1952; retired 3 January 1959.
26. While serving as Lieutenant in Command of the Captain Class frigate *Byron*, Burfield was involved in the sinking of the Type VIIC U-boat *U722* on 27 March 1945 west of the Hebrides and the sinking of the Type VIIC/41 U-boat *U1001* on 8 April 1945, south-west of Ireland. He was awarded a bar to his D.S.C. for his part in these actions.
27. ADM 156/252, pp.47-55.
28. ibid. pp.55-7.
29. ibid. pp.58-60.
30. ibid. pp.61-2.
31. ibid. pp.63-5.
32. ibid. pp.68-9.
33. ibid. pp.70-1.
34. ibid. p.2.
35. ibid. pp.74-6.
36. ibid. p.76.
37. ibid. p.78.
38. ibid. pp.83-4.
39. ibid. p.87.
40. ibid. p.88
41. ibid. pp.89-93.
42. ibid. pp.94-6.
43. ibid. p.98.
44. ibid. p.99.
45. ibid. p.100.
46. ibid. p.101.
47. ibid. p.103.
48. ibid. p.105.
49. Obituary of Commander 'Robin' Watkins in the *Daily Telegraph*, 5 May 1993, p.19.
50. See *Amazon to Ivanhoe* by John English (World Ship Society, 1993) for more information about the service careers of *Hero* and *Hotspur* post-1943.

Appendix V: Two Speed Destroyer Sweep

1. Friedman Norman, *British Destroyers From the Earliest Days to the Second World War*, (Seaforth Publishing 2009), p.193.

Appendix VI: Cablegram from Lieutenant Commander G.R.G. Watkins to his Wife, 13 April 1942

1. This cablegram was sent from Vichy-held Algeria and was therefore bound to be read by the French, the Italians, the Germans and the Admiralty. It was, consequently, written in the form of a code, e.g. home = Alexandria.
2. Mary Tothill was the wife of Commander Tothill who had been Watkins' CO during his time as First Lieutenant aboard Janus. Tothill would later be his 'Friend' during the court martial held on 9-10 March 1943 at Portsmouth.

Bibliography

PRIMARY SOURCES

The National Archives (TNA), Kew

ADM 1/10607	HMS *Havock*, Report of Proceedings off Dutch Coast, 9th to 15th May 1940.
ADM 1/12040	Loss of HMS *Havock*, 5/6-4/42; Report of Commanding Officer Lt. Cdr. G.R.G. Watkins.
ADM 116/3534	Spanish Civil War: Attack by government and insurgent aircraft on HMS *Blanche*, HMS *Royal Oak*, HMS *Gipsy*, HMS *Havock* and HMS *Hardy*. Submarine attack on HMS HAVOCK.
ADM 156/252	HMS *Havock*, Report of Grounding on Tunisian Coast 6/4/42; Lt. Cdr. G.R.G. Watkins DSO, DSC, RN, tried by Court Martial at Portsmouth, 9-10/3/1943.
ADM 167/88	Admiralty Board minutes 3104 of 9th October and 3106 of 1st November 1933.
ADM 199/361	Home Fleet Diaries.
ADM199/386	War Diary, Mediterranean, 10/6/40 – 6/9/40.
ADM 199/387	War Diary, Mediterranean, 6/9/40 – 20/12/40.
ADM 199/445	Mediterranean Operations, 1940 – 41.
ADM 199/473	Narvik.
ADM 199/474	Reports of Proceedings, Norway, 1940.
ADM 199/650	War Diary of the C-in-C Mediterranean Fleet, January to July 1942.
ADM 199/679	Naval Support for the Syrian Campaign.
ADM 199/799	Operations *Cultivate*, *Supercharge* and *Treacle*.
ADM 234/444	HM Ships Damaged or Sunk by Enemy Action, 3rd Sept 1939 – 2nd Sept 1945, 13/4/42.
ADM 358/458	Damage suffered by RN Destroyers at Second Sirte.
ADM 358/506	Cablegram from Lt. Cdr. G.R.G. Watkins sent to his wife.

David Goodey's Personal Archive

Lieutenant John Burfield, unpublished memoirs.
Log of Midshipman Derek Napper.
Personal notes of David Masterman Ellis dated 8/2/1988.

SECONDARY SOURCES

Official Reports and Histories

Destroyers and Flotilla Leaders 1914-1920, DNC Department copy no. 127; Richard Osborne's personal archive.

Naval Staff History Second World War, *Selected Operations (Mediterranean) 1940,* Historical Section Admiralty, 1957; Richard Osborne's personal archive.

Naval Staff History Second World War, *Naval Operations in the Battle of Crete 28th May-1st June 1941,* Historical Section Admiralty, 1960; Richard Osborne's personal archive.

Naval Staff History Second World War, *Selected Bombardments (Mediterranean) 1940-1941,* Historical Section Admiralty, 1954; Richard Osborne's personal archive.

Naval Staff History Second World War, *The Tobruk Run, June 1940 to January 1943,* Historical Section Admiralty, 1956; Richard Osborne's personal archive.

HMSO Publications

Admiral Sir Andrew Cunningham's Despatch to the Admiralty, sent on 7 July 1941, Supplement to *The London Gazette*, 18 May 1948 (HMSO).

East of Malta, West of Suez: The Admiralty Account of the Naval War in the Mediterranean (HMSO, 1943).

Roskill, Captain S.W., *The War at Sea 1939-1945 Volume I: The Defensive* (HMSO, 1954).

_____, *The War at Sea 1939-1945 Volume II: The Period of Balance* (HMSO, 1956).

Studies

Alliston, John, *Destroyer Man* (Greenhouse Publications, 1985).

Austin, Douglas, *Churchill and Malta's War 1939-1943* (Amberley Publishing, 2010).

Bagnasco Erminio *I MAS e le motosiluranti italiane 1906-1968* (Ufficio Storico della Marina Militare, 2nd Edition, 1968).

Barnett, Corelli, *Engage the Enemy More Closely: The Royal Navy in the Second World War* (Hodder & Stoughton, 1991).

Bertini, Marcello, *La Marina italiana nella seconda Guerra mondiale*, Vol. XIII, *I Sommergibili nel Mediterraneo*. Tomo III (Ufficio Storico della Marina Militaire, 1968).

Brown, David K. (Editor), *The Design and Construction of British Warships 1939-1945: Volume 1, Major Surface Warships* (Conway Maritime Press, 1995).

_____, *Nelson to Vanguard: Warship Design and Development 1923-1945* (Chatham Publishing, 2000).

Campbell, John, *Naval Weapons of World War Two* (Conway Maritime Press, 1985).

Cochia, Aldo, *La Marina italiana nella seconda Guerra mondiale. Vol VII La difesa del traffic con l' Africa settentrionale dal 1o ottobre al 20 settembre 1942* (Ufficio Storico della Marina Militaire, 2nd Edition, 1976).

Connell, G.G., *Mediterranean Maelstrom: HMS Jervis and the 14th Flotilla* (William Kimber, 1987).

Cope, Ron, *Attack at Dawn* (Clink Street, 2015).

Cunningham, Admiral of the Fleet Viscount A.B., *A Sailor's Odyssey* (Hutchison & Co., 1951).

Dickens, Peter, *Narvik: Battles in the Fjords* (Ian Allan, 1974).

English, John, *The Hunts* (World Ship Society, 1987).

_____, *Amazon to Ivanhoe* (World Ship Society, 1993).

_____, *Afridi to Nizam: British Fleet Destroyers 1937-43* (World Ship Society, 2001).

_____, *Obdurate to Daring: British Fleet Destroyers 1941-45* (World Ship Society, 2008).

Faulknor, Marcus, *War at Sea: A Naval Atlas 1939-1945* (Seaforth Publishing, 2012).

Friedman, Norman, *British Destroyers From the Earliest Days to the Second World War* (Seaforth Publishing, 2009).

Galea, Frederick R., *Call-Out: A Wartime Diary of Air/Sea Rescue Operations at Malta* (Malta At War Publications, 2002).

Gill, G. Hermon, *Royal Australian Navy 1939-1942* (Australian War Memorial, 1957).

Greene, Jack and Massignani, Alessandro, *The Naval War in the Mediterranean 1940-1943* (Chatham Publishing, 1998).

Grehan, John and Mace, Martin, *The War in the Mediterranean 1940-1944* (Pen & Sword Maritime, 2014).

Haarr, Geirr H., *The German Invasion of Norway April 1940* (Seaforth Publishing, 2009).

_____, *The Battle for Norway April – June 1940* (Seaforth Publishing, 2010).

_____, *The Gathering Storm: The Naval War in Northern Europe September 1939-April 1940* (Seaforth Publishing, 2013).

Hague, Arnold, *The Allied Convoy System 1939-1945: Its Organization, Defence and Operation* (Chatham Publishing, 2000).

Haines, Gregory, *Destroyers at War* (Ian Allan, 1982).

Hodgkinson, Hugh, *Before the Tide Turned: The Mediterranean Experiences of a British Destroyer Officer in 1941* (Harrap, 1944).

Holland, James, *Fortress Malta: An Island Under Siege 1940–1943* (Orion Books Ltd, 2003).

Hudson, Norma, *Sole Survivor, One Man's Journey, the Biography of John Norman Walton, the Sole Survivor of HMS Neptune* (The Memoir Club, 2007).

Ireland, Bernard, *The War in the Mediterranean* (Pen & Sword, 2004).

Lamb, Charles, *War in a Stringbag: the Classic Second Word War Fleet Air Arm* Autobiography (Bantam Books, 1980).

Nicholson, Arthur, *Very Special Ships: Abdiel Class Fast Minelayers in World War Two* (Seaforth Publishing, 2015).

O'Hara, Vincent P., *Struggle for the Middle Sea: The Great Navies at War in the Mediterranean Theater 1940-1945* (Naval Institute Press, 2009).

_____, *In Passage Perilous: Malta and the Convoy Battles of June 1942* (Indiana University Press, 2013).

Osborne, Richard, *The Watery Grave: The Life and Death of HMS Manchester* (Frontline Books, 2015).

Pack, S.W.C., *Night Action off Cape Matapan* (Ian Allan, 1972).

_____, *The Battle of Sirte* (Ian Allan, 1975).

Preston, Antony, *V and W Class Destroyers 1917-1945* (Macdonald).

Richards, Brooks, *Secret Flotillas Volume 2: Clandestine Sea Operations in the Western Mediterranean, North African & Adriatic 1940-1944* (Seaforth Publishing, 2013).

Rohwer Jurgen *Chronology of the War at Sea 1939-1945: The Naval History of World War Two* (Chatham, 2005).

Shores, Christopher and Cullm Brian with Malizia, Nicola, *Malta: The Spitfire Year 1942* (Grubb Street, 1991).

Simmons, Mark, *The Battle of Matapan 1941: The Trafalgar of the Mediterranean* (Spellmount, 2011).

Smith, Peter C., and Walker, Edwin, *The Battles of the Malta Striking Forces* (Ian Allan, 1974).

Smith, Peter C., *Eagle's War: The War Diary of an Aircraft Carrier* (Crecy, 1995).

Spooner, Tony, *Supreme Gallantry: Malta's Role in the Allied Victory 1939-1945* (John Murray, 1996).

van Crefeld, Martin, *Supplying War* (Cambridge University Press, 1977).

Woodman, Richard, *Malta Convoys 1940-1943* (John Murray, 2000).

Websites

www.naval–history.net.
http://www.unithistories.com/officers/RNofficersH.3html
http://www.wlb–stuttgart.de/seekkreig/42–04.ht

Index